Paul Benjamin

PEOPLE'S PADRE

PEOPLE'S PADRE

AN AUTOBIOGRAPHY BY

Emmett McLoughlin

THE BEACON PRESS   BOSTON

Copyright 1954

The Beacon Press

Library of Congress catalog card number: 54-6164

First printing, March 1954
Second printing, October 1954
Third printing, January 1955
Fourth printing, July 1955
Fifth printing, December 1955
Sixth printing, February 1956
Seventh printing, September 1956
Eighth printing, December 1956
Ninth printing, May 1957
Tenth printing, September 1957

The text of the letters in this book is accurate, and the incidents reported actually occurred, although in a number of instances the names of persons and places have been omitted or altered.

Printed in U.S.A.

To those people of Phoenix whom I have been privileged to serve.

And to my friends, especially our hospital trustees, whose faith in me has helped to make possible my transition from the priesthood to a much more fruitful citizenship.

Contents

Emmett McLoughlin

St. Anthony's Seminary, Santa Barbara, California, where the author studied from 1922 to 1927.

Santa Barbara Mission, where the author studied from 1928 to 1934, and where he was ordained on June 11, 1933.

Father Emmett in 1934, the first year of his priesthood in Phoenix. He is wearing a Franciscan robe, with its knotted cord.

Father Emmett's acolytes included Negro, Filipino, and Latin-American boys.

"Father Emmett's Mission" (St. Monica's Community Center), originally a store, grew into a church, a social hall, a clinic, a maternity center, and boys' and girls' club rooms.

St. Mary's Church, Phoenix. Father Emmett lived in the rectory from 1934 to 1948.

The breaking of ground in June 1943 for St. Monica's Hospital (later Memorial Hospital). At the left is Pat Shaughnessy; at the right is Ray Busey, a member of the hospital board and a former mayor of Phoenix.

Superintendent McLoughlin with three nurses.

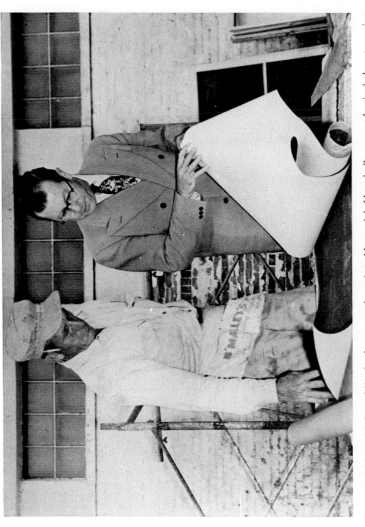

Superintendent McLoughlin looks over plans for Memorial Hospital's new physical-therapy wing for polio patients.

Superintendent McLoughlin with Memorial Hospital's X-ray machine.

Emmett McLoughlin at his home in Phoenix.

Emmett and Mary McLoughlin preparing a barbecue meal on their patio.

CHAPTER ONE

"A Priest Forever"

And by no means will it be lawful for them to leave this Religion according to the command of the Lord Pope, because according to the holy Gospel: *No man putting his hand to the plow and looking back is fit for the Kingdom of God.*

On Friday at noon, in every Franciscan monastery in the world, the above words from the Rule of St. Francis are read to every priest and every student for the priesthood. They are quoted as the infallible word of God, under the threat that any who looks back will suffer ostracism and rejection by his former fellow Catholics, the contempt of the non-Catholic public, and the curse of God.

Of the Roman Catholic priests who have put their hands to the plow, thousands have looked back. Conscious of the recriminations they knew they would otherwise face, a high proportion have slipped away from the communities in which they had sincerely worked and have sought security in the anonymity of distant cities.

This is the story of one who spent twelve years in a semi-nary of the Franciscan Order of the Roman Catholic priest-hood, worked for fourteen years in one parish, doubted for more than ten years — and finally turned back. He tried to make the break openly and honestly and to brave the storm in the same city in which he had worked as a priest. Five years later he has found that God did not curse him; that the wrath of his former co-religionists, though con-tinuous and vicious, has availed nothing; that the general public did not offer condemnation but congratulation; and that the Kingdom of God seems much nearer than it had ever been before.

"Thou art a priest forever, according to the order of Melchizedek." These words from the fifth chapter of Hebrews, pronounced by a bishop of the Roman Catholic Church over a young candidate for priesthood, officially symbolize his entrance into the aristocracy of Catholicism. In the eyes of Catholics the words not only give him the power to perform the vital functions of that Church — the offering of the mass and the forgiving of sins — but also, with an aura of reflected glory, elevate his family to the company of the privileged families of the Church. Those families feel more blessed than other families.

The parents of a priest, especially if they are immigrants, substitute the prestige of the priesthood for economic and social aristocracy. They boast almost as much of a son who is a priest as they would if he were the President of the United States. This is one of the reasons for the Church's ability to solicit a steady supply of young men each year into the Catholic seminaries of America. It is one of the reasons for the willingness of these young men to leave the freedom, the pleasures, and the opportunities of American life and give themselves to Rome.

The reason why a boy enters a seminary and the reason why he stays are different.

I have known hundreds of boys who entered the Franciscan seminary in Santa Barbara; but I have known none who entered with a realization of the high purposes of self-discipline, self-sacrifice, and self-annihilation that he must achieve before he is considered fit to be a worthy representative of this ancient church in a modern world. A boy between eleven and fifteen years of age is certainly too young to understand any of these disciplines. He enters for one of several reasons. His parents may influence him toward this end, effectively guiding him into a seminary as other parents guide their sons into law, medicine, or industry. Or perhaps a friend who has already entered urges him, with glowing accounts of the sports, the hikes, and the fellowship with a hundred other boys — and no meddlesome girls. Or perhaps he admires a parish priest, one who leads his Boy Scout troop and who gently and affably encourages him to follow in the footsteps of his idol.

It was a combination of all three forces that caused me to find myself at the door of St. Anthony's Seminary of the Franciscan Order, in Santa Barbara, California, in September of 1922. I was fifteen years old.

For more than a thousand years, my ancestors had been Roman Catholics. My parents were native Irish, born and reared on the barren soil of County Sligo in the province of Connaught, in the northwest of Ireland, a region so unproductive that many Irish themselves say that only goats can live there; an area so akin to hell in British eyes that Oliver Cromwell was ready to damn the Irish to " Hell or Connaught."

The Irish potato famine of 1846 had started the tide of immigration to America which eventually carried my father and mother, who had lived on neighboring farms in Ireland, to opposite coasts in America — my father to New York and my mother to San Francisco.

At first my father waited on table in the Astor House on Broadway. But later he forsook the Great White Way and the rear walls of Manhattan's firehouses — where he played handball with his relatives and fellow immigrants — to follow his childhood sweetheart to the Golden Gate.

Work was scarce in San Francisco at the turn of the century. Barney McLoughlin went up the river to Sacramento, where he found a job as a grocery delivery boy. Perhaps the Irish Catholic colony there attracted him. At that time and throughout my boyhood, it was almost a ghetto, suffering from the stigma of the railroad " push " of a previous generation. Sacramento was the western terminus of the joint construction drive of the 1860's from the east and west, which spanned the continent and ended with the driving of the golden spike in Utah in 1869. Imported Chinese labor had hauled the rails for the Central Pacific, laying the ties from west to east. Imported Irish labor had blasted the mountains, driving the spikes from east to west.

The Irish pushed past the golden spike in Utah, settled in Sacramento, summoned their sweethearts from Ireland, and proceeded to produce Irish-Americans in great numbers.

My father joined the Ancient Order of Hibernians, delivered groceries, and on every possible occasion rode the river to court his lady in a San Francisco rooming house. This might have gone on for years, as Irish courtships sometimes used to do, if the great earthquake of 1906 had not occurred. My mother was made homeless when her rooming house was dynamited by the Army to control the raging fire. She found shelter in a tent in Golden Gate Park. In order to reach her, Barney McLoughlin talked himself onto the " bread " train, stocked by the bakeries of Sacramento to keep the San Franciscans from starving, and got past the United States Army, which had thrown martial law around the stricken city. He found her, probably through the Irish Catholic police " grapevine," and convinced her that a quaking city was no place to live.

An Irish Catholic contractor had built the San Francisco city hall with empty barrels instead of reinforcing steel in the supporting columns. It netted him a greater profit on his investment — but he had not calculated on earthquakes. The city hall collapsed. In a temporary city hall, located in a Jewish synagogue, my father and mother obtained their wedding license. They went to a Roman Catholic priest and were married in April 1906. I was born on February 3, 1907, in Sacramento, California.

My earliest impressions were hearing about the persecution of the Irish by the English, and the sacredness of the ritual and the customs of the Roman Catholic Church. I can remember the mournful lullaby plaint of " The Wearing of the Green." I can remember also being taken to mass when I was barely able to walk, being taught how to say the rosary, cross myself, genuflect. During sermons in the old cathedral, I fell asleep innumerable times.

We lived "south of the tracks." I was the eldest child in a family of two boys and two girls. At the age of nine I was selling newspapers to help augment the family income. I also caddied on the Sacramento Country Club golf course, until a priest told me it was sinful to work on Sunday — even though the family income needed my small assistance.

While I was engaged in the intense boyish competition of a newspaper contest, an incident occurred that was perhaps a portent of my future work in social welfare.

A boy told me that there was a section of town where there lived wealthy young women who would subscribe to the paper. It was near the river, an old part of town, below Chinatown, close to the Southern Pacific railroad shops. I went down and rang doorbells. At every door a scantily dressed young woman responded. I told my story about the value of the Sacramento *Bee* for the well-informed citizen, and about the need of my poor family for a Thanksgiving or a Christmas turkey. Every young woman gave me a month's subscription. I won the first prize. It was not until later that I learned that I had canvassed the "red light" district.

St. Francis parochial school, with its inoculation of daily mass, daily religious classes, daily contact with priests and nuns, counteracted any remote danger of "worldliness." It was impressed upon me that, although I might sell papers with non-Catholic children, play with them, live near them, I must remember that they were not "our kind." Being neither Irish nor Catholic, they had only a remote and dubious chance of reaching heaven.

Attendance at a parochial school causes cleavages among Catholic and non-Catholic youngsters that sometimes are not healed. I was told that public-school youngsters were

" laying for " Catholics; frequently I carried rocks in my pockets for self-defense when passing a public school. One Sunday morning two Catholic boys joined me in a plot to avenge the faith by throwing a " stink bomb " into a Protestant church after we had returned from mass. My father overheard us and administered a stern lecture about fair play and American freedom of religion. He threatened me with an unforgettable beating if he caught me talking about such a plot again.

In spite of the efforts of a Franciscan priest to send me to the seminary of his Order at Santa Barbara, I first enrolled in high school at the Christian Brothers College. But three of my former schoolmates returned for vacation with such enthusiastic accounts of the mountains and the sea at Santa Barbara, of the hiking and swimming, of picnics and sports, that I joined them when they left by train for the fall semester.

When a boy enters a seminary, he begins twelve years of the most thorough and effective intellectual indoctrination the world has ever known.

It begins gently, with a blending of the legitimate pleasures of boyhood, the stimulus of competition in studies, and the pageantry of the forms of an ancient religion unseen in an ordinary parish church. It ends twelve years later, with a mental rigidity and acceptance of medieval superstitions and religious concepts as archaic as those of the Buddhist monks upon the isolated, frozen mountains of Tibet. It may surprise non-Catholic Americans to learn that the story of Tibet in Lowell Thomas' *On Top of the World* has its counterpart in the hundreds of Roman Catholic seminaries flourishing in the cities and countrysides of America.

The course of training for the priesthood is roughly divided into two periods. The first six years are spent in the junior seminary — four years of high school and two years of what would be considered college work. The senior seminary provides the last college years, devoted mainly to Catholic philosophy, plus four years of training in all the intricacies of Catholic theology. Between the junior and senior seminaries in religious orders (Franciscans, Dominicans, Vincentians), there comes a year devoted entirely to religious indoctrination. This is the novitiate.

The indoctrination in exclusiveness so characteristic of the Roman clergy begins in the junior seminary. Even though we wore ordinary American clothes and went on weekly hikes to the ocean, we were solemnly warned not to look at the " mermaids " on the beach. We could not go alone, either to the ocean, or to the mountains, or into the city of Santa Barbara. Our organized sports were always intramural.

We were being thoroughly trained in Catholicism. Dramatics were encouraged — but more often than not the plays were religious. Attendance at mass was daily and compulsory. So were community prayers, morning and evening. All our textbooks, even in high-school courses, were written by Catholic authors. No daily newspapers were permitted, and no non-Catholic magazines.

Even in our English lessons, our thinking was carefully guarded. The small school paper — the *Antonian* — was supervised by a priest. As its editor I knew that the subject matter of every editorial and of every article was chosen by the priest-adviser and carefully edited and " corrected " by him before publication.

All incoming mail was opened by the Prefect of Discipline, a priest; if he deemed advisable, the letters were confiscated. A letter addressed to one of my classmates by a woman was intercepted; it was an affectionate letter and signed with a girl's name. The boy was accused of carrying on dangerous and sinful correspondence with a woman. The officials would not believe that she was his sister until I corroborated his story and produced other students who had seen her visiting the seminary. (Such a violation of personal liberty is in America almost never condoned except in prisons and mental institutions.)

All outgoing mail had to be placed in the Prefect's office in unsealed envelopes. When I was in the senior seminary and about to be ordained, my brother was in the junior seminary. My mother was sick. In an attempt to cheer her up, he had written a flippant and jocular letter to the effect that he did not plan to attend my ordination but was planning to sneak out to a movie instead. The letter was intercepted. I was called to the Prefect's office and told that my brother would be dismissed for failure to appreciate the sacredness of the priesthood. When he insisted that he had merely tried to tease my mother, they relented.

Along with newspapers and movies, radios were forbidden for the use of junior seminarians. The priests in their supervised recreation hall were permitted a radio — but we were not admitted to that hall. When Notre Dame played the University of Southern California, we were allowed to listen to a speaker placed in the window and beamed to us outside. On the morning before these games we all prayed at mass that God would vindicate the Faith through the victory of Notre Dame over this Methodist university.

Not only were we gradually withdrawn from the world

but we grew to feel that the non-Catholic public disliked us and, if given the opportunity, would persecute us. Santa Barbara hoodlums were said to prowl our seminary grounds at night. We heard uncouth youngsters ridicule the brown-robed monks for wearing " bathrobes " on the city streets. In the late 1920's, when the Ku Klux Klan spread to California, the priests pointed out the big " K K K " set in stone and the burning crosses on the surrounding hills. We prayed for the grace to be willing martyrs at the hands of vicious non-Catholics.

During these junior years, the boy has no official ties binding him to the Church. He may leave the seminary at any time, without penalty. Many boys do so; and others are dismissed as being too worldly or intellectually unqualified for the intense indoctrination ahead. The impression is instilled, however, that any boy who voluntarily leaves jeopardizes the " pearl of great price " — the salvation of his soul. He constantly hears sermons, in church services and in the classroom, about the exalted dignity of the priesthood, about the principle of a vocation, about the possible anger of God against those who reject his calling: " No man putting his hand to the plow and looking back is fit for the Kingdom of God."

As a student in the junior seminary, I was permitted to spend the summer vacation at home. When I worked as a service-station water boy to pay for my clothes and tuition in the seminary, I tried hard not to be shocked by the lewd stories of the station attendants and by their flirtations with feminine customers. Then in my late teens, I had never touched or kissed any woman but my mother and my sisters.

One friend, who had quit the seminary, took me to dinner

at his home. On the way back, he gave a lift to one of the girls of the parish with whom he had developed an innocent friendship. My mother saw me arrive in the model-T coupe, sitting in the car with a girl. I had to endure the most severe upbraiding of my life. I was dedicated to God, my mother said; I should not even talk to girls. I must promise her — and I did — never to allow temptation to come so close to me again.

During a subsequent vacation, when I worked for the California State Fair, my mother ceased to worry because I labored with a gang of men. My job was the temptation-less chore of shoveling out cattle stalls.

With one magnificent gesture, the ceremony of entering the novitiate sweeps aside the centuries. The aspirant for the priesthood in the Franciscan Order finds himself, in spirit, walking the ancient streets of Assisi, eating in its hallowed monastic halls, and chanting the sixth-century hymns of Gregory the Great. One moment I stood before the Provincial Superior of the ancient Order in the dimly lit sanctuary of the church, dressed in my best twentieth-century clothes. In the next moment my coat was almost torn from my back and thrown violently across the church floor; over my head was dropped the hooded, rope-bound robe donned by St. Francis in the year 1206. My head was shaved, leaving only the circular band of hair distinctive of the ancient monks; for the entire year of the novitiate, this tonsure was to be worn. My shoes, socks, and underwear, symbols of modern life, were taken from me; in their place I received a coarse woolen " under-habit," flannel knee pants, and sandals.

To symbolize more effectively the repudiation of the

" old " man and the start of a " new " spiritual life, even our names were changed. I had been christened John Patrick. I was now named Emmett — or, in Latin, Emantus — in memory of an obscure saint in early Irish and French history.

To add to the effectiveness of the renunciation of the modern world, this ceremony took place in the ancient mission Church of San Luis Rey, near San Diego, built a century and a half ago by the bare hands of Indian neophytes, under the guidance of the Spanish monks. Not only had they brought from Spain the gold and silver robes, the incense, and the rituals of the centuries, but the very walls seemed to breathe the words of Thomas Aquinas, Duns Scotus, and the ancient Church Fathers of the first few centuries of Christianity.

During this year our seclusion from American life and our indoctrination in the " spirit " of the Catholic Church became so intensive that I came to feel that I alone was a true Christian, privileged to commune with God. I believed that the American way of life was pagan and sinful, a rebirth of the Roman Empire and destined to the same disgraceful doom in the ashes of history. I came to believe that the American government was to be tolerated though wrong — tolerated because it gives unlimited freedom to the Roman Catholic Church, wrong because it gives freedom to other churches. I believed that the ideal form of government was the one in which I was living in the seclusion of my spirit — the era when the Papacy made kings because the power to govern came from God to the king through his " representative," the Pope. My boyhood concept of civics — of the rights of man to the processes of law and of government through the consent of the governed — faded away under the constant repetition of the teachings of Thomas Aquinas and the moral theologians. The Constitution of my country and the laws of its states dimmed into trivialities in comparison with the all-powerful Code of Canon Law of the Roman Catholic Church. I became in all truth a citizen of the Church, living — by accident — in the United States.

During this year (it was 1928), I voted for the first time. I felt that it was a worldly act. But Alfred E. Smith was running for President of the United States and we were told that we must vote — and for whom.

Such intensive indoctrination was unknown to the Western world outside the Roman Catholic Church until it was copied by Fascism, Nazism, and Communism. The training for the priesthood goes on, after the novitiate year, for six more years. We were no longer permitted to visit our homes, even for vacations, unless a death occurred in our families. Even such a visit was permitted only by consent of the Father Superior (called the Father Guardian) and of the Father Provincial of the Province. (The Province — a geographical division of the Franciscan Order — in this case comprised the states of California, Arizona, Utah, Oregon, and Washington.)

The process of indoctrination in all seminaries is intensified by the use of the Latin language. All textbooks of Catholic philosophy and theology are in Latin. The lectures by professors (at least in my day) were in Latin. Examinations were conducted in Latin. We reached the point where we were thinking in Latin, the language of the early centuries of Christianity. Subconsciously we were living not in the age of presidents and politicians, of labor unions and capitalists, but in the age of masters and slaves, of kings and serfs, of Popes, representing God, and the faithful, who meekly acquiesced in their decisions as coming from the throne of God himself.

The chains with which the religious orders of the Roman Catholic Church bind their priestly aspirants to a lifetime of service are the three vows of obedience, poverty, and chastity. The first " simple " vows, binding for three years, are pronounced at the end of the novitiate year. I had just completed a solid year of intense seclusion. I had been confined to the monastery grounds. I had taken part in daily conferences on the sacredness of the " religious " life. I had seen few people except my companions and a chosen group of exemplary priests. I had been swept to such an emotional height that as I recited the sacred vows I was oblivious of the Order and of the Roman Catholic Church. In my own mind I bound myself directly to God in a dedication of love.

The vow of obedience is the most important of the three. It identifies all ecclesiastical superiors with the Church, and it identifies the Roman Catholic Church with God. Every command by the Superior of a religious community or by a church pastor, no matter how petulant, how ill-advised, or how unjust, must be considered as a command from God himself and must be obeyed as such under the penalty of sin.

The young monk must learn obedience even as a dead body " obeys " the will of him who places it in any position. Obedience must be so complete, according to the early Franciscan teachers, that if the Superior ordered us to plant the cabbage upside down, with the roots in the air, we should do so — because God would reward our obedience by mak-

ing the cabbage grow in spite of the Superior's mistake.
When the command is given with the phrase " under Holy
Obedience," refusal means a mortal sin. The robe of every
Franciscan monk is girded with a rope. One strand hangs
from his side. It has three knots on it symbolizing the three
vows — poverty, chastity, and (the bottom knot) obedience. The young Franciscan is trained that when the Provincial Superior greets him he must kneel on one knee and
kiss the lowest knot on the Superior's cord, and then his
hand. It is the token of complete, abject, unreasoning
obedience.

The vow of poverty means the abnegation of all worldly
possessions. Through this vow, the monk swears that so
long as he lives he shall not own a single material thing —
not a suit of clothes, a bed, a book, a fountain pen, a package
of cigarettes, or a crust of bread. He may use some of these
things — but only by permission of his Superior. The
Order itself is bound, by Canon Law, to the strictest poverty. It must not own property, automobiles, furniture,
money. These things it uses only at the pleasure of the
Pope; and it must relinquish them all if he should so command. The Rule of the Franciscan Order goes farther.
All property used by both the organization and the individual must be of the quality owned by the poorest private
citizens. Monasteries must be simple in construction,
meager in furnishings, minimal in conveniences. Clothes
must be few and of the poorest quality. Food must be of
the plainest, suitable to the table of men who eat merely
for sustenance and who also through the sense of taste
mortify their flesh to keep it " under subjection."

As student monks, preparing for the priesthood, we lived
according to this ideal of poverty. We were not told that

most priests and officials of the Order ignored it. We wore used, patched, and threadbare robes, some formerly used by monks who had died. Our beds were cots without modern springs, covered with straw pads. Each cell was furnished with a table, a chair, and a crucifix.

Our communal meals were served in an atmosphere of medievalism, of poverty and austerity. The monks were seated at a U-shaped arrangement of plain, varnished tables. The Superior and the older priests were seated at the head table. The student monks occupied the side tables, while the lay brothers were relegated to the humbler locations near the kitchen. Solemn, lengthy prayers, rumbled through in semi-conscious rote, preceded the appearance of food. The priests, beginning with the Superior, were served first, and what remained was passed along in large platters.

Our meals were eaten in silence. One of the students, stationed at a pulpit, read in Latin from the scripture, from the Rule of the Order and its " by-laws " and penalties, from some devotional treatise, or from the biography of a saint. On exceptional occasions, the Superior granted permission for *colloquium* — pious conversation.

A hallowed custom at the end of the meal was the passing of a small urn of toothpicks to all the brethren. It was started by the Superior to indicate that he had finished and that the rest should not be far behind. One of the lay brothers who cared for the dining room had heard so much about poverty that he believed it extended even to toothpicks. Noticing that many of them seemed dirty and frayed, we put pencil marks on toothpicks as we used them. They appeared again and again. The brother had been salvaging them as he emptied the garbage. Even the Superior admitted that neither St. Francis nor the Pope wanted poverty carried that far.

The vow of chastity binds the priestly enthusiast to a life of celibacy. It reinforces all the laws of the Roman Church concerning sex, with the additional penalty of the violation of a sworn vow. The student priest must learn to believe that chastity and celibacy are the most sacred of virtues, the most divine, the qualities that above all others mark him among all men in the world as a genuine follower of Christ.

He must learn to crush the desires of the flesh by fasting, self-denial, and even physical pain. Many Americans have read of the ascetics and hermits of the early and middle ages of Christianity who mortified the flesh by wearing hair shirts, fastening chains about their waists, and sleeping on boards or in bare coffins. But it might surprise these Americans to know that in the senior seminaries for Franciscan priests in the United States there hangs, inside the door of each cell or bedroom, a scourge or whip. It is made of several strands of heavy cord, each knotted at the end. Each Monday, Wednesday, and Friday evening at 5:45 o'clock we closed the doors of our cells; to the chant of the " Miserere " we disrobed and " scourged our flesh to bring it into submission." The Superior patrolled the corridors to listen to the sounds of beating — the assurance of compliance.

We were made to read the treatises of medieval recluses who advocated bathing in one's underwear to reduce temptation.

In the name of spirituality, customs were developed in us that were designed to prevent the temptations of the flesh.

One such is *custodia oculorum* (custody of the eyes). Modesty and chastity — we were taught — are protected by a deportment characterized by keeping one's eyes on the ground, even while walking, so that one does not see the faces or upper parts of the bodies of the passers-by. This is intended, of course, to prevent susceptible young monks from being tempted by the forms and faces of passing young women.

We were warned also of the danger of "particular friendship." In our innocence we understood this to mean too much fraternization with some particular fellow student. But we soon learned that a student would be warned or punished even if he were merely found in the room of another.

The distinction between the licit and the illicit was so elusive in our minds that we could not discern it; we believed everything pertaining to sex was sinful. I was twenty-three years old and a student of philosophy when I had a romantic dream. I was embarrassed to confess it. I didn't know whether it was sinful. I didn't dare discuss it with a fellow student — any such discussion would be reported and immediately and severely punished. After several days of mental torture, I drove myself to the point of talking to the Superior. He told me that the dream was not sinful if I did not give voluntary consent to it.

We were warned constantly about the danger of any association with women. The saints had characterized them as tools of the devil, devils themselves in beautiful forms, instruments permitted by God to exist and test man's virtue of chastity.

One of my duties, while a theological student, was to guide tourists through the weathered corridors and towers of Santa Barbara Mission. The donations of these visitors, mostly non-Catholic, provided the revenue that supported the monastery with its seventy monks. On one occasion, I guided a group of Methodist Epworth League members through the mission towers. The Superior was waiting when I came down. He questioned me in detail as to the number of guests and particularly the number of girls. It had been a mixed group of forty-five. He reprimanded me for being in the tower with such young women and added: " You must always remember that all women are vicious and malicious." He stopped with a start when I innocently asked: " Was your mother? "

Gradually, imperceptibly, the student's idealism of a God of Love becomes blended with fear — fear of authority, fear of sin, fear of the ever-threatening fires of hell.

He must learn humility. Like the saints of old, he must efface himself, he must submerge his personality and his individuality in the vast, world-wide design of the Roman Catholic hierarchy. Again and again, in sermons, prayers, and meditations, he steels himself to go on, to study, to persevere, remembering always the words he is not permitted to forget: " No man putting his hand to the plow and looking back is fit for the Kingdom of God."

He is forbidden to talk except at certain hours of the day. He must arise at dawn to meditate on the iniquity and the omnipresence of sin. He must recite the hourly sections of the Divine Office. Failure to comply with any of these regulations is a sin and may plunge him forever into hell.

As a lay Catholic, I had known of sin. In my catechism lessons I had been taught the difference between mortal (deadly) and venial sin — the former so serious that it meant hell forever, the latter a milder offense that would mean an indeterminate time in the fires of purgatory until the soul became cleansed and fit for the awesome presence of God.

I had been taught the Ten Commandments. I had been taught the six commandments of the Church, which required mass every Sunday, confession, reception of the sacrament once a year, fasting and abstinence on appointed days, compliance with marriage laws, and financial support of the Church. All these commandments bound the Catholic under the penalty of damnation.

But I had never known there were so many sins. It was a mortal sin for me, as a Franciscan, to wear shoes without specific permission. Because the founder of my Order, St. Francis, said so, it was a mortal sin for me to ride a horse. This is because in the thirteenth century only the rich could afford horses; they were a luxury and Franciscans were sworn to poverty. (St. Francis, of course, knew nothing of trains, automobiles, motorcycles, scooters, or airplanes. As he did not condemn them, it is no sin for a Franciscan to use them.)

A priest is taught that if, in his offering of the mass, he ever fails to place in the wine the drop of water symbolizing the union of the divine and the human nature in Christ, it means hell. He sins mortally if he says mass without two lighted candles, or if those candles are not at least 51 per cent beeswax. If he eats a bit of meat on Friday, if he drinks one drop of water (or beer or whisky) after midnight before saying mass, if he eats more than two ounces of breakfast on a "fast" day, he is doomed to an eternity of torment — unless he can confess and receive absolution before he dies.

Moral theology is the study of sin — of sins of thought,

of sins of deed, of sins of omission. It is the study of the
" divine " power of the Pope and the Church, the power
to inflict the penalty of sin on any action or lack of action
which may be deemed necessary for faith or morals or the
preservation of the Church. It reaches its culmination in
the official declaration that if anyone " *thinks* contrary to
the spirit of the Church — *anathema sit*." (*Anathema sit*
means literally " Let him be cut off." It is the official form
of conclusion of every hierarchical denunciation, whether
the decision of an official council or of the Pope himself.)

When we began our course in philosophy, however, we
were told in our classes in logic that we must now think for
ourselves. The existence of God, the immortality of the
soul, the need for religion, must be proven from reason
alone. The Bible was to be ignored. We were to be taught
according to the form of scholastic philosophy, which had
been developed by Thomas Aquinas on the basis of Aris-
totelianism, but in the history of philosophy we would
learn the systems of thought developed by all the great or
alleged great thinkers of the world.

This we were told after we had already spent six years
in intensive Roman Catholic mental discipline. We now
thought we were mentally free. We were temporarily
" agnostics," gamboling in the pure air of unrestricted
mental research.

We did not suspect that we had been already conditioned
against non-conformism. We were like puppies running
around in a wire enclosure — thinking they had escaped the
leash.

We were still monks. We meditated on the sins of humanity and the " truths " of the Church. We attended daily

mass and we recited the scriptural quotations of the Divine Office. This atmosphere prevented the slightest deviation while we progressed through a " free " philosophy and by the light of our own " reason " came to the " irrefutable " conclusion that there was a God, that we had souls, that God had inspired the scriptures, that Christ was divine, that he had founded a " church " — and that the Roman Catholic Church was it.

To emphasize the illusion of free thought, we were encouraged to debate various aspects of philosophical and scriptural questions. But the debates went only so far. We argued evolutionism against creationism — but never the existence of a creator. We debated on whether the whale had swallowed Jonah literally or figuratively — but never on whether our Bible was infallible. We took sides on the manner of reconciling the freedom of human will with the foreknowledge of God — but we did not debate the freedom of the will itself.

It did not occur to us even to want to debate the forbidden issues. In our preconditioned minds, they were not issues. They were simple, accepted, proven truths.

I do not recall having ever seen, in our seminary library, a volume of Nietzsche, Freud, Jung, Schopenhauer, Santayana, Hume, Locke, Berkeley, or Karl Marx. Our Roman Catholic textbooks set up straw men with carefully chosen quotations and to our delight knocked them down and confounded the heretic. In our minds we had mastered and refuted all modern philosophy.

We had studied contemporary religion and modern thought in the same manner that a student in Moscow must study American democracy.

For ten years we covered the history of Christianity.

All we knew of the *Decline and Fall of the Roman Empire* was that it must be false because it attacked the Papacy. We never saw H. G. Wells's *Outline of History* – but we were prepared to refute it. We knew the historical arguments for the primacy of Peter and swallowed it whole — without reading a word against it.

Even in American history, which is so recent that it is difficult to distort, we were given a false picture. The American Republic was portrayed to us as the outgrowth of Roman Catholic doctrine. We were taught that Deist Benjamin Franklin, Unitarian Thomas Jefferson, and other founders of the country borrowed their ideas of freedom and self-representation from Robert Bellarmine, a contemporary Italian cardinal of the Roman Catholic Church.

The 45,000 Roman Catholic priests in America are divided broadly into two groups — " secular " and " regular." " Secular " is from the Latin *seculum* (the world). " Regular " is from *regula* (a rule). The secular priests are those who live in the " world " and are directly under the authority of local bishops. The regular clergy comprise all of those who are under the " rules " of the very many religious orders or " congregations."

The members of most of these orders are monks, friars, or brothers. To become a monk or a friar, one must assume the vows of a particular religious order. He may or may not subsequently become a priest by the reception of ordination. Centuries ago the term " monk " referred only to those who lived alone in isolated cells within a larger enclosure (a monastery). Friars were those who lived together as brethren in a friary. Officially, Franciscans are " Friars Minor " (the Lesser Brethren), and their residences are "friaries." But custom now permits the terms to be used interchangeably, as I do throughout this book.[1]

Historically the orders came into existence either through the individuality and personality of a religious leader in the Church or in response to some specific need. The Benedictines descend from the group who followed St. Benedict in the Dark Ages. The Jesuits formed the intellectual spearhead of the Counter Reformation against early Protestantism. The Maryknoll Fathers were founded a generation ago in New York to train missionaries for the Far East and the Orientals of California.

The orders of the "Church Militant" are sometimes compared to the branches of the American armed services — and their members frequently display the jealous loyalty evident at times among soldiers, sailors, and marines. In their origin, at least, this comparison had some validity. The orders performed different functions within the Church: the Jesuits maintained schools, the Benedictines farmed and wrote books, the Franciscans preached among the poor. But as the centuries passed, the original objectives either became outlived or took a subordinate place among the general objectives of the Roman Catholic clergy. Now practically all orders have local parish churches and priests who work as chaplains in hospitals or teach in Catholic schools.

This general uniformity in the work of all priests, secular and regular, has its counterpart in the similarity of their training. The education of all priests throughout the world is under the supervision of the Vatican. Very little leeway is permitted in curriculum, either in the various countries or among the orders. Most philosophical, moral, and dog-

---

[1] One of the largest Franciscan friaries in the United States, the one in Washington, D.C., is formally known as "The Monastery."

matic textbooks are written by Jesuits, and the volumes by
Davis, Genicot, Donet, Tanquerey, and Vermeersch are as
familiar to all priests as Webster's dictionary.

During our seminary days we had received a double indoctrination. One was in Roman Catholicism. The other
was in Franciscanism. We were taught the history of the
Order and the great deeds of the sons of the lowly Francis
of Assisi who, since 1206, had been the most numerous,
the most learned, the most devoted priests of the Roman
Catholic Church. The robe or " habit," we were taught,
was so much more sacred than that of other religious orders
that we should kiss it as we donned it. We wished we had
lived in the golden years when Franciscan monks had
founded universities in Europe, died in the persecutions under Queen Elizabeth in England, spread in inexhaustible
numbers over the realm of the Spanish Empire, and brought
Roman Catholicism behind the swords of the Conquistadores to Mexico, Colombia, Peru, Argentina, Central America, California — and Tucson, Arizona. I believed that
Franciscans were better preachers than the Dominicans,
better teachers than the Jesuits, and, of course, better priests
than the ordinary secular clergy. Like the Pharisee in the
Temple, I " thanked God that I was not as the rest of men,"
that I was not only a Roman Catholic, not only a priest, but
— above all — a Franciscan.

The rules for both junior and senior seminarians were so
strict — no smoking, no movies, no newspapers, no talking
after bedtime, no leaving the grounds without permission,
no shirking the additional work of washing dishes, cleaning
floors, or scrubbing toilets — that violations were inevitable.
In the junior seminary, the punishments took the form of

withdrawal of picnic privileges, writing of special themes, standing or kneeling in the corner in front of the student body. A common penalty was working on the "chain gang"; whole classes were frequently punished in this manner. In my day the "chain gangs" built basketball and tennis courts and leveled off a baseball diamond. A more severe penalty, though not uncommon, was beating. The offender, at night, in the dormitory, in a spot where all the boys could hear and many could see, was forced to kneel at the side of the bed; his bare buttocks were beaten at the whim of the priest in charge with a rod or a rubber hose till his spirit was chastened and his pride was broken.

In the senior seminary, young men between the ages of eighteen and thirty were humiliated by campusing, confinement to their rooms, or exclusion from the community recreation room. If they reached the dining room after community prayers were finished, they were forced to kneel in the center of the floor with arms outstretched and head bowed until the Superior gave a signal permitting them to rise, state their excuse, and join their fellow monks in the simple, tasteless meal.

This subservience in the monasteries takes the form of a caste system reminiscent of medievalism. The priests, the students or clerics, and the lay brothers are not permitted to intermingle. They live in separate parts of the building. In the Santa Barbara Mission, where we spent our years of philosophy and theology (the senior college years), the priest-professors enjoyed the sumptuous library and lounge, with its radio, the daily papers, current magazines, and a constant supply of wine and liquor. Only priests might enter it. The students' recreation room boasted a phonograph, Catholic magazines, and religious books. The lay brothers, who milked the cows, raised the vegetables, cooked the food, cleaned the church, answered the door, and who were virtually the slaves of both the priests and the students, were confined to their own barren assembly room, containing a few chairs, a table, a few ultra-pious magazines, and their meager ration of tobacco and snuff.

The transcript of credits for my junior and senior years (which, as mentioned in a later chapter, I obtained under threat of a lawsuit after leaving the priesthood) indicated that I had been a good student. I received B as a low grade only twice in the entire twelve years.

It never occurred to me to doubt the accepted and " infallibly " defined dogmatic or moral teachings of Roman Catholicism. But I was prone to argument, and I was frequently accused of inclining towards " modernism " and of holding theories such as human evolution that might be " suspicious of heresy."

I did in the last four years frequently rebel vociferously against the childishness of the discipline imposed upon us. Our entire class was over twenty-one years of age. I was the eldest; in my last year, as the senior, I was official spokesman for the fifty or more theological students. I had to ask humbly for permission for *colloquium* at meals, for an evening of recreation, or for ice cream if we were permitted a picnic at the ocean. (Relatives of the students frequently gave a few dollars for ice cream for the whole student body; but the money could be spent only by special permission of the Superior.) On one occasion the priest forbade the ice cream because it had not been available fifty years before when *he* had been a student. " The Franciscan Order," he said, " forbids innovations." My Irish background overcame my humility. " If that's the way you feel," I asked, "why don't you throw out that electric bulb and get yourself a candle? "

We did not get the ice cream.

This same resistance to progress was conspicuous in care of the sick. The constitution of the Order provides that rooms in every monastery be set aside for the sick, and that an " infirmarian " be chosen to nurse them. The German Franciscan priests had persisted with a remarkable and ancient medical theory. In the infirmary of the Santa Barbara Mission was a cabinet filled with hundreds of bottles, each labeled as a cure for a specific disease. There were different pills for pneumonia, gout, hay fever, arthritis, headache, cancer, heart trouble, and sprained ankles. The pills all looked like saccharin tablets. Once, when I was sent to the infirmary with a minor ailment, I rebelled when the good brother tried to make me take the appropriate pill. I opened all the bottles, took a pill from each, and shocked him by swallowing them all, to prove they were useless. He reported me to the Father Superior as an uncooperative patient. He said the combination of pills would kill me — but I didn't even have a stomach-ache.

We were not permitted to smoke — for disciplinary, not moral, reasons. The priests and the lay brothers, however, smoked cigarettes or pipes or chewed snuff. The Provincial Superior alone could give permission for smoking. This he would do only when " health " reasons justified it. Some of the young monks actually received permission to smoke because it was " beneficial " for their hay fever or sinus trouble. I had no ailments except varicose veins. I wanted permission to smoke merely because I enjoyed it. Three times I appealed to the Very Rev. Novatus Benzing. His reason for refusing was: " Women who smoke can't have

babies." My protestations that my vow of celibacy made
his argument pointless did not move him. So I smoked as a
personal protest against childish discipline.

With a classmate I took up gardening in my leisure time
as an escape. We agreed to maintain the " Sacred Garden "
of the Mission — a spot so dedicated that all women except
royal queens and wives of United States Presidents were
barred from it. We built a hothouse and raised most of the
shrubs and trees that now grace the mission and seminary
grounds. We specialized in cacti and obtained a peculiar
satisfaction out of producing rare specimens from seed faster
than any commercial nursery. When we could get away
from the monastery, we visited the botanical gardens, nurseries, and neighboring estates where the owners had imported unusual cactus plants from Germany, Central America, and the Andes. The most famous students of the Cac-
taceae were Germans. They wrote in German and Latin
and named the plants in Greek — three languages with
which we were familiar. We became the botanical trans-
lators among the Santa Barbara horticulturists and prepared
a glossary of the Greek names of cactus species and varieties. The exotic beauty of the Selenicereus, the varieties
of the Epiphylla, and the sheen of the African Mesembry-
anthemum carried us into a world of beauty that enabled us
to forget enforced prayers, meaningless silence, and physical
scourging.

But we were not unhappy. After years of seclusion and
indoctrination, we knew no other world. We were unaware
of our indoctrination of fear. We thought it was love. We
were constantly told so. We had come to accept celibacy
— the doctrine that prohibits priests and nuns from marry-

ing — as supernatural. The simple pleasures granted us — permission to talk to one another at times, an occasional picnic — satisfied souls that had become not merely childlike, but even childish. We belonged to what we firmly believed to be the only enduring organization in the world — the Roman Catholic Church — and through it we belonged to God. The teachings of Catholic theology and Catholic philosophy, presented with all the finality of authoritarianism, seemed logical and proven. Interpretations of the scripture were right because the Church said so. The Church was right because God said so. After all, had not God granted infallibility to the Church and to the Pope? The scripture said so. It all became an easy, simple form of logic. It was so simple, direct, and apparently true that there was no need to disturb one's mind arguing against it.

As the years went by and ordination approached, we dreamed instead of what we would accomplish once we were ordained priests.

We enthusiastically gathered about any visiting priests on sabbatical leave from the missions of inner China. We listened to the tales of priests stationed in large American cities and vicariously joined them in their mighty bouts with the devil, lifting sinners from the gutters of sin and despair. We prayed that we at last would be the ones to undo the work of Luther, Calvin, Wesley, and Joseph Smith, and bring the ignorant back so that there might at long last in the plan of God be " one fold and one shepherd."

It is my firm belief that every young man of the thirteen of us who knelt before Archbishop Cantwell on ordination day in June 1933 was so thoroughly indoctrinated in his belief in the Roman Catholic Church that he sincerely believed that his was the greatest privilege given to mortal man, that nothing else mattered, neither friends, nor family, nor country — only the culmination of his dream of many years to hear the archbishop pronounce the awesome words, " Thou art a priest forever, according to the order of Melchizedek." To himself and to all the Roman Catholic world he was *alter Christus* — " another Christ."

CHAPTER TWO

"Unto the Least of These"

Ordination to the priesthood and the celebration of his first low mass and first solemn high mass bring the young priest gifts, congratulations, adulation, and the devout veneration of the Roman Catholic laity and leave him floating on a cloud that he feels will carry him, after a life of good works, directly to the throne of God.

During my years of theological study, I had become a favorite of a venerable elder statesman of the Roman Catholic Church of North America, the Most Rev. Orosco y Jiminez, Archbishop of Guadalajara, in Mexico. He had had the distinction of being the object of the animosity of the late President Elias Calles, strong foe of the Roman Catholic Church in Mexico. Three times he had been exiled to the United States — the first time in a cattle car, finally by plane. He was known to all the hierarchy of the world, and he was a confidant of the Pope. Before my ordination he had asked my Franciscan superiors if he might take me to Rome — but the permission was refused. I later learned that it was refused only because of the fear that I might enjoy the trip.

My first mass was recited on June 12, 1933, in a Mexican Catholic church in Los Angeles, to the accompaniment of a full Mexican orchestra, a packed congregation, and goats bleating in the yard outside. The friendly archbishop preached a fiery Spanish sermon about my future as a great leader of Holy Mother Church. After the mass he made me sit in front of the communion railing while the entire congregation filed past and, on bended knee, kissed the palms of my hands. In a more restrained American fashion, this scene was repeated the next Sunday in my home parish, St. Francis, in Sacramento, amid the congratulations of my boyhood acquaintances, my parents' friends, and relatives, including many that I had never heard of before.

The archbishop gave me two flowing albs (the garment worn under the chasuble at the mass) made of exquisite Mexican lace. These, like all the money I received as ordination gifts, were confiscated by my Superior upon my return to Santa Barbara.

Through a special dispensation which must be renewed periodically, the members of many religious orders are ordained at the end of the third year of their four-year course of theology. Before our final year at the senior seminary we were priests " without portfolio." We could and did " say " mass. But we were forbidden to hear confessions, to baptize, or to preach sermons; to do so would have been a sin. We had the inherent power, but to exercise it legitimately we had to have " faculties " — the delegation of pastoral authority by the bishop for the *cura animarum*, the " care of souls."

A priest can function as a priest only in the diocese (a geographical division of the United States set up by the Pope of Rome and placed under the jurisdiction of a bishop) of which he is a member and to whose bishop he has sworn absolute obedience. If he leaves that diocese or has a falling out with his own bishop, he is ecclesiastically and economically helpless. The effect of this type of control over the freedom of priests can readily be realized. A priest may be " a priest forever " but he is not a priest *everywhere*.

In June 1934, the members of the Provincial Council met to decide to which posts we were to be assigned. The Council comprises six priests, including the Provincial himself. They have full authority, subject only to the General of the Franciscan Order in Rome and to the Pope, to make all decisions affecting the life and future of every priest, student, and lay brother of the Order in the Province. They can order the members of the Province from a given friary to any other friary in any other state within the Province. They can take away " faculties." They can punish any member by confinement, " exile " to the desert missions, or other assignments designed to break the human spirit.

The Franciscan Order boasts of its " democracy." The Provincial and his Council are not appointed by Rome — as is the case with some religious orders, notably the Jesuits — but elected. This democracy, however, is more apparent than real. The Provincial Council is elected by the " guardians " — the Superiors of the local Franciscan communities. The guardians, in turn, are appointed by the Council. The same form of " democracy " applies to the Papacy itself. The Pope is elected by the College of Cardinals — and the cardinals are created by the Pope.

But to us, the thirteen young priests champing at the bit to win the world for Christ, the meeting of the Provincial Council seemed to be a gathering of our kindly elders pondering the best assignment for our benefit and for the glory of God.

The decision scattered us over the western states. My assignment was to St. Mary's Church, in Phoenix, Arizona. To a narrow-minded native Californian, it came as a shock. The China missions would have been preferable; after all, there are millions of Chinese. But who in California had heard of Arizona — and did people live there?

The Provincial Superior, in informing us of the decisions of the Council, told me I was being sent to Arizona as a punishment. He said I had been too stubborn, too insistent upon dispensations from discipline for both myself and the other students. The Provincial Council hoped that the heat and hard work of Phoenix would temper my disposition. I and the rest of the class, he said, should imitate the most docile of our group, Father K. Father K., incidentally, became the first of the class to quit the priesthood. He left from St. Mary's in Phoenix, went to Utah, and joined the Mormons.

Each of us had received a new, black, mail-order suit of clothes. We were given a railroad ticket and only enough cash for our meals. I arrived in Phoenix on June 30, 1934. My apostolate had begun.

Phoenix turned out to be a wide, new, wonderful world, filled, to a young priest, with sin and corruption and a multitude of souls needing salvation. My days were occupied with teaching religion to schoolchildren, conducting various devotional services, performing marriages, preaching sermons, and hearing confessions of the penitent. The Grim Reaper continued to harvest, and as a young priest I was sore put at times to console the bereaved and to vindicate, in the face of all forms of tragedy, a kindly, all-wise Providence.

St. Mary's Church, the oldest in Phoenix, had been founded in a tiny adobe chapel in 1882. The original congregation had been almost entirely Mexican. The strong man of the parish's half-century history had been the Provincial Superior who had sent me to Phoenix, the Very Rev. Novatus Benzing. He was a stern, Prussian type of German taskmaster, who exacted full compliance with Church discipline from his parishioners, from his subordinate clergy, and from himself. One of the generation of "priest-builders" of America, he built during his long tenure a huge rectory, a grammar school, a high school; and he replaced the adobe chapel with an elaborate two-story structure which was actually a double church, accommodating a thousand people above and six hundred in the lower church.

The Mexican Roman Catholics, whose parents had built the old adobe and who themselves had contributed heavily to the new edifice, were relegated to the basement. By the time I reached Phoenix, the Mexicans had built their own church a half-mile away. But, among the people and some sympathetic priests, the bitter memory still persisted of the Spanish-speaking priest (one of my former teachers, half-English and half-Mexican) standing in front of the church directing the worshipers: *Mexicanos abajo!* — "All Mexicans downstairs!"

In 1934, six priests ministered to approximately one thousand parishioners — the largest Catholic congregation in the town.

My assignment was that of "co-operator" or assistant, and my duties were any that the pastor might assign. The routine functions were to say mass daily (and at least twice on Sundays), to hear confessions every Saturday afternoon and evening, to teach assigned classes in catechism, and to preach whenever directed. I was rarely allowed to choose a sermon topic: it was assigned by the pastor or, in later years, by the bishop. As a further insurance against modernism or heresy, regulations of the Province required that during our first three years in the ministry sermon manuscripts were to be sent in advance to the office of the Provincial.

As the youngest priest of the parish, I was also given the time-consuming and troublesome chores that the senior clergy did not relish. I became the Roman Catholic chaplain of all the rest homes of this health-seekers' paradise, of the Arizona State Hospital for the Insane, and of the county poor farm. Six years as chaplain of St. Joseph's Hospital and as confessor of most of the nuns in Phoenix gave me an insight into the procedures and ethics of Catholic hospitals that helped in later years when I planned and administered a hospital.

Since leaving the priesthood, I have been questioned more often about confession than about any other teaching or commandment of the hierarchy. What do people confess? Do they really tell the details? Are they sincere? How often do they confess? Does the priest charge them for confessing? More jokes, of both the parlor and the backroom complexion, are circulated among both Catholics and Protestants about confession than about any other practice of Roman Catholicism. To many Catholics the sacrament of confession is a comforting moral bath, to others a dreadful ordeal, and to non-Catholics an intriguing mystery.

Surprising as it may seem, the hearing of confession is the most boring chore that a priest performs. I was completely sincere in hearing confessions, as most priests probably are;

but the monotony of most confessions is anything but exciting. It is a custom in all parochial schools for the children to receive communion on the first Friday of each month. This custom has its origin in a story of a vision of Jesus Christ received by a nun in which promise was given that anyone who received communion on nine consecutive "first Fridays" was guaranteed sure passage to heaven.

The schoolchildren confess the Thursday before. In a large parish all the priests spend the whole day listening to accounts of all the pranks that youngsters play. "Bless me, Father, for I have sinned. I fought with my brother." "I disobeyed my mother." "I teased my sister." "I stole cookies." "I threw rocks at other kids." "I cheated in school." "I laughed in church." Occasionally the half-listening priest comes up with a start when some eight- or nine-year-old confesses that he violated the Sixth Commandment — the Seventh in the Protestant churches — "Thou shalt not commit adultery." Further questioning usually elicits the information that the child has performed the act of voiding or defecation behind a fence or in a neighbor's garage.

The confessions of adults are usually as colorless as those of youngsters. Roman Catholics who confess weekly or monthly are generally the very devout, whose sins are confined to gossip, lack of charity, wrangling with neighbors and relatives, careless distractions while attending mass. People habitually guilty of more serious sins usually confess only once a year, to comply with the commandment which enjoins them to perform their "Easter duty."

There are some sincere adult Catholics who have difficulty with drunkenness or the sins of the flesh. And they will confess these same sins time after time, sometimes week after week. Some, both men and women, touch on these offenses vaguely, hoping the priest will miss the point and spare them from the vituperative lecture that many priests give. Others brazenly confess extreme sexual misbehavior as though they enjoy the retelling and are daring the priest to do something about it.

Priests themselves enjoy the old story of an elderly lady who calmly confessed, " I had illicit relations with a man."

" How recently did this happen? " asked the priest.

" Oh, fifty years ago," the little lady replied.

" Have you ever confessed this sin before? " inquired the puzzled priest.

" Oh, yes, Father, but I just love to talk about it."

Non-Catholics have the impression that Catholics must pay for their sins when they confess. This is true — but not according to the usually accepted idea. Catholics must do penance. The priest may impose any penance he wishes — a box of candy to a wife who has been wronged, an apology to one defamed, restitution to a person defrauded, prayers for the soul of one who has been murdered, or a cash donation to the " poor box." But usually the penance is confined to prayers, the recitation of a few " Hail Marys " or " Our Fathers," or rosaries. The rosary is the recitation of five " Our Fathers " and five decades of " Hail Marys," counted off automatically on a circle of beads.

During the fourteen years that I sat in confessionals, I was told of everything from flirting to murder.

A special excommunication is inflicted on the priest who uses the confessional for purposes of seduction. But there

is none for the woman who confesses the intimate details
of an "unfortunate" evening. Many priests willing to tell
the frank truth would admit that such confessions do
perturb them. I have heard such confessions — and I have
heard the confessions of many priests who have heard such
confessions.

The work of the Lord went on in all sincerity, through
Phoenix winters so delightful that they attracted the world,
and summers so hot that a famous Arizona member of the
cloth quit the Protestant ministry with the remark:
"Preaching in Arizona is useless. The weather is so hot
the residents have no fear of hell."

Among my duties were those of chaplain at the Arizona
State Hospital for the Insane. There the priest's function
was not to try to convert the insane, or even to forgive their
sins — since they were presumed incapable of committing
sin — but rather to furnish them with the last rites on their
deathbeds. This ceremony, extreme unction, did not require consciousness or mental competence on the part of the
patient. It assumed that the Catholic — or the non-Catholic,
if the rite could be performed without anyone's objecting
— would, if he could think, realize that the Roman Catholic
religion is the "true church" and that he would want its
"sacraments." He would presumably want his sins for-
given. Extreme unction automatically accomplishes this
forgiveness, and also guarantees that the recipient has died
as a good Roman Catholic. Many bishops of the United
States require the performance of this ceremony before they
permit burial in a Catholic cemetery.

In 1935 most of southwest Phoenix, though densely popu-
lated, was outside the city limits. Physically it was a fringe

area, " south of the tracks," between the warehouse district and the city dump, permeated with the odors of a fertilizer plant, an iron foundry, a thousand open privies, and the city sewage-disposal plant. Its dwellings for the most part were shacks, many without electricity, most without plumbing and heat. They were built of tin cans, cardboard boxes, and wooden crates picked up by the railroad tracks. In these shacks, babies were born without medical care; they often died because of the extreme temperatures (up to 118 degrees) in the summer or froze to death in winter. Southwest Phoenix helped Arizona attain the highest infant death rate in the nation. Officials of the United States government awarded it the distinction of being the worst slum area in the United States.

The people who lived in the area were the rejects of a lusty, sprawling, boasting cow-and-cotton town that was trying hard to become a city. It was trying to compete for the tourist trade with Miami Beach, San Diego, Tucson. It was trying to bolster the social status of its citizens by shunting across the tracks the immigrants from Oklahoma, Arkansas, and Texas and by veneering itself with the gloss of a symphony orchestra, a Little Theater, and a necklace of resort hotels.

Phoenix did not know — or pretended not to know — that it had slums. But in them lived the Negroes, the Mexicans, the " white trash." There, in 1935, were prostitutes and outlaws, the glassy-eyed victims of denatured alcohol, and the innocent children of minority groups, forced by the " better element " to be born and to live in the slums. The area was often called " The Bucket of Blood " because of its stabbings and shootings.

To a social worker the neighborhood was a cesspool of

poverty and disease, of syphilis, of gonorrhea, of grotesquely deformed venereal babies, of blindness arising from contamination in the birth canal, of women being delivered in one-room shacks by untrained midwives and neighbors, while their children looked on. To a young, shocked, enthusiastic priest, it was an opportunity and a challenge.

I had been called into the neighborhood to minister to a Negro boy dying of tuberculosis. In the same family thirteen children had already died of tuberculosis. The boy was born a Baptist but he died a Roman Catholic. His parents were Baptists, his neighbors were Baptists. I received hearty encouragement from my Superior and my bishop to wean them away from a denomination that has done more for the Negro than any other in America. The Church was willing to advance money to help me do it — providing I paid the money back.

In the center of the neighborhood, a grocery-store building — robbed so often that the chain operating it could not continue to suffer the losses — was up for sale. It was to provide the nucleus of an effort that grew into social work, recreation, medical clinics, paved streets, three housing projects, one of the largest hospitals in Arizona — and my renunciation of the priesthood and Roman Catholicism.

The first step was, of course, the building itself. My childhood experience with newspaper contests helped me now. I entered a subscription contest for the local diocesan Catholic paper. When I won, the $600 prize became the down payment for the grocery store. Dinners, bazaars, barbecues, gambling, panhandling, and begging provided the funds and materials to remodel it into a church and social hall.

The church did not fare as well as the social hall. The

white Catholics of Phoenix contributed well. At the time I congratulated them for their missionary interest. Later I realized that, in spite of Roman Catholicism's protestations of " one Lord, one faith, one baptism," they wished a separate Negro church and Negro school lest they might have to worship together before a common altar. The opposition came from priests, nuns, and laity when I tried to gain acceptance of Negroes in the Knights of Columbus, parish societies, the parochial school (where only a token few were taken), and the Catholic school of nursing.

Most Negro children are graceful dancers. I installed a juke box, which packed the social hall more effectively than the Pied Piper of Hamlin. Many youngsters played and danced till they were too tired to fight or steal or molest. Juvenile delinquency dropped.

There were still the health problems. The most acute was the lack of maternity service. I solicited the aid of St. Joseph's Hospital with the argument that a home delivery service would supplement the training of its medical interns. The state of Arizona had no prenatal clinic and was anxious to establish one. But we had no room.

Adjoining our property was a barber shop. The owner of the building was a Roman Catholic. He became " sold " on the thought of a medical clinic dedicated to the memory of his deceased daughter and gave me the property. We evicted the barber and hauled a truckload of wine and whisky bottles to the city dump.

This building we remodeled into the first maternity clinic in the history of Arizona. Free home deliveries by registered nurses and doctors were offered to all women in the neighborhood — and readily accepted. The doctors, fresh from learning the latest techniques of their medical schools, adapted themselves to the primitive situation by bringing babies into life in shacks and tents, and under bridges. They worked without the benefit of running water, electricity, or sterile equipment. The program centered around the ability, humor, and yeoman service of a sturdy Iowa nurse, Daphne Michael, who accepted the job of mother to the whole blighted area. Twenty-four hours a day, seven days a week, she was on call. A born nurse, a jolly woman, a white angel to the Negroes, she alone, of all white people of Phoenix, men or women, could walk unthreatened and unharmed among brawls, street fights, and bloodletting on the unlighted lanes. She could order the Negroes to quit their fighting and get her a lantern, build a fire, fetch water for boiling from the nearest canal — because Sadie was twisting in anguish and going to have a baby.

But too many of Sadie's babies had ophthalmia neonatorum, gonorrhea of the eyes, or congenital deformity due to syphilis. A venereal clinic, again the first in Arizona, had to be established.

Two physicians, Dr. Leo Tuveson and Dr. Sebastian Caniglia, offered their services. The State Health Department offered the laboratory tests and the neoarsphenamine and mapharsen for treatment. But Sadie and her sisters and their husbands or their equivalents did not like the stabbing needles of blood tests or treatments.

As I had heard of pigs being raffled in Georgia as an inducement to mass treatment of syphilis, I raffled a baby alligator which a friend had given me. For every treatment the patient was given a free chance. Second-hand radios, begged from local department stores, provided further bait — and many were won by people without electricity. The

patient load increased, and soon the line of sufferers with
" bad blood " stretched to the next corner.

My fellow priests demurred. Syphilis, they held, was the
punishment of God on the sexually promiscuous; by providing a cure I was interfering with the curse God had
placed on license. (I never told them, or my Superior, that
during the Second World War I permitted the Army to
operate in our clinic building a prophylactic station for
Negro soldiers.)

During these early years in the development of this center, my man Friday was a tall, light-complexioned, lanky,
lazy, affable, lovable, fearless old Negro named Tom Franklin. He was the father of the dying tubercular boy who had
been the occasion of my entering the neighborhood. He
would wear any cast-off shoes and pants, but he paid at least
fourteen dollars for his Stetson cowboy hat. He had an
inexhaustible store of tall tales about his own past. He had
been treasurer of a Louisiana Negro Baptist church and had
stolen the treasury. He claimed to have murdered a man
and to have jumped to the safety of the Oklahoma Terri-
tory. He openly bragged that he had wrangled horses
and cheated customers in the gambling booths of Bill
Cody's Famous Wild West Show. He had been bootlegger
to judges and to " the Law " in Oklahoma and kept them in
office by hauling truckloads of Indians from precinct to precinct and voting them all as Negroes. He swore he could
make six-year-old bonded bourbon in a half-hour with
iodine and an electric needle better than any stored in a
government warehouse.

Tom Franklin was crowding seventy when I met him.
He had become scrupulously honest and had embraced

Catholicism. He became my janitor, watchman, custodian, sacristan, counselor, assistant, advocate, and personal body-guard — all for free. When our grocery store was remodeled, he slept on a pile of lumber, his sprawling Stetson over his handlebar mustache and a long-barreled, Oklahoma six-shooter under his head. He lectured the " canned heaters " on the evils of " rot gut " and waved them on with his gun when they tried to sleep in the budding church. He lazily shot at the youngsters who climbed the fence — but later explained to me that he had shot high; it took too much energy to chase them, and he was getting old. He would talk for hours with people waiting to see me, describing the greatness of the 101 Ranch, explaining how he cheated in horse trading by filing the teeth of an old nag and blowing air into the veins of his neck to fatten him up, and ending with a lecture on the greatness of the Roman Catholic Church and Father Emmett. He protected the girls on the playground and escorted the nurses to their cars after evening clinics, his six-shooter dangling in his hand with its trigger cocked. Tom even protected me.

One evening, as I stood conversing in front of the mission, a young Negro snapped open a switch knife, touched my stomach, and swore he would avenge the wrongs done by white men to his race by cutting me to bits. Unseen and unheard, the big revolver was jabbed into his back and the quiet voice of Tom Franklin came from beneath the broad brim of the old Stetson hat: " Get along, boy, before I blast you into hell."

We were in depression years, and people were hungry. Negroes were the " last hired and first fired." WPA salaries could not feed large families. In Los Angeles lived a man who had survived on soup kitchens and later had suddenly

become rich when oil was found on his property. He
remembered his soup-kitchen days. He sent truckloads of
food to St. Joseph's Church in Los Angeles. At Christmas
he bought clothes for children, hired chefs to prepare a
sumptuous meal, and sent everyone home with a bulging
basket of food. A friendly priest told him of me and my
effort. Two days before Christmas I received a truckload of
premium ham and bacon. Southwest Phoenix — poor, dis-
eased, and ostracized — ate high on the hog for several days.

The WPA of the early Roosevelt era needed projects.
We needed material help and personnel. The mothers of
the slums needed clothes, bedding, and care for their children, so that they might go north of the tracks to scrub
floors, wash, and cook for seven dollars a week — in order
that their own offspring might survive on sow belly, chitter-
lings, and grits till good times came again or the Sweet
Chariot might swing low and carry their undernourished
spirits into a more Christian world.

We gathered old clothes. I begged bales of cotton. A
kindly bureaucrat provided help. We started a day nursery for the tots of working mothers and a sewing room for
mothers who had so many children they could not leave
home to work. The whole neighborhood stayed warm with
comforters made in " Father Emmett's Mission." Youngsters went to church and to school in clothes made over
from the cast-offs of the rich or the pretended rich. The
Phoenix city council and the Community Chest had begun
to help.

It was inevitable that this activity on the part of a white
Catholic priest should produce a reaction among certain
Negro religious leaders. It did. I was accused of stealing
the money. A mass meeting of the preachers of the section

was advertised in handbills characterizing me as the "voice of Jacob but the hand of Mussolini." I was denounced as buying converts with ham and bacon, and forcing Negroes under my power by giving them clothes inoculated with syphilis germs which spread the disease and then brought them into my venereal clinic. A committee was sent to the Honorable R. C. Stanford, governor of Arizona, with the demand that I be deported from the state.

Instead, we acquired more adjacent property. An old lady lived next to our community center — a Catholic and an eccentric person, who saved matches in cans and water in buckets. She willed her property to me, and a few months later was murdered by a sex fiend. I was accused of the murder. Another neighbor's house burned down. The owner, a Negro preacher, accused me of arson. I was in San Francisco at the time, but the chief of the Phoenix fire department told me that I had allegedly arranged to have my Negro ball team set the fire while I was out of town.

Our land was developed into the only floodlighted playground in southwest Phoenix. From it softball teams, of both boys and girls, went out to defeat all opposition in the city. The players were Negroes. I was told by prominent Catholics that the "niggers" were feeling their oats. The police department called one evening to inform me that most of my senior team were guests of the local bastille. On entering the cell block, I found my boys still attired in their Kelly-green uniforms, each embroidered with the identification "Father Emmett's Mission." (They had chosen green because of my Irish ancestry.) I demanded the reason for their arrest. They had been caught stealing. On their way home from a game, they had passed a produce market. One of the boys had " lifted " a watermelon. A cop had seen him. Why had the whole team been locked up? The desk sergeant admitted that my team had defeated the police team so often that this seemed the only way they could get even. A bit of Irish temper unbecoming a clergyman effected their release.

Most of these boys of my many teams have remained in Phoenix. They served in the armed forces and returned to raise their own families. I meet them frequently in the lodge rooms of the colored Elks, and we invariably reminisce. Only one boy of the entire group has gone bad. " Fats " became a city bus driver. Barnes is now a deputy sheriff. Thompson joined the police force. O'Neal became an athletic director in the Army. Before D-day, when the American Army was twiddling its thumbs in England, Ford Smith, one of my former pitchers, organized a Negro team in London and challenged the whole white Army. Ford pitched and won the game. He returned to Phoenix after the war to join the city recreation department and to continue to pitch for the Phoenix Senators.

I am a member of both the Negro and the white lodges of the Elks. (Church officials severely reprimanded me for joining. Priests must avoid membership in groups not under Catholic control.) When the Phoenix group of the I.B.P.O.E. of W. attempted to borrow some $40,000 to build a more adequate new structure, the local banks were very reluctant to make the loan. One vice-president asked me if I would grant the loan if I were in his position. Yes, I said. Would I attest that the colored Elks would pay back the loan? They would pay it off before maturity, I answered. Within two years after they got the ten-year loan, it was paid off.

When their new clubhouse was dedicated, on August 24, 1946, the program referred to me as " the good padre of the slums, champion and friend of the needy and unfortunate and in fact, of all men, irrespective of race, creed or religious denomination." The records of the Phoenix lodge show:

At the Mortgage Burning Ceremony of Wm. H. Patterson Lodge #477, I.B.P.O.E. of W., Honorable J. Finley Wilson, Grand Exalted Ruler, took the opportunity not only to compliment but to confer a life-time membership on Father Emmett McLoughlin, O.F.M.[1] This degree was conferred in recognition of the work of Father Emmett in improving the lot of the underprivileged and his cooperation with the Wm. H. Patterson Lodge in fostering its charitable contributions. J. Finley Wilson declared that, as Grand Exalted Ruler, with all power invested in him by the Grand Lodge, he hereby declared and conferred the degree of Honorable lifetime membership on Father Emmett McLoughlin. Done the 22 day of February, in the year of our Lord 1948.

When I lost my wallet to a pickpocket on a fiesta day in Mexico, the loss of the colored Elks' golden membership card meant more to me than the loss of the money.

The only other white man to receive this recognition was my close friend Ray Busey, one of the original members of our hospital corporation, a trustee ever since, and at that time the mayor of Phoenix.

After five years, the work in southwest Phoenix was solidly established. "Father Emmett's Mission" — officially, St. Monica's Community Center — was an institution.

I had to humiliate myself, to beg, to accept insults, to wait in offices, to explain the needs of the poor, to be brushed off like an unwanted salesman, and to persist for the sake of my

---

[1] " O.F.M." is the abbreviation for Order of Friars Minor.

people till I was tossed the crumbs that would send me on
my way. A fellow priest suggested that while passing
through San Francisco I might appeal to the president of a
drugstore chain for medical supplies. I did. He listened to
my plea for the poor of Phoenix. In an impatient manner
he informed me that the drug company was not concerned
with the health of the people of Phoenix and would contribute no drugs; and would I please leave, as he had business to attend to. I stood on the curb on San Francisco's
ancient Mission Street. The Ferry Building looked cold
in the swirling fog. The clanging streetcars echoed the indifferent spirit of a large city.

I felt somehow that I was facing a crisis, that if I accepted
this rejection I had lost my initiative, that I must conquer
some obstacle if I were to retain the courage to battle the
odds necessary to succeed as a crusader. Down the street
loomed the ugly gray shape of the main offices of the Southern Pacific Railroad. Its president and vice-president were
Roman Catholics. I asked for an appointment with the
vice-president. He knew Phoenix. Our venereal clinic
was near his railroad tracks. His porters and dining-car
waiters were all Negroes. I knew that cleaning up syphilis
could protect his employees and his passengers, and that
a donation of $2000 would finance the clinic for a year.

He was sympathetic but said that company policy prohibited such donations. If they gave in Phoenix, how could
they refuse in Bakersfield, Stockton, Glendale, Yuma,
Tucson, El Paso, and Tucumcari? " But," he continued, " if
the railroad could haul anything for you . . ." I regained
my confidence. I thought of my mother's piano, untouched
for years, the possible beginning of an orchestra for the
youngsters at the mission. My mother consented, and the

Southern Pacific hauled the instrument a thousand miles from Sacramento to Phoenix, with daily telegraphic reports as to its whereabouts and safety.

Now we needed trumpets, clarinets, saxophones, and bass horns. The National Youth Administration was conducting a project in the state of Virginia for the reconditioning of discarded musical instruments. They were available, but the recipient had to pay the freight. The Southern Pacific did not reach Virginia. But I was chairman of the local county chapter of the American Red Cross. Gladly I accepted an offer to attend the national convention in Washington, D.C. The NYA agreed to crate the instruments and truck them to the capital. I got in touch with Arizona and California delegates, borrowed their railroad tickets, and checked the crated instruments as personal baggage. Everybody was happy — especially the Negro children when the WPA music project furnished teachers and a band was organized. Soon the green-and-white uniforms of Father Emmett's Mission Band were part of every parade, even that of the Ancient Arabic Order of the Mystic Shrine.

Dr. Thomas Parran, a Roman Catholic, Surgeon General of the United States Public Health Service, described the varied services of St. Monica's Community Center as the most dramatic and successful example in America of the co-operation of public and private agencies. Besides his agency we had support from the Surplus Commodity Corporation, the Farm Security Administration, the Works Progress Administration, the National Youth Administration, the Arizona Department of Health, the Maricopa County Health Department, the City of Phoenix, St. Joseph's Hospital, and the Phoenix Community Chest.

Praise also came from within the Roman Catholic Church. The reactionary Brooklyn *Tablet,* on October 15, 1938, said of the project:

Phoenix, Ariz. Oct. 7. Launched only three years ago, St. Monica's Community Center here, which ministers to the spiritual and physical needs of the poverty-stricken Colored population of this city, has become one of the most interesting settlement projects in the Southwest.

Under the direction of Rev. Emmett McLoughlin, the center, known to residents as Father Emmett's Mission, has extended its activities into various fields of welfare work and has merited the praise of the public authorities.

Franklin D. Roosevelt's startling statement that one-third of the nation was ill clothed, ill fed, and ill housed was painfully true of Phoenix. It became apparent that playgrounds, social halls, clinics, doctors, nurses, and orchestras could merely treat the symptoms of a sick neighborhood so long as the basic disease remained. That disease lay in the miserable conditions under which these people lived. Children would not go home when the home was a tin shack with no electricity or running water. Mothers were not interested in maintaining a household when they had to carry water from an irrigation canal to wash their dishes. Fathers could face neither themselves nor their families when their wages, garnered from picking cotton, shining shoes, or the WPA were so meager that they could rent nothing better than a hovel and when a segregated society forced them to live in a ghetto of squalor. The beer joints, bars, and pool halls were not so much havens of relaxation as avenues of escape and forgetfulness. In 1938, there were more than eight thousand sub-standard dwellings in Phoenix.

The United States Housing Act was passed by the Congress in 1937. With the aid of an architect, Leslie J. Mahoney, and a reporter, Bob Macon of the Phoenix *Gazette*, I embarked on another crusade. We first had to convince the state legislature. To do that we had to convince the constituents that Phoenix really had slums.

Bob Macon ran a daily headline story with photographs. I took motion pictures of the leaning shacks, " one-holers," and congested firetraps. One of them was actually a horse stable on a fifty-foot lot, which had been converted into one-room shelters housing twenty families — of people, not horses — at $20 per month per family.

I showed the pictures to and pleaded with Baptists, Methodists, Catholics, Presbyterians, Orthodox and unorthodox Jews, Kiwanians, Rotarians, Lions, the PTA, the YMCA, the YWCA, and the man on the street.

When the legislators met in January of 1939, I was appointed chaplain of the state House of Representatives. I violated the neutrality of my appointment by arguing public housing with representatives from every part of the state.

I pleaded for public housing every day before the session started, and threatened to forget to bless the members if they didn't pass the enabling law. Those senators who good-naturedly reminded me that chaplains were forbidden to lobby for any bill made no move to eject me even though I brought the issue into a prayer which, as I recall, ran like this:

O God, who has inspired thy Son to say, " The foxes have holes and the birds of the air have nests but the son of man hath not where to lay his head," be pleased to bless these representatives of all thy people. Bless in particular those whose constituents are forced to live in the manner of the Master because of poverty and the greed of their fellow men. Pour forth thy wisdom upon these thy servants that they may be guided in their deliberations toward laws that will enable thy children to live in homes of decency and to praise thee with dignity. Amen.

In the last hour of the last day, as adjournment drew near the enabling law was passed, and federal funds for eradi-cating the slums became possible in Arizona.

The Phoenix city council immediately appointed a hous-ing authority, and the mayor named me as chairman.

The fight had just started. Funds must be secured, sites located, property purchased, architects chosen, materials decided upon, commercial greed and graft beaten away from a $2,000,000 project.

The Phoenix Real Estate Board came to life when it realized that this " socialistic " sin had been committed in its own bailiwick. Roman Catholic owners of slum bonan-zas put pressure on the clergy, and the clergy put pressure on me. I was about to destroy an incentive to sanctity, they said; poverty and deprivation were conducive to self-sacrifice, self-sacrifice fostered holiness; the contemplated new homes would give poor people luxury, and luxury led to sin. But I had come to believe that, although lilies may grow in the alley, and a saint may have arisen occasionally from the slums, still citizenship, decency, and religion flour-ish best when a home is not a shack and sanitary facilities mean something more than an outside faucet and a hole in the ground.

Three sites were chosen for projects to accommodate more than six hundred families. All three were in slum areas, but the cries that rose to the city council would have led bystanders to believe that we were about to tear

down the country club. The property owners demanded
public hearings. The dogs that barked showed who had
been hit. Several were Roman Catholics. Some were also
Irish. They had complained for years of the grinding, ex-
ploiting tactics of the British. Now they were caught own-
ing properties in slum areas, covered with shacks, from
which they extracted rents that returned their investment
within a year. No money was needed for maintenance. A
single outdoor water faucet would do for twenty families.
A single outside toilet would suffice. Because it rarely
rained, roof repair was unnecessary. And none of the
shacks was ever painted.

The golden goose was about to be slaughtered. And if
it were, the clergy was told, what would happen to their
church collections? I presided at a meeting in the city hall
after the police had taken a shotgun from one irate citizen.
I heard myself denounced as a disgrace to the clergy and as
a renegade Irishman who had out-Cromwelled Cromwell.
The other members of the housing authority stood behind
me. The sites were approved. We condemned the properties and tore down the shacks.

The houses were built — without graft. Construction
costs were the lowest in the nation: $1750 per house, for
houses of concrete and brick, roofed with tile. Rents were
as low as $10 per month.

The projects opened as America went to war.

Families moved in from the shacks and the tents to live
according to the American standard, with a toilet, a heater,
and a refrigerator. They learned to respect property. Juvenile delinquency dropped, families were stabilized, and
less-privileged Americans raised their heads in public. A
blue star hung in a window of almost every home. A boy

from the slums had gone to fight for his newly found American way of life. As the war went on, all too many of those blue stars turned to gold.

We had helped give those boys of the slums a way of life worth dying for.

CHAPTER THREE

"A Corrupt Tree"

When the housing projects opened, I had been a Roman Catholic priest for seven years. I had said mass every day. I had heard confessions every Saturday. I had preached a sermon every Sunday. People, Catholic and non-Catholic, were kind enough to tell me that I had become firmly rooted in the religious, economic, and welfare life of Phoenix. I was called a good priest. The daily newspapers called me "the people's padre." The Spanish-language newspaper, *El Sol*, had headlined a picture of me in two-inch type across the front page: " EL SANTO DEL SOUTHSIDE DE PHOENIX! " — " The saint of the southside of Phoenix." The Negro weekly, *Arizona Sun*, spanned its front page with the caption " GUARDIAN OF THE SOUTHSIDE OF PHOENIX."

But inwardly I had become a miserably unhappy priest.

Gradually, as the years went by, it began to occur to me that something was wrong. I observed that in many cases the spark of religious fervor and enthusiasm in the work of the priesthood did not seem to weather the years. Middle-aged and older priests seemed, for the most part, resigned but apathetic. They said mass, they preached sermons, they heard confessions — but they did it as a job, not as a religious dedication. As I came to recognize this attitude of apathy in other priests, I realized that the same attitude was developing in me. The fire that burned through my soul on ordination day — that fire to make the world Catholic — was hardly a flicker of its former intensity. I no longer cared if the world ever became Catholic. Something was wrong.

Every priest is supposed to meditate daily on the truths of religion, his own moral life, and his work for the salvation of souls. Once a year he must make a " retreat " — a stepping back from his active daily routine to a contemplation of his purpose in existence and in the priesthood. I was thought by my confreres to be a " worldly " priest — one interested more in housing, health, and hospitals than in sermons, sin, and salvation. But I did meditate. I realized that my past, my present, and possibly my soul were tied to the Roman Catholic Church. I had to go on. I had been taught all my life that the Roman Catholic Church was the Kingdom of God on earth. But I was losing faith. Was I losing faith in God? No — for I saw him everywhere, in his heavens, in his nature, and in the eyes of the baby I was privileged to help bring into the world through our clinic. Was I losing faith in the Church? Certainly I *was* torn between what I had been taught in the seminary and what I learned from my own experience of the practice of the Church.

Since the days of Lord Duppa, the remittance-man pioneer of central Arizona who envisaged a fabled, Phoenix-like metropolis on the ruins of an ancient civilization, and before the days of air conditioning, people in Phoenix have slept under the stars during the hot summer months. The builder of St. Mary's Church added a practical, non-ecclesiastical feature — an open porch fifty feet above the ground. The Arizona air is so clear that at night the stars seem to crowd each other out of the heavens; and on summer evenings, alone, I watched those beacons in space, tried to count the silent falling stars, and pondered over my own soul, its relationship to the Catholic Church and to my search for God. "By night I sought Him whom my soul loveth. I sought Him but I found Him not. I will rise now and go about the city in the streets and in the broad ways I will seek Him whom my soul loveth."

To me, since early boyhood, the Roman Catholic Church had been the representative of God on earth. I believed it. My parents died believing it. My ancestors in Ireland had believed it so strongly that they had been willing to be slaughtered by Cromwell, had gone through the potato famine, and still boasted that seven hundred years of persecution by the world's greatest empire could not take from them the thing that was more sacred than their national existence — their allegiance to the Roman Catholic Church, and to the Pope of Rome.

I had sincerely and without restraint given my life for twenty years to the Church. Should I continue to give my life to a system that could involve the exploitation of my years of service for the political aggrandizement of the hierarchy?

My dissatisfaction at the time was not due to any doctrinal doubts. I did not disbelieve the doctrine of the Trinity, the divinity of Christ, the seven sacraments, baptism, mass, or even confession. I did not yet disbelieve the infallibility of the Pope, the historical succession of the bishops, and my own power to forgive sins.

My first disillusionment arose from the inconsistency between word and action of the Roman Church and the Franciscan Order — from their failure to put their ideals into practice.

I had misgivings about abstract doctrinal matters — but no well-defined doubts, because they did not touch my daily life or the lives of the poor with whom I worked. Still naive, I obeyed the papal law of reading no book that questioned a Roman Catholic doctrine.

I was living every day with the Church's moral code, trying to apply it in my own life and that of my people.

I had left the seminary believing that charity was a characteristic of the Church, that it meant a kind word as well as a crust of bread, and that it applied to all men.

I thought that poverty meant detachment from the chains of material things and that money was intended as a means of survival and not as an end in itself.

I had been taught that the Church was the " mother of learning " and had held high through the centuries the light of Christian education, and that the countries she influenced were the enlightened ones of the world.

I had been taught that rosaries, medals, relics, and the ceremonies of religion were inducements to prayer and devotion and not superstitious idols themselves.

I had believed that the Church's teachings on divorce, mental sin, birth control, and celibacy would produce moral lives and spiritual freedom.

The Roman Catholic Church preaches love. " Faith, hope and love, and the greatest of these is love." But the young priest leaving the protective shelter of a seminary to enter the active ministry in a parish is soon shocked by the lack of charity he encounters. He finds this lack first among the clergy themselves. Suspicion and distrust of pastors and Superiors is the rule and not the exception. The Superiors, imbued with the doctrine that their decisions are those of God, exercise their power frequently, more with the spirit of a top sergeant than that of a " servant of God."

It is a common saying among the Catholic laity that whenever a priest becomes popular and successful he is transferred elsewhere. A co-worker of mine in the Phoenix parish, Father Kilian Pryor, was invited to speak before labor groups. He was invited again and again. He organized a credit union, with the advice of the president of the state federation of labor. Word went to the bishop from certain fellow priests and prominent lay Catholics that Father Kilian was dangerously friendly to labor. He was ordered out of the diocese in 1948. We had been intimate friends for many years. He knew that I was on the verge of quitting the priesthood, and had argued with me that I should never leave. But in his own new assignment he found himself the pawn in a dispute between the Franciscan Order and his new bishop. In eventual disgust he gave up his post. He is doing well as an executive in industry.

One of my classmates was outstandingly successful in youth work in San Francisco. He organized among the young Catholic workers an American counterpart of the Jocist movement in France. It was designed to bring practical Catholicity into the daily lives of youth, in their studies, their jobs, their recreation. He was too successful. After years of fruitful activity, he received a sudden order to leave the city and was assigned to a parish in Spokane, Washington. When my own relationship with the Order was becoming strained, he wrote: ". . . I just made a tour of California, from San Diego to the northern border, and talked to all the priests to say goodby to the boys. The general impression is that what is desired in the priesthood is a low-grade mediocrity — lots of little pawns . . . yes-men with no individuality or ambition or dreams."

An even more intense antagonism generally prevails among the various religious orders, and between them and the secular clergy — especially the bishops. The story is told of a Jesuit and a Franciscan who stood on the edge of a canyon. The Jesuit called out, " *Quae est Franciscanorum regula?* " (" What is the rule of the Franciscans? "). The echo came back, " *Gula, gula* " (" Gluttony, gluttony "). To which the Franciscan called out, " *Diabolus est Jesuita!* " (" The Devil is a Jesuit! "). And the echo, " *Ita, ita* " (" Yes, yes ").

In general, bishops have little use for the religious orders. They can't control them as effectively as they can their own secular clergy. In fact Rome, through the Sacred Congregation of the Religious, has set up controls to protect the orders from losing their best parishes to the bishops.

It is a common practice for bishops to reserve the wealthier neighborhoods for their own secular clergy, while relegating to the religious orders the less prosperous areas. If by chance an order should build a financially successful parish the bishop is apt to take it away — unless the order has circumvented him by having the parish rights approved in Rome.

The power of the bishop over his clergy is as unlimited as that of a monarch in the Middle Ages. Only the right of capital punishment is denied him. It will come as a surprise to most Americans to know that there are institutions in the United States to which priests are sent by the bishops without any trial. One is in Oshkosh, Wisconsin, operated by the Alexian Brothers. Another, supported by the hierarchy, is in Jémez Springs, New Mexico, near Albuquerque. The "crimes" for which priests are sent to those institutions are generally alcoholism, insubordination, or lapses in the realm of celibacy.

A devout Franciscan, well known in the San Francisco area for the high spirituality of his sermons and writings, injudiciously stated in a sermon that he believed sex education would be advantageous for Catholic youth. He was reported to ecclesiastical authorities, ordered to recant, and summoned to Rome. He was deprived of the priestly powers of saying mass, preaching, and hearing confessions, and reduced to the status of a lay brother. During many of the years I was stationed at St. Mary's he was there, a servant of the clergy, cooking their meals and living within himself in solitary communion with God.

The lack of charity among Catholic clergy and laity toward non-Catholics is appalling. This will be evidenced in many of the letters from Catholics that appear in a later chapter. The following story may be extreme, but it is true. An aunt of mine lives in a large city in the United States. Early one cold morning, returning home from daily mass, she found a bottle of whisky on a bannister near the sidewalk. She slipped it into her purse and in the safety of her home examined it. The seal had been broken. She hurried to her Irish Catholic grocer. He advised her against drinking it because it might have been poisoned by a Protestant and left as a trap for a Catholic. She kept the bottle. Finally, a man knocked on her door looking for work. His name was Irish. She gave him the job of painting the front steps. As he worked, she inquired into his religious background and found, to her dismay, that he was a Protestant. As she pondered over this disgrace, he complained about the nippy cold day and confessed that a good shot of whisky would help him paint better. She hurried inside, got the bottle of possible poison, and gave him a generous drink. " If it had killed him," she said, " it wouldn't have mattered because he wasn't a Catholic anyhow." She drank the rest of the bottle herself.

I had been reared to feel that non-Catholics were to be tolerated but not trusted. The Roman Catholic Church teaches — despite its American hierarchy's protestations to the contrary — that only Roman Catholics can enter heaven. A side door to the kingdom is left open for non-Catholics who are " invincibly " ignorant and therefore would be Catholics if they were not so stupid. Hence, we were taught, the only salvageable Protestants were the morons who could not perceive the logic of the faith. Intelligent Protestants were, therefore, going to hell with malice aforethought because their ignorance could not be " invincible " or morally excusable.

The strictness of this doctrine is unpopular among Catholics in America. The Jesuit Father Feeney, of Boston, was excommunicated because he held to it. But it is clearly stated in the decrees of the Council of Trent, the depository of Roman dogma. It is taught to every Roman Catholic priest in his course in theology. When he denies in Catholic publications and before his faithful that this is an official doctrine, he speaks falsely.

My forays into social work, public health, community

co-operation, labor relations, and housing brought me into association with thousands of non-Catholics. I found them friendly, informed, sincere, religious, intelligent, and much more interested in and willing to sacrifice for the " under-dogs " — the forgotten men and women — than were the members of my own faith and its clergy. They were certainly not " invincibly " ignorant, nor could I believe that those good, sincere people were destined to hell. My friendship with them weaned me from the smug exclusive-ness of Roman Catholicism. I felt that they were just as good as I and any other Roman Catholic, and in the eyes of a common God possibly a great deal better. This reali-zation of the intelligence, devotion, and moral integrity of most Protestants was a shock to me. This certainly explains the reason why the hierarchy does not want its clergy to form any intimate acquaintance with them.

The development of our community center and my cam-paign for public housing had led to frequent invitations for speeches at local public high schools, at the Phoenix Junior College, and at the Arizona State College. I was always re-ceived courteously, listened to attentively, and questioned intelligently by students who showed much more dignity and desire to learn than those I had taught in the Catholic high schools. My experiences made it impossible for me to believe the hierarchy's denunciation of the public-school system as unmoral, irreligious, materialistic, and contributing to juvenile delinquency and adult crime in America.[1]

In the early 1940's it was my privilege to be invited to New York to collaborate with Nathan Straus on a book about public housing. As it would have been sinful for

[1] See, for instance, the discussion in *Our Sunday Visitor*, September 4, 1949.

a Franciscan to stay in a hotel without special permission,
I was given a room in the St. Francis rectory on Thirty-
first Street in downtown New York. It was Passion Week,
the week before Holy Week which, with all the beautiful
ancient pageantry of the Roman Catholic Church, com-
memorates the death of Christ. Services were being held
throughout the day. I listened to a beautiful sermon about
the love of Christ for humanity and his death for the salvation of all men. Outside the massive church door, middle-
aged women with stacks of Father Coughlin's paper were
screaming headlines of hate and bigotry toward Jews. I
went to the pastor's office and complained about this patent
inconsistency and lack of charity. He politely told me it
was none of my business — and that it was a good source of
revenue. Furthermore, he added, Coughlin was right and
the Jews deserved it.

I described the incident to Mr. Straus, and a few days
later found the counterpart of the story in his office. As
we were working, I wearing a clerical suit with a Roman
collar, several rabbis came in. They saw me and stopped
in astonishment. What was Nathan Straus, a Jew, doing
with a Roman Catholic priest? He took them into an
inner office and after a few moments came back and introduced them. When they left, he told me that he had explained that I was from the west and not in sympathy with
Father Coughlin and the anti-Semitism which was apparently characteristic of the eastern Catholic clergy. That
visit is delightfully recalled in Mr. Straus's book *The Seven
Myths of Housing*.

One of the cornerstones of Roman Catholic teaching is
the doctrine of the Mystical Body of Christ. It is based

on the words of St. Paul, " For ye are all children of God by faith in Jesus Christ. For as many of you as have been baptized into Christ have put on Christ. There is neither Jew nor Greek, there is neither bond nor free, there is neither male nor female; for ye are all one in Christ Jesus." The doctrine means that all Christians are a part of the same entity, united in a real — though so-called " physical " — way with Christ himself. Hence, any offense committed against a fellow Christian of whatever race, sex, or station in life is an offense against Christ himself. The doctrine is further strengthened by Christ's own words: " When I was hungry, ye fed me. When I was thirsty, ye gave me to drink. When I was naked, ye clothed me. Inasmuch as ye have done it unto one of the least of these my brethren, ye have done it unto me."

It had always seemed to me that the most obvious application of this doctrine was in the field of race relations. Within Catholic institutions and organizations, segregation was to me the most inconsistent thing in the whole pattern of the Church's theory and practice. In most parts of the country there was not even the excuse of local custom to justify it. There was segregation in parochial schools even where it was non-existent in the public-school system.

No Negro student was admitted to St. Louis University, and a young Jesuit priest was hastily transferred back to California when he recommended that the student body protest. There was segregation in Notre Dame University even though the student body wanted it abolished; for years I angered my fellow priests by rooting against Notre Dame's football team even when they were playing Southern Methodist University and the University of Southern California (Methodist).

Racial segregation was still more incongruous to me because it could be abolished so easily. A few words cabled from the Pope to the Apostolic Delegate in Washington, and on to the American hierarchy, could, within twenty-four hours, abolish all racial segregation in every Catholic university, school, and nursing school in the land. It has been said that the Pope wouldn't dare thus antagonize the American bishops. He risked such antagonism, however, when he ordered every priest to withdraw from Rotary clubs.

Protestant churches do not have a perfect record either (although they are making steady and sometimes spectacular improvement). But the Protestant denominations do not have all-powerful hierarchies that could abolish this evil with the stroke of a pen.

How could I believe in the Mystical Body of Christ — and refuse to accept a Negro into a school, a church, or a hospital? How could I live with myself if I remained part of a Church that not only ignored, but in practice denied, what it so solemnly taught?

The fact that sisters' hospitals refused to teach nursing to white and Negro girls together came as a shock to me. In 1941 a Phoenix Negro Catholic girl wished to become a nurse. I promised to arrange the details and got in touch with the nun who was director of nurses in St. Joseph's Hospital. She refused. She stated that such a radical practice could not be carried out. It would not be tolerated by patients, doctors, or other nurses. "But how about the teachings of our Church," I pleaded; "don't you believe in the Mystical Body of Christ?" She claimed she did, but that it didn't matter; the girl would not be admitted. I lost my temper and swore to the Sister of Mercy that I would build a hospital myself. I would build a nursing school that would take in girls from all over America, black and white, red and yellow, and prove to all the nuns and priests and bishops that the teachings of Christ could cease to be mere empty words and become living realities. I stalked out of her office, leaving her stunned, in her black robes of archaic piety.

The next day she called me by telephone. She asked if I still felt that I could build a hospital and nursing school. I insisted that I did. She suggested that I consult a psychiatrist — and hung up.

Still trying to help, I wrote to the Colored Graduate Nurses Association of New York. I found that only fourteen nursing schools in the United States admitted both colored and white girls. None of them was under the auspices of the Roman Catholic Church.

The practice of segregation on the part of the Roman Catholic hierarchy was and is a direct violation of its own official promulgation. The bishops, in their annual meeting many years ago, issued this statement: " We owe a special obligation of justice to see that they [the Negroes] have in fact the rights which are given them in our Constitution. This means not only political equality, but also fair economic and educational opportunities, a just share in public welfare projects, good housing without exploitation and a full chance for the social advancement of their race."

This inconsistency between teaching and practice in the matter of race was the first clear proof to me that the Roman Catholic Church, at all levels, was failing to live up to its own ideals. To me it could not be inconsistent and be of God. This was without question an evil fruit of the tree of Catholicism. Its evil was not superficial nor due to an outside influence such as the " human element " — blamed for all shortcomings in the clergy or the laity. The evil was inherent in the fruit. The rottenness reached back to the roots of the tree and to me con-

demned Catholicism with Jesus' own words: "A corrupt
tree bringeth forth evil fruit."

In general, young Catholic boys interested in the priesthood do not choose a religious order because they prefer its
history, traditions, or ideals. They are too young to iden-
tify the Dominicans with preaching, the Franciscans with
poverty, or the Jesuits with education. They join those orders because of personal contact with Dominicans, Franciscans, or Jesuits.

My identification with the Franciscan Order had, of
course, taken place during my seminary days. Through
it all, like a golden thread in the robe of the Order's glory,
was woven the ideal of Franciscan poverty.

As a youngster I had known nothing and cared less about
the vow of poverty. I had seen and known poverty. To
help our family eat, I had mowed lawns, watched babies,
sold newspapers, and picked up beans one at a time in the
wake of threshing machines. I had not liked poverty.

But I was taught that poverty was a spiritual, sacred thing.
The Rule composed by St. Francis himself stated: "As pilgrims and strangers in this world, serving the Lord in poverty and humility, let them go confident for alms, nor should
they be ashamed because the Lord made himself poor for us
in this world. This is the sublimity of the highest poverty
which has made you, my dearest brothers, heirs and kings
of the kingdom of heaven: poor in goods, but exalted in
virtue."

The general conventions of the Order, with the consent
of the Pope, had strengthened the Rule by the detailed regu-
lation of the "constitutions." Regarding poverty they
state:

135. The poorness of the garments must always be attended to, as well in the price as in the color; roughness and poverty must always be present in them.

144. The Friars shall walk in open sandals, to the exclusion of any other covering for the feet of any material whatsoever. The sandals must be entirely free of all vanity and singularity. It shall be lawful to use boots, shoes, leggings or slippers, only in case of necessity and with the permission of the Superiors.

151. Let the Friars sleep on a straw mattress, placed over bare boards or on an inflexible iron framework. With the Superior's consent, however, weak old men and the sick are permitted to use hair mattresses. The Friars shall not sleep without the habit or at least without their tunic, drawers and cord.

296. . . . They shall take diligent care that the furniture of the convent be in accordance with the seraphic poverty which we have professed.

299. Let the superfluous and vain use of things be completely eliminated and let all the Friars, especially the older ones, by whose example the others are led, be content with few and poor things as become the servants of God and the followers of most holy poverty.[2]

It was obvious to me from the time of ordination that poverty, as taught by St. Francis and as practiced in the Middle Ages, was not entirely suitable to the mode of life in the United States. St. Francis might well have forbidden toilets, electricity, refrigerators. As I grew older in the priesthood, it seemed that some older monks had made poverty a fetish. Poverty became a goal in itself, rather than a means to the detachment from wealth in order that priests might devote themselves more freely to serving people. On the other hand I saw in the Franciscan monasteries an almost complete ignoring of the constitutions on poverty.

[2] For all quotations from *The Rule and Constitutions of the Friars Minor*, I have used the edition published in 1936 by the St. Anthony Guild Press.

To me the great inconsistency lay in the protestation of poverty to the monks and the laity in sermons and exhortations — while those ideals and the constitutions were completely ignored by some of the officials of the Order.

During depression years, while the poor used lard or margarine, the monks ate butter. Regardless of cost no inferior grades of meat were tolerated. One of our Superiors would not allow the cook to use processed cheese because a consumer survey had judged it inferior to naturally aged cheese. The monasteries had the conveniences of the better classes — not the austerities of the poor.

The Rule and the constitutions were specific regarding the prohibition of the use of money:

On the Prohibition of Money

231. It is a basic precept of our Order that the Friars shall receive money neither of themselves nor through an interposed person. While we may have the use but not the ownership of necessary things, we can have neither the ownership nor the use of money. Hence any handling whatsoever of coins or money which is not purely natural, that is, in any commercial way, no matter to whom the coins or money may belong, is absolutely forbidden us.

232. Whoever, therefore, shall have procured, received, expended or carried coins of money, or whoever shall have substituted another to receive money to be used for his own needs or the needs of others, or shall have money deposited with himself or with another, shall be subject to the punishments decreed against proprietors.

233. Boxes or receptacles for receiving pecuniary alms, even those offered for masses, are absolutely forbidden both in the church and in any other place. Nor are the Friars allowed to solicit money in our churches, even during a sermon, for themselves, for the church of the Order or for the convent.

241. The Friars, whether prelates or subjects, are not allowed to buy, sell or commute anything juridically, nor to enter upon other contracts nor make deeds of any kind in regard to the use

of money, without the syndic or his substitute. If at times it should be necessary for the Friars to make out a promissory note for money received by the syndic or his substitute, let it be couched in words not repugnant to our Rule, as if the Guardian were merely to say that some money had been received.

This section of the Rule and the constitutions, although read to and instilled into student monks, is simply and completely ignored by many Franciscan priests and officials in the United States. Those boxes so explicitly forbidden in Section 233 are very prominent in Franciscan churches. The syndic referred to in Section 241 is supposed to be a layman who volunteers his services to handle money from collections, alms, and poor boxes. Personally I had never heard of such a syndic appointed for any church or monastery. Priests count the collection, accept mass offerings, collect the profits from fairs, bazaars, and bingo games, and make bank deposits just as casually as the owner of the corner grocery.

The constitutions are very explicit regarding legacies and estates:

307. Since our Order is incapable of possessing immovable goods, we are, therefore, not allowed to receive perpetual legacies, perpetual offerings or any revenues.

310. The Friars, under pain of excommunication, to be incurred ipso facto, shall not demand from the heirs before any judge the annual offerings or the legacies, either by themselves or through the Syndics. . . .

311. In virtue of holy obedience, we enjoin that no Friar induce anyone to leave new legacies to the convent or to the Order.

In spite of these very plain regulations, the Franciscan Order and its churches and monasteries will and do accept

every legacy, revenue, or estate offered them. They also
go to the courts of the land whenever necessary to protect
their threatened " rights."

One such case, occurring in Santa Barbara, had all the
color of Spanish monastic antiquity, the grandees of old
Mexico, and the bitterness of an American court battle.
Near Santa Barbara live many descendants of the soldiers
who accompanied the missionaries from Spain in 1767.
Some of those soldiers received land grants in early California, and the United States has recognized those claims.
On one of these claims, owned by an elderly Santa Barbara
woman, oil was discovered. She became wealthy. When
the Franciscans and the Jesuits learned she had no heirs,
they became competitively solicitous about her spiritual
welfare. Though she had neglected her " duties " for years,
no one had been concerned until now. The Franciscans
won. She willed the revenue of the oil wells to the Order.
But then a young man with an eye to the future moved into
the picture. She married him outside the Catholic Church,
but did not change her will. When she died, the young man
sued to break the will and claim his rights as surviving
spouse. The Franciscan Order fought back. A compromise was reached, and the officials of the Order — in spite
of St. Francis, his Rule, and his ideals — are still receiving
the revenue of " black gold."

The ideal of poverty did not seem important to me, but
the inconsistency of the leaders of the Order was very important. I tried to follow ideals of service to humanity, especially the poor and the socially disenfranchised. To those
ideals and the time they required I had sacrificed many of
the formalisms of the Order and of the Roman Catholic
Church. The recorded miracles of Christ were all for the

physical betterment of his fellow man. I felt that feeding a starving family was more pleasing to him than eating at a set time in a monastery; providing a shack with heat more sacred than wearing bare sandals; putting clothes on the backs of the naked more vital than wearing a Roman collar; and heeding the prayer of an unattended woman in labor more reverent than gathering at dawn to nod sleepily through a silent meditation.

For such aberrations from the narrow line, I was frequently and severely reprimanded — reprimanded by the same officials of the Order who in total disregard of the most solemn tenets of St. Francis built million-dollar seminaries, bought luxurious resorts for " retreat " houses, and air-conditioned their Phoenix monastery with refrigeration while their parishioners were sweltering in the desert's summer heat.

In Franciscan churches and in those of the secular clergy, the race for money goes far beyond the abuse of the ideal of poverty: it approaches greed. There are always churches and schools to build, shrines to be developed, and priests to be sent to visit their relatives in Ireland. Every priest who is sincere deplores the financial exploitation of the laity that is permitted — even promoted — by the Roman Catholic hierarchy.

The Church has no law on tithing, but the various methods of financial extraction are as complex and effective as federal taxation. Votive candles in the church, which vicariously keep God mindful of us when we are busy elsewhere, cost from a dime to a dollar. Receipts from medals, rosaries, statues, crucifixes, triduums, novenas, retreats, and special services all increase the level of the exchequer. While local merchants complain about the diversion of money to horse races, dog tracks, and slot machines, they say nothing of the near-by bingo games of large parishes which weekly drain thousands of dollars from normal channels of business. They are afraid to.

The bishop can order a special collection taken up at mass for any reason, and this he does on many Sundays throughout the year. There are hundreds of shrines throughout the country dedicated to Mary or some saint, all in need of funds to carry on the sacred cause. Literally millions of letters are sent to the faithful, offering the prayers of the organization and enclosing a blank for the expected contribution.

The most sacred ceremony of the Roman Catholic religion is the sacrifice of the mass. Catholics are taught that it is the renewal of the Lord's Supper, the application to the faithful of Christ's sacrifice on Calvary, the constant atonement at the throne of God for the sins of mankind. The early Christian martyrs burrowed into the bowels of the earth to perform this rite in safety. The passing centuries enriched it with ancient vestments and symbolical ceremonies. When kings and emperors, for whatever reason, turned their wrath against the Roman Catholic hierarchy, priests and people rallied, and — come imprisonment or death, in forest caves or thatched cottages — the mass went on. It was the heart of Roman Catholicism, and the slogan passed from generation to generation, " It's the mass that matters! "

But the mass, too, has succumbed to the dollar. Mass can be offered for any " good " intention — recovery from illness, the preservation of a job, the securing of a husband. But, more than for any other purpose, the faithful are taught that mass is efficacious for the souls of the dead. The average Catholic is known not to be a saint and presumed not to be a devil. Hence he passes upon his demise neither to heaven nor to hell, but through the long cleansing process of purgatory. His friends can effectively pray for him, but the mass, being a renewal of Christ's sacrifice on Calvary, is far more effective. Though the mass, theoretically, may have the power to atone for *all* sins, the Church teaches that God may not wish to apply the entire value of the mass to a given soul. Therefore it is wise to have many masses said for the deceased. Some Catholics in their wills leave thousands of dollars for thousands of masses for their own souls.

The fee for a low mass is one dollar. A low mass is recited, not sung. The offering for a high mass is from five dollars up. This provides singing of parts of the mass by the priest and parts by a choir. A solemn mass requires three priests, and the fee is from twenty-five dollars up.

It is a shocking thing to visit urban eastern churches and observe high masses whipped through in thirty minutes, with the priest chanting so fast that even an expert in Latin can hardly follow, and with the choir consisting of one person who doubles as organist and singer. Some of these churches will perform ten or twelve high masses a day.

The *Official Catholic Directory* for 1952 lists 44,459 priests in the United States. A minimum of arithmetic will show, since priests normally recite mass every day, that, even if each priest performed only one $1 mass per day, the total contribution by the faithful would be $15,000,000 a year in mass fees alone.

Mass fees, or "stipends," are sent to priests all over the world. The priest saying the mass usually has no idea of the intention or of the person for whom he performs the mass. He does it *ad intentionam dantis* (for the intention of the giver) — and accepts the fee. The devout faithful walk into a church in New York, pay the fee for a mass, and expect it to be recited in the church they attend — while actually it may be recited six months later by a priest in China. The clergy reserve the leeway of a full year within which to perform the rite.

Additional funds are garnered by the " remembrances at mass." A very fine theological line is drawn between the " intention " of mass and a " remembrance " at mass. When a mass is offered for an intention, only one fee may be accepted. But a priest may accept any amount of money for various remembrances from any number of people and discharge these obligations at one mass by one mental note, " I wish to remember all those that I should remember." He may do this even at a mass for which he has already accepted an " intention " fee. Hence a layman must know ecclesiastical jargon in order to get his money's worth. If he gives $500 and states " for 500 masses " he will get 500 masses — probably in Europe or in some poor parish in Alabama. The high masses and better-paying low masses are kept in the home church. But if the man gives $500 to be " remembered at mass," it will be accomplished the next morning. I adopted a policy when someone casually said, " There's a ten dollar bill for masses," of noting in the mass book, " $10.00 — 10 masses." For whatever the mass might be worth, I didn't want the people cheated. If I had noted, " $10.00 — masses," only one mass would have been said.

Remembrances at mass are employed by " wildcat " shrines which advertise through mailing lists and Catholic papers and magazines. And they are used officially by the hierarchy in the annual celebration of All Souls' Day. A week or two prior to the feast, which falls on November 2, forms are either passed out to all the faithful at the regular Sunday mass or mailed to the parishioners. The forms are bordered in black and contain the usual quotation from the book of Maccabees, " It is a holy and wholesome thought to pray for the dead, that they may be loosed from their sins." (This quotation may be unfamiliar to Protestants, because the two books of the Maccabees are not recognized in the King James version of the Bible.)   On the forms, Catholics list the names of their departed parents, relatives, and friends, and with their financial contributions drop them in the collection box the Sunday before All Souls' Day.   The lists, minus the money, are placed on the altar, and at every mass during the month of November the priest nods toward the bundle and asks God to release from purgatory those souls whose names he has not even read.   Most priests, nuns, and laymen take this whole financial procedure so much for granted that they never think of its commercialism, its incongruity, and the distance their Church has come from the days when it was said, " It's the mass that matters! "

Another lucrative source of revenue, especially for the bishops, is in the fees paid for the granting of marriage " dispensations "; for the Vatican claims absolute authority over the marriages of all baptized people — both Catholic and Protestant.

The Church has an exclusive right and a right independent of the State of ordering everything that regards the valid and licit celebration of Christian marriage. . . .   It belongs to the supreme ecclesiastical authority alone to decide when divine law forbids or annuls marriage.   This authority is vested in the Pope acting personally, or in an Ecumenical Council [a general council of all bishops called and ratified by the Pope] or through one of the Sacred Roman Congregations [a bureau or department of the Vatican] by special mandate or specific approval of the Pope. . . . All baptized persons, even heretics, schismatics and apostates [Baptists, Methodists, Presbyterians, etc.] are subject to the marriage laws of the church, unless it has expressly and in set terms exempted them in some particulars. Thus the Roman Church exempts non-Catholics, when they marry among themselves, from the impediment of disparity of worship.[3]

The most common impediments (circumstances which make marriage invalid or illicit) are " disparity of cult " and " mixed religion." Both forbid marriage between Catholics and non-Catholics. The power to dispense from these impediments and thus to " legalize " the marriage is delegated by the Pope to local bishops.

The Vatican and Catholic publications emphasize the number of dispensations and " declarations of nullity " that are granted without charge. But they avoid mentioning that the fee is so routinely demanded that it is stated in the form letters suggested for the use of priests in requesting dispensation from the bishops. The following models are taken from *Moral Theology*, by the Rev. Heribert Jone·

Your Excellency:
John Smith, a Catholic of St. Mary's parish, wishing to contract marriage with Bertha White, baptized in the Lutheran sect (*or* an unbaptized person), humbly begs a dispensation from the impediment of mixed religion (*or* disparity of cult). The reasons are . . .
I herewith enclose the promises which in my judgment were made and signed in all sincerity.
Enclosed find $. . . . . as alms.

Respectfully,
Rev. James Brown

---

[3] Davis, Henry (S.J.), *A Summary of Moral and Pastoral Theology* (New York: Sheed and Ward, 1952), pp. 399–400.

Your Excellency:

John Smith of St. Mary's parish, and Bertha White of St. John's Parish (*or* both of St. John's parish) humbly pray that Your Excellency grant a dispensation from one publication (*or* two *or* three) of the banns.

The reasons are as follows . . .

Enclosed please find $. . . . . as alms.

Respectfully,

Rev. James Brown [4]

The latter form shows that Catholics must pay even to avoid having their names announced to the congregation three times at consecutive Sunday masses. Historically the purpose of this " publication of banns " was to give the congregation ample time to express possible objections to the marriage; but in modern times it is merely a useless delay. In my experience, the banns were dispensed with more often than announced — and in each instance an additional five dollars went to the bishop.

The bishop sets the amount of " voluntary alms." It varies from five or ten dollars for the routine dispensation from the banns or from the " mixed religion " impediment to hundreds and even thousands of dollars in cases necessitating reference to Rome and the annulment of previous marriages.

I can recall working on a case that lay undecided in Rome for a long time — until I met a count from Albania who knew an Italian cardinal. A generous donation uncovered a legal solution for the couple involved. They still live in Phoenix.

The form letters quoted from *Moral Theology* indicate that reasons must be given to justify the action of the bishop or the Pope. Reasons always acceptable are called canonical

[4] Pages 567–569.

— that is, based on the Canon Law of the Church. One authority lists fourteen of the more common ones, including the following: " Excellence of merits such as defense of the faith, or *generous alms to the Church*, or learning or conspicuous virtue in the petitioners or their parents. . . . The necessity or the benefit of perpetuating a noble or a *wealthy* family." [5]

Another thing that made me question the value of Roman Catholicism was its encouragement of superstition. Southwest Phoenix of the 1930's was blighted not only physically but also mentally. Harder to kill than the spirochete of syphilis were the superstitions and taboos of ignorance: A water chestnut carried in the left rear pocket prevented disease. . . . A woman in labor had only to put a sharp knife under her bed to cut the pains. . . . The child with one toe on each foot and one finger on each hand, who hopped like a frog, had been formed that way because his mother had dreamt of frogs. . . . Fresh bacon rind rubbed on a baby's bald pate was a safer preventive of disease than the immunizations of our clinic.

Sometimes a sick youngster failing to respond to the skills of our doctors was taken to the neighborhood voodoo priestess, who climaxed her incantations by gluing her own photograph on the infant's feet and charging fifty dollars to guarantee a cure.

On September 12, 1952, a Mexican Catholic killed an elderly Mexican woman in Guadalupe, a few miles southeast of Phoenix. He had accused her of being a witch and of refusing to return the photograph of his wife through which she had cursed the wife with blindness. The sheriff's

[5] Davis, *Summary*, p. 440.

deputies found her house filled with statues, crucifixes, and a sacred shrine surrounded by photographs of more than two hundred people, many of whom she had " hexed."

The man was accused of first-degree murder. The trial, held in Phoenix in April 1953, reminded me of all the malodorous superstition and abysmal ignorance of the Salem witch trials of the seventeenth century, and of the Roman Catholic Inquisition of the Middle Ages.

The legal defense was temporary insanity due to a " hex " of the witch. A parade of Mexican Catholics testified that the murdered woman had been a well-known witch and imposer of wicked hexes. Evidence was given of the gradual blindness of the defendant's wife, and the inability of modern medicine to cure her.

Two Phoenix psychiatrists, one an ex-Catholic, stated in their opinion to the court that the defendant was " suffering from a delusional system inculcated by certain not uncommon cultural beliefs." They said that " his anxiety increased until his action was inevitable. . . . The guilt rests with a society that condones practitioners of such arts." One of those psychiatrists later told me that by " cultural beliefs " and the " society that condones " they both had meant the Roman Catholic Church and its four centuries of tolerance of superstition in Mexico. He added that scarcely a week passes without his being called to treat a patient who has been " hexed."

The people we served were Negroes and Mexicans. They had native intelligence, but they believed these superstitions. This I found understandable among the illiterate element of the Negroes. Two generations had not been enough to throw off the mental shackles of slavery.

But, if all I had been taught was true, ignorance and superstition among Mexicans was inexcusable. Roman Catholic historians tell proudly of the conquest of Montezuma by Cortes at the dawn of the sixteenth century. With the Conquistadores had come the priests, most of them Franciscans, who founded the first university in this hemisphere. Catholic historians tell of hospitals and especially of schools that offered learning to all. Yet after four hundred years of Church dominance in Mexico the people it had " educated " were ignorant beyond belief. (In 1953 President Cortines of Mexico announced his determination to reduce the 50 per cent illiteracy rate among his people.)

In the Mission of San Xavier del Bac near Tucson are carried on the same superstitions that American tourists find repugnant in the national shrines of Mexico. Mexicans and Indians make pilgrimages from Tucson and other near-by communities, usually on foot. They crawl on their knees through the church to the ancient wooden reclining statue of St. Francis Xavier (one of the original members of the " learned " Jesuits). The early Mexican custom was to make nude statues similar to our store-window mannikins; the people would then make clothes for these saints — simple garments for week days and elaborate gowns of gold and silver for Sundays and feast days. On the cloth robes of St. Francis Xavier the Arizona pilgrims pin their " votive " offerings — either gifts promised if a favor is granted or an advance gift showing good faith in bargaining with the saint. These offerings are tiny metal figures from one to two inches in length, sold by Mexican silversmiths. They are the figures of babies, arms, legs, hands, heads, or women's breasts. They indicate that the petitioner wants a baby, or has broken a leg or an arm, or has a *mal* — a disease.

The Franciscan priests who care for this mission do

nothing to discourage this hopeless practice. In fact, when St. Francis' robe is overburdened, the priests remove the offerings so that pilgrims can start in again. I have seen a priest stir up a barrel of these offerings with a broom handle.

As chaplain of the local jail, I was shocked at the percentage of Roman Catholics among the unwilling guests. Wondering if the same incidence prevailed in other jails and penitentiaries, I found a study written by a Franciscan, the Roman Catholic chaplain of Joliet Penitentiary in Illinois. He discovered that the Catholic percentage among prisoners in America is about twice their percentage in the total population.

If the Roman Catholic Church is the mother of learning and of holiness, how could this be? Priests answer that these prisoners and gangsters do not represent *American* Catholicism but are mostly Irish, Polish, Italian, Spanish, and Mexican — unfortunate immigrants from backward countries. This is the stock answer to the question of Roman Catholic crime and illiteracy in America. It will be found routinely in the " question boxes " of the hierarchy's publications. But it set me thinking along dangerously heretical lines.

I thought of my own ancestry. Both of my parents had come from Ireland. They had been steeped in superstitions — that holy water kept away lightning, that blessed medals warded off disease, that rain on a fresh grave was a blessing from God. They spoke more in genuine belief than in poetic fancy when they recited the age-old tales of the " giant's causeway " and of the fairies, banshees, and leprechauns. What, in seven centuries, had Ireland, under the domination of the Roman Catholic Church, produced besides a few poets and not enough well-known scientists to count on the fingers of both hands?

I thought, too, of Italy. How could its own Pope, preaching the inalienable dignity of the human soul and its value before God, bless Mussolini's planes as they swept out to annihilate the Ethiopians? Both Mussolini and Hitler had been reared as Catholics. Why, then, were they not excommunicated? Was not their tyranny worse than the reading of a forbidden book? Was it the design of the hierarchy, including the Pope, to educate the laity only to the point of believing that the Church and its representatives could do no wrong? Did it seem necessary to keep lay Catholics and the lower clergy indoctrinated in a blind belief in papal infallibility so they would not realize the inconsistency of the Pope's blessing of Mussolini in Ethiopia, of Franco in Spain, of Perón in Argentina — and of democracy in America?

Accidentally I received first-hand knowledge of the backwardness of the Latin-American priesthood. Surgeon General Parran once took me to a Washington reception being given by the Under Secretary of State, Adolf Berle, for the national health officers of the Latin-American republics. He introduced me to the doctors as the secretary of the Arizona State Board of Health. They were astounded to find a priest interested in health. When they learned that I spoke Spanish, I received invitations to almost every Central and South American country. Catholic priests, they said, obstructed their health programs, particularly the control of venereal disease. Those priests, like some of my own superiors, contended that syphilis was God's punishment and should not be interfered with. The Latin American health officials wanted me to convince their clergy that sanitation, clinics, and health education were not anti-Catholic.

I was not yet mature enough to analyze my own " education " or to question the veracity of Roman Catholic historians. But I was living with evidence that the " mother of learning " had been sterile so far as the people of Mexico, Italy, Spain, and Ireland were concerned.

Another thing that became more clear as my years lengthened in the priesthood was that some of the Roman Catholic teachings affecting the moral lives of its members, far from bringing them closer to the religious peace of life which is divine, actually tore their lives asunder, ruined their families, and in many cases drove them into neuroses and even insanity. These Catholic teachings, instead of being based on the laws of nature (which are ultimately the laws of God), actually, as shown by their consequences, are *against* the laws of nature. Therefore it seemed to me that these teachings were wrong. Among these unrealistic doctrines are the Roman Catholic teachings on mental sin, divorce, and the celibacy of the clergy and the nuns.

Children entering parochial schools at the age of six — and from then on — are taught that it is just as sinful to *think* about a wrong as to *commit* it. The desire, according to this doctrine, is morally equivalent to the act: to wish to kill is as sinful as murder itself; to covet someone's automobile is equivalent to stealing it; to desire another's wife will merit the fires of hell as surely as adultery itself.

The catechism itself says plainly: " The Sixth and Ninth Commandments forbid *all* immodesty in *thoughts*, desires, words and actions." [6]

[6] Geierman, Peter, *Convert's Catechism of Catholic Doctrine* (St. Louis: B. Herder Book Co., 1951), p. 53.

At the age of adolescence and thereafter, as any honest priest must admit, this doctrine causes not only confusion but mental and moral crises that may be, and frequently are, psychologically disastrous. The sincere Roman Catholic boy or girl at the age of twelve or fourteen is so filled with the fear of hell that he — or especially she — wants to avoid any shadow of sin. Many of these youngsters, and some not so young, can't distinguish the fine theological lines between the consciousness of sex or sex curiosity, and the deliberate mental intention to exercise the functions of sex. They feel that any thought of sex or contemplation of their own bodies is a deadly sin.

The moral textbooks call these mental conflicts " scruples." The scrupulous person will spend an hour confessing his sins of thought — and then confess that he has sinned again by thinking of these thoughts on confessing them. He will go to confession every day, trying to cleanse his soul, becoming constantly more involved, frantic, and sometimes almost hysterical. I went through this stage myself, and a member of my family was on the verge of insanity because of it. It happens to thousands of Roman Catholics. Can this be construed as in accordance with the law of nature and its God?

The hierarchy, by its official endorsement of separate maintenance, recognizes that many couples have made tragic mistakes in their marriages. It is the prohibition of remarriage that is so contrary to nature. These faithful, if they hope to reach heaven, must be resigned to a life of celibacy as rigid as that demanded of priests and nuns. They must avoid not only remarriage, but any relation with men or women that might tempt them to forget that they must remain unmarried until death. Every priest, if he will speak honestly, can name married couples in his parish who live under the same roof merely because of the disgrace — and frequently the loss of Catholic business — if they should divorce, but who still give nature its rein in clandestine affairs. They know of others, young, handsome, and beautiful, who have separated as to " bed and board " and, merely because of the fear of eternal condemnation, have withdrawn even from harmless social life, have become psychoneurotic, bitter inmates of a church-made mental hermitage.

In the Bible's story of creation, God is quoted as saying, " It is not good that man should be alone; I will make him an helpmate for him." The Roman Catholic rule of the celibacy of the clergy was not a rule of the ancient Church; it was optional. It became a universal law for the Latin Church about nine hundred years after the death of Christ. (Today, however, the Pope permits marriage among the clergy of the Eastern rites subject to Roman rule.) The reasons for this law are twofold. The religious reasons are that Christ was celibate and that he said, " He that will be perfect, let him sell what he has, and give it to the poor and come and follow me." Also, in the Book of Revelation, virgins seemed to be closer to the throne than others: ". . . for they are virgins. These are they which follow the Lamb whithersoever he goeth. These were redeemed from among men, being the first fruits unto God and to the Lamb." The practical reasons were, and still are, that it is cheaper to support single men than those with families; that the celibate clergy can be transferred more easily to other parishes or distant points around the world; and, most important of all, that priests will remain far more subservient to the dictates of the hierarchy if they don't have wives with whom to share their confidences and doubts — wives who might question the divine origin of the bishop's orders.

Many a young man who perseveres to the day of ordination to the Roman Catholic priesthood believes that celibacy is above nature, divinely instituted, and that he can and will be true to its vow. After all, from early boyhood he will have seldom talked to a woman and never had a date.

But in his later pastoral work he is inevitably associated with women, who constitute a large percentage of his flock. They, too, have spiritual problems, and sometimes they seem to act as though a young priest needs a bit of belated education in the facts of life. Priests frequently flatter themselves that they are the forbidden fruit that entices the modern daughters of Eve. It is a fact that most priests who leave the Church and marry (and there are thousands of them) marry Catholic women of their own parishes.

The Roman Catholic priest is supposed to teach his parishioners how to live in marriage, when marital relationships should or should not be had, how to solve the big and little problems of conjugal life. His word is final, above that of the trained counselor, the family physician, or the psychiatrist.

But the Roman Catholic priest can no better teach or counsel people about marriage than the paint salesman can advise the artist, or a stonecutter guide a sculptor. The blind cannot teach art. Those born deaf cannot conduct symphonies.

The Roman Catholic priest actually knows nothing about marriage except that sex is involved and lots of little Catholics are its desired result. The priest, in his thinking, contrasts celibacy with marriage. Celibacy means simply the inhibition of sex. Marriage, to him, means the satisfaction of its urge — little more.

Many things happen in marriage besides the act that leads to procreation, but the Roman Catholic priest's ignorance makes him unequipped to advise others about them. He has no concept of the softer, enduring, satisfying, non-sexual aspects of marriage, such as the intellectual complement between two people, the emotional balancing between a man and a woman.

Many a priest knows only that for the sake of a vow he thought he made to God he has gone through years of rising physical frustration. He has fought off a force crying out for satisfaction. He has prayed, meditated, and read, hoping for the surcease promised by the hierarchy: " My grace is sufficient for thee."

Frequently, in the night, his own temptation recalls the stories of the ancient hermits in the African deserts, fighting off the visions of devils in the shapes of beautiful women. He remembers, too, how St. Francis himself stripped naked in the snow and rolled in the brambles to try to extinguish the flame of concupiscence, and finally gave it vicarious satisfaction by his formal " marriage " to Lady Poverty.

Even the Roman Catholic Church recognizes that, next to the law of self-preservation, the most powerful human force is the law of procreation of the species. It has been said among the Roman Catholic clergy for years that the reason the unfinished Vatican Council — interrupted in 1870 by the Franco-Prussian War — has never been reconvened is that the Latin-American and African clergy, through their bishops, were planning to demand abolition of clerical celibacy. The Vatican would rather not complete the Council than risk this loss of control over the mass of priests and nuns.

The life of a priest is an extremely lonely one. If he lives in a large rectory, he is still lonely. Other priests are not interested in him or in his doubts and scruples. If he is the only priest in a solitary parish or a desert mission, he is still more alone.

As his years slip by and the memories of the seminary and its rigidity fade away, the realization may dawn that his life is not supernatural but a complete mental and physical frustration. He sees in his parish and his community the normal life from which he has been cut off. He sees the spontaneous childhood which he was denied. He sees the innocent, normal companionship of adolescence which for him never existed. He performs the rites of matrimony, as starry-eyed young men and women pledge to each other the most natural of rights and pleasures. He stands alone and lonely at the altar, as they turn from him and confidently, recklessly, happily step into their future of home, family, work, the troubles and the successes of a normal life.

More than anything else he seeks companionship, the companionship of normal people, not frustrated, disillusioned victims like himself. He wants the company of men and women, young and old, through whom he may at least vicariously take part in a relationship with others that has been denied him and for which, at least subconsciously, the depths of his nature craves.

No priest who has heard priests' confessions and has any respect for the truth will deny that sexual affairs are extremely common among the clergy. The principal concern of the hierarchy seems to be that priests should keep such cases quiet and refrain from marriage. "If he had only let the affair run its course and hadn't married and gotten himself excommunicated, we could have hushed it up," an official of the Order told me concerning the first of my classmates who left the Church and the Order. The same remark was made about another priest (also one of the original thirteen of my class) who is now married and owns a chain of service stations in the West. Another clerical schoolmate decided that the companionship of a nun was preferable to the difficult work of converting Indians on the Arizona desert. When the sister became pregnant and demanded marriage, my schoolmate consulted the bishop. His Excellency offered to transfer the nun out of the diocese if the priest would stay put. The priest refused. The last I heard, they were married and living happily in Chicago. Similar incidents could be enumerated indefinitely.

The number who rebel against the frustration and unnaturalness of this form of life is far greater than anyone realizes. No one knows how many priests have quit the Roman Catholic Church in America. I know of approximately one hundred. Most ex-priests do not reveal their identity for fear of persecution by the hierarchy. There are no official records, as far as I know. The bishops and the orders are so jealous of one another that they do not reveal the " defections " in their areas. Of the thirteen priests in my class, four, to my certain knowledge, have " looked back " and have doffed their clerical robes; that is about 30 per cent. My observation is that this percentage has held approximately true in all groups of priests that I have known or have heard of. On this basis, of the 45,000 priests in the United States in 1953, about 13,500 would sooner or later leave the hierarchy and return to normal life.

Many a priest who remains in the priesthood relaxes into a life of passive laziness. He has no challenge and no incentive. He is secure. The parish and its people will feed and clothe him. He need not struggle and save for the future. He says mass every morning. He teaches the catechism to children as a matter of rote. He recites the Divine Office. His lunch is served and, in the manner of churchmen in Latin America, he takes his afternoon nap. Later he visits the sick or plans the next bazaar. He prays again and has his dinner. He plays cards or, if his Superior or pastor will permit, leaves the rectory to visit parishioners.

There are sincere people in every parish who believe that their priest should have some recreation even though the pastor or bishop might frown upon it. If the reverend father tipples a bit too much, they will put him to bed or sneak him back to the rectory and swear that he never had a drink. Alcoholism among the clergy is embarrassingly common — the sacramental wine being always available. One priest I knew commonly said, " The Pope won't let me have a wife, so I have married this bottle."

I do not wish to imply that everything is wrong with the Roman Catholic religion, or that there are not a great many priests and nuns who obey both letter and spirit of the Church's laws. There are sincere priests within the fold, just as there are sincere ex-priests without it. Many of those within are doing mighty deeds of good, comforting the sick, helping the poor, consoling the bereaved. There are thousands of nuns who are burning their lives out in sacrifice to God in the Roman Catholic orphanages, hospitals, and parochial schools of America, unaware of the inconsistency of their own racial attitudes, of the narrowness of their in-

doctrination, of the harm their hierarchy's policies can bring
to humanity.

Every Roman Catholic has heard of aberrations from the
code of the Church by laymen or priests. He hears, though,
only of isolated instances. His priest-friend tells him that
these events, if true, are to be deplored as that thing called
the " human element " of God's Church. He points out
that such sins have occurred all through history. After all,
wasn't Judas a traitor and didn't Peter betray Christ? Pope
Alexander VI had children. Cardinal Richelieu was a pro-
totype of political Machiavellianism. But in spite of these
" exceptions " the Roman Catholic Church has survived the
centuries, and because it has survived — the Catholic is
taught — it must be divine. The priest neglects to tell his
parishioners that on the basis of this argument sun-worship
and Judaism should be even more divine than Romanism
because they have survived longer.

But for me the lack of charity, the avarice, the inconsistencies, the transgressions of priests could not be shrugged
off with a meaningless phrase — the " human element."
They were an essential element, a natural and universal
flowering of the seed.

I came to the irrevocable conclusion that the Roman Catholic Church had misrepresented itself to me. It had claimed
that it was the " bride of Christ," that the Pope was God's
representative on earth, that its teachings were the depository of eternal truth. I could not personally investigate all
the alleged sources for the claims of the Papacy to infallibility. There are no original documents. The only priest
I knew who had gone to Palestine to study Roman Catholicism at its source had quit the Church to teach in the University of California.

I could not yet break down the logic upon which the claims of the Roman Catholic Church to the exclusive possession of truth are based. But I was personally convinced that doctrines of the Roman Catholic Church, if sincerely believed, and the hierarchy's laws, if rigidly adhered to, were productive not of peace of mind but of anguish of soul — not of normal creative life but of barrenness of spirit and bleakness of ignorance.

Though I could not examine the roots of this tree that had spread itself across the earth through the centuries, I could examine the fruit to see if it were firm and unblemished, to see if it seemed to be of God. " A good tree cannot bring forth evil fruit; neither can a corrupt tree bring forth good fruit. By their fruits ye shall know them."

CHAPTER FOUR

The Hall of Judgment

I did not know what I believed. I was still — by heredity, by feeling, by lack of any other conviction — a Roman Catholic. The abstract doctrines of the Church still seemed true to me, but the hierarchy of the Church was beginning to seem false.

During these years I kept my doubts to myself. I joined my fellow priests in complaining about my pastor, my Provincial Superior, the bishops, and especially the arrogant cardinals of the United States. We condemned all of these as ecclesiastical politicians, deplored the " donations " made to Rome in return for promotions, and attributed the rash of " scarlet fever " to every priest who aspired to the red robes of the bishopric.

But doctrinal or moral doubts were heresy. There are many priests desiring to curry favor with the hierarchy who will report any apparent moral discrepancy. In some religious orders, priests are even assigned the duty of spying on fellow priests and reporting to " headquarters." If a dictatorship, communistic or fascistic, should take over in America, it would not seem unfamiliar to the Catholic clergy. They are watched by the laity and the clergy alike;

they dress in a garb that spotlights them under the gaze of public curiosity; and their self-consciousness, engendered by years of seclusion, causes them to feel and to fear that their every step and misstep is immediately known to those who have the power to control and discipline them.

The hold of the Roman Catholic hierarchy over most of the clergy, as I have observed it, is not the bond of love, or of loyalty, or of religion. It is the almost unbreakable chain of fear — fear of hell, fear of family, fear of the public, fear of destitution and insecurity. I firmly believe that, in place of the 30 per cent of the clergy who probably leave the priesthood today, fully 75 per cent would do so if it were not for fear.

The doctrines of heaven and of hell are, together with the existence of God and the immortality of the soul, the fundamentals of all conservative religions. The Roman Catholic descriptions of heaven are so entrancing that millions have been persuaded to endure injustice, slavery, and ignorance on earth lest they sin and forfeit the " promised land " hereafter. Catholicism's picture of hell — a seething cauldron of endless fire, created by the eternal wrath of an angry Old Testament God — is also so vividly and so constantly portrayed that it strikes terror into the souls of pious Catholics.

Little children going to confession at the age of six fear hell more than parental anger. Adolescent boys and girls, conscious of sex and its curiosities, unable to distinguish that curiosity from " mental " sin, see themselves hanging over that pit of fire until they can hurry to confession and cleanse their souls. Young married women, burdened physically and mentally with the nightmare of constant pregnancies, refuse their own and their husbands' wishes and undermine their families because of their fear that birth control means eternal torment. And that same fear of hell makes sincere, healthy young priests eat out their hearts, their minds, and their sanity rather than turn back from the plow toward a normal life.

Most priests, torn between the intellectual realization that they have been misled by the hierarchy and the fear of family reaction, hesitate and live on through barren years in the priesthood. My parents were dead, but I had sisters and a brother, who was also a priest, aunts and uncles, and a swarm of cousins — all Irish and all Catholic. From them and their friends I could expect nothing but repudiation if I took my hand from the plow.

Every priest is taught through the years that anyone who leaves the priesthood will be not only cursed by God but rejected by the public. The priest believes that people will sneer at him as one who has violated his solemn promises and therefore cannot be trusted with responsibility. In Catholic circles mention is never made of ex-priests who are successful — but only those who have strayed, who have starved, and who have groveled back to the hierarchy, sick, drunken, broken in spirit, begging to do penance for the sake of clothes on their backs and food in their bellies.

The standard Jesus set for salvation was not the wearing of a Roman collar, the recitation of the rosary or of the Divine Office. It was not the building of a church or a shrine, or the practice of poverty, or the non-practice of birth control, or the practice of celibacy. It was not the wearing of a robe, or sprinkling with holy water, or anointing with oils, or fasting in Lent, or abstaining on Friday, or eating in common, or kissing a knot on the end of a cord. Jesus gave men one standard: " Inasmuch as ye have done it unto one of the least of these my brethren, ye have done it unto me."

Here I found my God. I buried my doubts and my fears in working harder for the housing of the poor, the betterment of public health, and the promotion of the hospital I had dreamed of — a hospital that would care for the poor and prove to the world that people of all races could study, work, and live together.

In 1941, at the height of the national military-preparedness program, Phoenix became the hub of a surrounding wheel of Air Force training fields — drawn by the desert climate, cloudless skies, and unlimited visibility. By day and by night, the air was filled with the roar of training planes.

Military personnel, civilian engineers, contractors, workers, and their families poured into the small city. The community facilities of Phoenix, particularly the hospital accommodations, were overwhelmed. The hospitals, geared to the town of the 1930's, had 365 beds for 50,000 people. In 1941 there were still 365 beds — but for 140,000 people.

The highest bidders — the substantial citizens, the " friends of the friend " — got the beds. Too often, the Mexicans, the Negroes, the poor whites died. Ambulances and police cars, with sirens wailing, roamed in vain through the night, from hospital to hospital and small-town rest homes. The Phoenix police, the sheriff's deputies, the Arizona highway patrol, and the local newspapers bore bitter testimony against a community that let its people perish for lack of a bed and a dollar.

I had told the nun at St. Joseph's Hospital that somehow I was going to build another hospital. It would have a nursing school to take white girls and black girls, red and yellow, and prove that Christianity, if tried, could work. It would also take the wounded and sick from the streets and the highways, and — before asking their finances and banking references — give the medical aid that might save their lives.

Then came Pearl Harbor. The Lanham Act passed by the Congress provided money to help states and communities meet the shock of shifting wartime populations. The Federal Works Agency advanced funds to build sewage-disposal plants, water-filtration systems, school additions, recreational facilities, and hospitals.

Surgeon General Parran, who had already befriended our community center, now became enthusiastic about both my aims: an interracial institution and immediate care for the sick and the injured. He was especially interested in our venereal clinic, for he had written a history of syphilis, *Shadow on the Land*, and he had been the first person to defy the taboo of society by using the word " syphilis " on a national radio broadcast. He suggested an application for an appropriation of Lanham Act funds. But he did more: he sent the regional officials of the United States Public Health Service to Phoenix to help me prepare the application and prove the need of another hospital in Phoenix.

The syphilis problem, strangely enough, helped build the hospital.

Our original plans called for an inadequate fifty-bed institution on three city lots adjacent to the community center. But the acceptable Public Health Service plan for the fifty beds required a full city block.

While we were looking for the property, a ruling came from Washington that community facilities financed under the Lanham Act could be built only with the approval of the War Department. The closest installation of the Army, Navy, or Air Force was to be its representative. Luke Field was the closest.

Early in 1942 the incidence of venereal disease in Phoenix and at Luke Field was the subject of embarrassing public discussion. Sulfa drugs were being surreptitiously used by infected fliers. When plane crashes and deaths occurred, the drugs were blamed. The commanding officer of the air base blamed the venereal disease of his men on the promiscuous women of Phoenix. The health authorities retorted that the lecherous Air Force was contaminating the purity of Phoenix womanhood. The Army ordered all of Phoenix " off limits " to military personnel. This decree insulted the city council, the chamber of commerce, the luncheon clubs, the churches, the PTA, and the USO.

The tension was most intense at the time when I had an interview with the commanding officer of Luke Field. I presented our problem. Phoenix needed more hospital beds. We could not provide them unless he and, through him, the Ninth Corps Area command in Salt Lake City approved. The tough, rough-spoken colonel (who later became one of the leading generals in the defeat of the Japanese air force) was willing to make a deal. He would recommend approval on condition that the proposed bed capacity be doubled and that half the beds be reserved for the treatment of the female syphilitics of Phoenix. I agreed. His endorsement quickly went to Washington through the Ninth Corps Area of the United States Army.

Nine months after this dream child was conceived, on August 10, 1942, while I was in Sacramento, a telegram informed me that the President of the United States, Franklin Delano Roosevelt, had approved the hospital and appropriated the money for its construction. The hospital was born.

My return to Phoenix was greeted with a full-blown revolution. The daily newspapers had mistakenly announced that the hospital was to be "for colored and Mexican residents" exclusively. Handbills had been scattered across the neighborhood:

MEXICANS, SPANISH AMERICANS, MEMBERS OF THE LATIN RACE IN THE STATE OF ARIZONA

Since the Mexican or Spanish American race has always distinguished itself and does distinguish itself by its independent spirit, always proud to belong to the great Mexican family without mixing with other races;

Therefore, we, the undersigned, energetically protest that we be made equal to other races or mix with them, and, therefore, to prevent this impending evil, without any offence to the Rev. Father Emmett, we call a PUBLIC MEETING.

The purpose of the meeting was to petition the Arizona congressional delegation to have the hospital appropriation split. Half was to be given to me for a Negro hospital. The other half would go to the "committee" for a clinic and hospital to be used exclusively for members of the Latin race, regardless of their place of birth.

This move, if successful, would have destroyed our interracial plan and would have made each of the divided appropriations so small that neither group could have had more than an ineffective clinic. The congressional delegates, however, would have to try to please all their constituents. I determined that the new request must never reach Washington. I got in touch with my Latin American friends, who thronged to the meeting. One of them was elected chairman and called on me to speak. I pleaded for unity among all people " south of the tracks " and explained that the hospital was for all races — as everything American and Christian should be. A motion was made from the floor requesting approval of the project as planned. There were several hundred people present. The vote to approve was unanimous.

In the center of the slum area was a vacant fourteen-acre, six-block cotton field. The price was $9000. We had nothing. Barbecues and bazaars brought in a few thousand dollars. A worker in our community center, Miss Jean Donnelly — who taught catechism to the youngsters, played the organ in church, and made layettes for all the mothers who delivered through our clinic — assumed the herculean task of writing to every person in the city directory who lived on a prosperous-sounding street. By the time the plans and specifications were ready, the property had been purchased.

But now we found ourselves blocked by the most formidable obstacle of all, the War Production Board. The President's approval and the appropriation of cash meant nothing to this jealous guardian of the nation's lumber, wire, nails, pipes, steel, radiators, toilets, and bathtubs. Without its priority rating, nothing could be built. The WPB rejected our project as not essential to the war effort.

With the help of our Senators we won a reconsideration. But we had to prove all over again that the existing two hospitals were overcrowded, that the shortage of beds was endangering the lives of defense workers and therefore threatening the effectiveness of our ships at sea and our planes in the air.

It was at this point that the latent jealous opposition of

the nuns came into the open. Among the details of the WPB questionnaire were twelve questions to be answered by the existing hospitals. They covered statistics for 1940, 1941, and 1942 as to bed capacity, patient days, and percentage of occupancy. The Methodists' Good Samaritan Hospital readily answered the questions, but the Sisters of Mercy at St. Joseph's Hospital refused. (The nun in charge was the one who had suggested the psychiatrist when I told her I would start a hospital.)

We had formed a hospital corporation, and fortunately one of the trustees, Henry Wright, was Arizona director of the War Production Board. I turned to him now to pry the necessary information from the reluctant Sisters of Mercy. For days the hospital switchboard said the sister in charge was out of town. When Mr. Wright finally reached the sister by telephone, she told him that all the statistics the government wanted could be obtained only by special permission. (The hospital capacity and occupancy figures for every hospital in the United States appear annually in the *Journal of the American Medical Association*.) After Mr. Wright's firm insistence, she consented to answer the government's questions.

When the official questionnaire reached the WPB, the Good Samaritan Hospital showed an average occupancy in 1942 of 91 per cent — a percentage far above the safe level that would provide for emergencies or catastrophes. St. Joseph's, the older and more popular hospital — which turned poor patients away throughout the year with the excuse that all its beds were filled — told the government that its occupancy in 1942 was only 78 per cent. In the

WPB report, the nuns said their capacity was 246 beds — though in the *Journal of the American Medical Association*, March 27, 1943, they had reported only 200 beds. (Five years later, when the Sisters of Mercy appealed to the people of Phoenix for $1,500,000 to build a new hospital, they stated that their hospital contained only 190 beds.)

A declining occupancy percentage would indicate that there was no bed shortage in Phoenix. If no shortage, no need for a new hospital. If no hospital, no interracial nursing school, and therefore no embarrassment.

The War Production Board, ignoring the report of the Sisters of Mercy, issued a priority rating for the construction of the new hospital.

This action by the nuns was not a surprise. I had been Roman Catholic chaplain of that same hospital for enough years to expect this pattern of behavior.

The nun is one of the most remarkable products of the Roman Catholic Church. She is an absolute slave; one whose willingness to offer her life should fill Communist leaders with jealousy; one from whom the hierarchy conceals her slavery by the wedding band on her finger; one who believes that in shining the bishop's shoes, waiting on his table, or scrubbing the floor, she is gathering herself " treasure in heaven." She is the one who makes possible the Church's hundreds of hospitals; the one who teaches in its thousands of parochial schools and orphanages; the one who (with her 156,695 sisters in 1952) does the drudgery behind the scenes in the hierarchy's drive to " make America Catholic." She is also a woman, with all the desires, instincts, loyalties, and hatreds of which a woman is capable; subservient to her " man " through her indoctrination of her " wedding " to Christ; often catty and gossipy toward her sister nuns and hospital student nurses; maternal in her hoverings over priests and children; matriarchal in her petty politics for the control of her hospital or convent; and magnificent in her spirit of abasement, poverty, and self-annihilation on behalf of God and the Roman Catholic Church.

In many seminaries in the United States, nuns — living in walled-off sections to prevent contact with the priests or seminarians — spend their lives performing the domestic services of cooking, laundry, and cleaning. During the persecutions of the Roman Catholic Church in Mexico in recent decades, many nuns sought refuge in the United States. The Bishop of Tucson, the Most Rev. Daniel J. Gercke, offered some of them refuge in his episcopal mansion. He dispensed with his servants. The Mexican nuns took over all the household duties. If he merely rang a bell, a nun slipped in with bowed head to receive his orders, and on bended knee kissed his episcopal ring in appreciation for the privilege. As a dinner guest in his home, I personally witnessed this scene.

The stories of underground tunnels connecting priests' rectories with sisters' convents and of the bones of new-born babies found in the nunnery walls are, of course, so much " hogwash." I have heard of only one romance between a priest — my schoolmate — and a nun.

A priest would have little chance to feel romantic about a pretty nun. The face framed in a nun's veil is all he can see. Nuns are always chaperoned and travel in pairs to prevent any possibility of romance. For the same reason most of them may not leave their convent after dark, except when traveling with the permission of their Superior.

Nuns do love priests — but with the love of a mother, not the love of a paramour. This affection often embarrasses priests. When nuns dine their clergy, they hover like moths, obsequious in their servitude — while the priests would prefer that they either sit down to eat or leave.

After I left the priesthood, several nuns across the country adopted me as their " prodigal son." They wrote for years, giving me advice on how to return to the Church, how to confound the devil, assuring me of their prayers, and always signing their letters, " Your loving mother in Christ."

There is no cruelty I know that surpasses that of nuns toward ex-nuns. An ex-nun once came to me looking for a job as a nurse. Her background was fascinating. She had entered a Belgian convent as a nursing nun. Her father was a doctor, chief of staff of St. Vincent's Hospital in Antwerp. After one year she asked to be released from the convent. She was told that if she did — even though the Code of Canon Law of the Roman Catholic Church provides that any nun under " simple " (temporary) vows must be released upon application for such release — her father would be dismissed from the staff of the hospital. In Belgium, which is almost entirely Catholic, the stigma of Church disapproval is worse than an indictment under civil law. If she persisted in leaving the sisterhood, her family would be disgraced. Her younger brothers and sisters would not be able to make honorable marriages, and her father would lose his position. So she remained a nun.

She was sent to the Belgian Congo, and there as a missionary nursing nun spent six years, fighting the dangers of the jungles. After seventeen years of subservience to the

hierarchy, she stepped out into freedom. Her father had
retired, and her brothers and sisters were married. She was
released with forty dollars and her written promise that
she would never demand recompense for her seventeen
years of service or any written documents proving that she
had ever been a nurse.

The day she left the convent, Hitler's planes were bomb-
ing Brussels. A direct hit struck a theater, killing and
wounding three thousand people. Still a nurse by instinct,
she went to work, dragging out the wounded and saving
their lives. She became a nurse first in the Belgian army,
then in the American occupation forces, and finally an
executive nurse, organizing health programs for D.P. camps
of 10,000 people at one time. When an American woman
sponsored her entry into America, she wanted a climate like
Africa's — and naturally came to Arizona.

But no one would give her a position. The Arizona State
Nurses Association was sympathetic and referred her to me.
I secured for her a year's temporary permit and placed her
in charge of all our out-patient clinics. I found her one of
the most competent nurses I have met in eighteen years of
association with hospitals.

She had documents from the United States army of occupation attesting to her ability as a nurse. She had statements
from the Belgian government. She had testimonials from
the government of the Belgian Congo. But, because she
had left the sisterhood, she had no certificate that she was a
nurse.

After her year under the temporary permit, the Arizona
State Board of Nurse Examiners — one of whose members
was a nun — studied her background. After a perfunctory

examination, they refused to register her as a nurse and ordered me to fire her. She applied to the California Board of Nurse Examiners and was immediately granted a certificate as a registered nurse — though California nursing standards are certainly not lower than those of Arizona.

Some nuns overcome their frustration by becoming Amazonian matriarchs. They outwit the bishop and clergy and are tyrants to the nuns and nurses under them.

It is very seldom that anyone, priest or layman, is invited behind the outer doors of a sisters' convent. But I had that privilege on the occasion of the feast day of the Sister Superior of St. Joseph's Hospital, the most sincere, gracious, and thoroughly Christian of all the hundreds of nuns I had met.

I was ushered into a large room. Around the table sat more than twenty nuns. On the table were piled gifts not only from the ones present but also from nuns in all the hospitals, convents, and schools of the Sisters of Mercy in the southwest. All the gifts I noted were handmade, exquisite examples of various forms of needle work, wrought through tedious hours of patient skill while the nuns were conversing, praying, or meditating. They were things that the Sister Superior could not, as a nun, possibly use, articles that she would have to give away, but things that showed the desires of the givers and pointed to a hidden but unquenchable instinct. For most of the gifts for the Sister Superior were baby clothes.

Construction bids for our hospital were opened in Washington, D. C., in the spring of 1943. I was on hand. Only half the battle was won. The hospital was assured, but not

a nurses' home or a nursing school. The Federal Works
Agency was willing to advance the money, but the War
Production Board again said "No."

In the innermost recesses of one of the "temporary"
offices constructed during World War I, I found the man
who said "No." He was Everett Jones, one of the ablest
hospital administrators in the country, who had been borrowed to head the WPB hospital division and to guard the
dwindling reserves of the nation's resources. I paraded all
my arguments across his desk — bed shortage, nurse shortage, the Negro nursing potential. The answer was still
"No." Materials were too scarce. I wanted to know
what I had to do to make him say "Yes." Suppose I could
secure the most critical materials through second-hand
channels, suppose I could find all the electric wiring,
switches, outlet boxes, fixtures, water pipes, steam pipes,
toilets, radiators, wash basins — without priorities — would
he then approve the construction? Maybe, but he didn't
think it was possible.

Neither did I. But I knew one man who had never heard
of the word "impossible." He was an almost legendary
Horatio Alger success myth of the middle west, owner of
Chicago's radio station WLS and of the powerful *Prairie
Farmer* magazine. He also owned the Arizona Network
and was one of my hospital trustees. His name was Burridge D. Butler.

Mr. Butler was a very old man when I first met him.
Someone had dared me to approach him. I was told that
when he saw my Roman collar he would curse vigorously
and throw me out. At the time, I was trying to promote
floodlights for our playground. He did curse — but when
I responded in kind he bought the floodlights.

He was a large, heavy man, tall and dignified, even as he

approached his eighties, an overpowering, irresistible, insulting, rough-spoken, driving master with one of the biggest, most generous hearts in all America. The son of a preacher, who concentrated more on the gospel than on his family, he had seen his mother die in privation, and he had quit school to feed his family while his father tried to nourish other people's souls. He was a deeply religious soul who vociferously hated all religions, and he became a very rich man who hated the rich. He attended meetings of business executives — and condemned them for cheating the poor. He said " No " to every appeal — and then helped found and finance the Boys' Clubs of America. He drove his employees — but if they got sick he supported them for life. He disclaimed all interest in minority groups — but when I spoke of our hospital he broke down in tears.

As a youngster he became a newspaper office boy; at the age of forty he sold eleven newspapers and retired. His first wife had been a schoolteacher. When he began courting again, the beautiful woman he pursued refused him at first, because she thought he never changed his socks. After their marriage she learned that he had no time for trivialities and that when he needed socks he bought a gross — same size, same color. He bought shirts, suits, and Oriental rugs in bulk quantities, too.

Mr. Butler had offered to give me his Phoenix radio station, KOY, if I left the priesthood.

This was the man I sought when the federal government turned me down. I stopped in Chicago on my way back from Washington. Mr. Butler listened, swore, and telephoned the president of the Northern Illinois Power Company, telling him to gather his engineers, meet with me the next day, determine what the nurses' building would need — and to get it.

Back in Phoenix, truckloads of material poured in from Chicago. We located the pipes, the radiators, the toilets, the fittings. Everett Jones and the War Production Board capitulated.

In 1948 Mr. Butler died in the hospital he had helped to build. On the wall of my office, on a nail from which once hung a crucifix, there now hangs a gnarled Irish shillelagh. It belonged to Burridge Butler. It is a constant reminder to me of a great, gruff man who had never heard of the impossible.

On February 14, 1944, at a ceremony which included local and state officials as well as Bishop Gercke of Tucson and representatives of the United States Public Health Service, St. Monica's Hospital began its proud history. The nursing school opened on October 1 of the same year. A warning to nurses and doctors was posted in the emergency room: EVERY PATIENT BROUGHT TO THIS HOSPITAL MUST BE GIVEN EMERGENCY TREATMENT BEFORE ANY FINANCIAL QUESTIONS ARE ASKED. Ambulances no longer wailed through the night with no haven to reach. City police, sheriff's deputies, highway patrolmen clustered in the emergency ward. "Thank God," they said, "that we have this hospital."

A Negro girl became the office posting-machine operator, a Japanese girl was my secretary, a Mexican girl handled the switchboard. An ambitious Negro janitor, Arthur Rosser, became a fully qualified X-ray technician. He later organized the Arizona branch of the American Registry of X-ray Technicians and served as president of both the Phoenix unit and the state organization. He is now employed by the United States Indian Service as supervising X-ray technician for the western states.

The opening class of regular student nurses included white, Negro, Japanese, Mexican, and Indian girls. (We added a special class of four girls who had completed two years of training in other schools.) Among them were no racial arguments. By admitting Negro girls as student nurses, we had done what no Roman Catholic nursing school up to that time had even tried. Christianity and democracy had succeeded.

The Los Angeles Catholic *Sentinel* of June 19, 1947, stated:

Standing as a beacon light in the sea of racial intolerance, prejudice and bigotry, and as a monument to the courage, vision and loyalty of its founder to the principles of brotherly love, is St. Monica's Hospital School of Nursing in Phoenix.

At about the same time Mrs. Eleanor Roosevelt told our student nurses:

I think it is a grand thing you are being trained together and I think it is important that all of us as citizens of the United States realize that it is the people who count. . . .

I think a group such as this, going out into the world, has a great opportunity to do not just a job as nurses, but as citizens of a country.

In *The Saturday Evening Post* of October 18, 1947, Milton MacKaye in his article on Phoenix said:

Father Emmett is an uncompromising enemy of segregation. He does not believe it is Christian. At St. Monica's no line of color or creed is drawn among patients, and in the nurses' training school white, Negro and Spanish-American girls work together on terms of equality.

In *Inside U. S. A.*, published in 1947, John Gunther wrote:

One Catholic priest, Father Emmett McLoughlin, a Franciscan, has a considerable reputation for his work " south of the tracks" in Phoenix among the Negroes, encouraging Negro education and welfare and proselyting them.

The staid Paulist magazine, the *Catholic World*, in June 1947 published an article about my work entitled "The People's Padre," by Joseph Stocker. The article stated:

The hospital, the mission, the clinics, and the housing developments — are the living monuments to a priest's compassion for the little fellow and to his conviction that man is not born with intolerance but acquires it.

But shortly after the opening of the hospital, the Bishop of Salt Lake City visited the institution. As he stopped in the foyer, he said, " Father, this is a good work. But you cannot go on with it. It is too unusual for a priest. You are and will be a thorn in the side of the nuns who have a hospital in this same city. You will be forced out by your superiors in the hierarchy."

Another man, a famous priest of a religious order, echoed the bishop's words on his visit. " You can't succeed," he told me; " clerical jealousy will get you. This is too different. I organized a boys' choir that became nationally famous. They couldn't stand it. They got me. If you don't prepare, they will get you too."

At the time I was not only superintendent of the hospital but also president of the board of directors. I took the priest's advice and prepared for the eventual showdown. When it came, four years later, thirteen of the sixteen men on our board of directors were Masons. St. Monica's Hospital — now called Memorial Hospital — was never a Church institution under the jurisdiction of the hierarchy. It was and still is owned by a non-profit community corporation.

The first break with the hierarchy came as the first class

of student nurses approached graduation. They were four girls, three of whom had been dismissed from Catholic hospitals for petty disciplinary reasons. The Arizona State Board of Nurse Examiners ruled that they could not take state board examinations because the nursing school had not been approved. The president of the Board of Nurse Examiners was a nun — an official of the Roman Catholic nursing school in Tucson, which barred Negroes.

We filed suit in Superior Court against the Board. The bishop of the diocese asked me to withdraw the suit; the spectacle of a priest suing a nun would embarrass the Roman Catholic Church. But I refused to back down, and the trial took place. Our principal attorney was a Roman Catholic.

At that time there were no written standards in Arizona for the approval of a nursing school. The sister, under oath, stated that our school could not be approved because its records were not satisfactory. Cross-examination of the nun brought out the fact that her Board had no way of knowing whether our records were satisfactory or not — because they had not examined the school's records. The judge stopped the trial. He gave the Board a deadline and ordered it to approve our school — or he would do it by order of the court.

In February of 1946, on the second anniversary of the hospital's opening, the Sunday edition of the *Arizona Republic* ran a feature about it, with a front-page story and headlines: " FATHER EMMETT'S FAMED HOSPITAL BECOMES PHOENIX HAVEN OF MERCY."

The tension was increasing. We needed $30,000 to construct a laundry and boiler plant. A hierarchical superior came to Phoenix on an official visit to check the conformity

of all Franciscan priests to the rules of the Order. Knowing
that the Order, in spite of its avowal of poverty, had the income from California oil wells, I asked him to loan us
$30,000. He not only refused but denounced me as being
too worldly, un-Franciscan, and embarrassing to the sisters'
hospital. I pointed out that our hospital was at least caring
for all emergency cases whether they had money or not,
and that the sisters' hospital had not been willing to do this.
"The Catholic Church," he said, "has no responsibility to
these people. As far as I am concerned, they can die in the
streets. They are the responsibility of the city."

Here was a man whom I was supposed to respect and
obey as God's representative. I thought of the verse from
First Corinthians, " Though I speak with the tongues of men
and of angels and have not charity, I am become as sound-
ing brass or a tinkling cymbal."

Some months later, a long-distance telephone call informed me that the Provincial Council was in session. They
demanded my immediate presence.

The Franciscan Order, forbidden by its Rule to own anything, and in theory restricted to the use of poor, simple,
modest buildings, had purchased one of the most luxurious
mansions on the Pacific coast, above the Palisades north of
Santa Monica, high on a hill overlooking that strip of shore-
line famous to all who have ever heard of Hollywood — the
fabulous Malibu Beach. The structure itself was as ornate
as the Waldorf-Astoria. Its rambling rooms stepped from
one level to another in a profusion of beauty and luxury.
The glazed tile on some of the floors was said to be worth
$100,000, and the whole estate $500,000. The kitchen was
beautifully tiled – floor, walls, and ceiling. One spontaneously reached to feel the texture of the library's huge gor-

geous Oriental rug — only to find it made of tile. The stair-
ways, the corridors, the porches, the driveways seemed a
varied, unending fantasy of glazed beauty. The building
was used as a " retreat " house, whence people could come
from the noise, confusion, and sin of Los Angeles, to rest,
pray — and meditate on the passing glory of all things
material.

In the library, the six elders of the Provincial Council
were in session. My interview was brief. It was not a trial,
or a hearing, or a lecture. It was a recital of charges and an
ultimatum. They said I was failing in the spiritual life; I
was not attending morning meditations. They charged I
was not joining the brethren in the recitation of the Divine
Office. I was late for the common meals — if I attended at
all. I had become a worldly priest, careless in the wearing
of the Roman collar and neglectful of the spiritual duties
toward my Negro parishioners. All of this decadence, the
spokesman emphasized, was due to the hospital. Its construction and especially its administration were a material,
unspiritual work, unbecoming a Franciscan priest. The
Provincial Council had decided that I must relinquish my
post and turn the institution over to a lay administrator.
The Council wished merely an expression of my priestly
obedience.

As the brown-robed, gray-haired, portly monk spoke, I
thought of the bishop who had warned me and the priest
whose famous choir had been dissolved: " This is a good
work, but you will be forced out by your superiors in the
hierarchy." I thought, too, of another, whom, in my own
way, I had tried to follow in his work for the poor and who,
twenty centuries ago, stood quiet while " the chief priests
accused him of many things."

I told the Provincial Council that the hospital was poor, that I served without salary, that as soon as the finances were improved I would try to find someone to take my place. This statement satisfied them, and I hastily slipped out through the great carved oaken doors.

A Franciscan priest drove me back to the Los Angeles municipal airport. The plane would not leave for another two hours. I wanted a chance to think. I slipped off my Roman collar and put it into my brief case; I found a quiet restaurant which served the employees of the neighboring aircraft manufacturers. Then I mentally re-created the scene and tried to understand it. Six priests, sons of the poor St. Francis, with the hems of their brown robes blending, like draperies in a king's palace, into the intricate patterns of exquisite tile on the floor — with the huge fireplace and the exposed oaken beams of the roof, the whole picture could have been a scene from a castle in the days of King Arthur.

Was I a bad priest? I didn't always wear the Roman collar. I didn't eat meals on time. I missed morning meditation. I took into our nursing school colored girls sent by nuns who could not get them into schools of their own orders. My hospital was giving medical care to 20,000 people a year. All that, said the Father Provincial, standing in this scene of regal luxury, was too worldly a work for a Catholic priest.

Was my work too worldly? I no longer heard the chatter of the changing aircraft shifts. My mind slipped back to St. Monica's Hospital. I saw the graduating classes of my student nurses, their parents and relatives. I saw Indian parents from the western reservations, shy, unexpressive, polite, awkwardly clothed, but proud as the American eagle itself because their daughter could go back to the reservation hospital and care for the members of the tribe. I saw Negro parents from Texas, Louisiana, Mississippi, and Alabama, embarrassed at being among so many white people, trembling with emotion as they heard the white chief of the medical staff praise their daughters as excellent nurses; their warm handshakes and their tears were still vivid. I saw white parents, too, proud that, vicariously at least, they had lived through a test of democracy and love.

" One Lord, one faith, one baptism. One God and Father of us all, who is above all, and through all, and in you all."

In their new, smart, starched uniforms they stood before me, white girls, black girls, yellow girls, red girls, with the highest average nursing grades in Arizona — grades above the national averages.

At the graduation ceremony, the director of nurses fastened a pin on each girl's uniform — the symbol of our school, a pin I had designed. Between the upraised wings of the Phoenix, on a field of gold, was the Latin word *Surrexi* — " I have risen." Around it was first the white band of nursing, then a band of the turquoise blue of the Arizona skies. Together the girls stood before me, and with emotion repeated the words I had written to explain their school pin:

I have risen.
I, who proudly wear the emblem of St. Monica's School of Nursing, have risen. Dim in the mists of the fabled Egyptian antiquity, the Phoenix bird rose (as the ages passed) from the heat of its own ashes to repeated new and greater life.

I have risen.

So too from the desert ashes of past civilizations of the great southwest, reaching back beyond the ken of men, has the city in which my school is situated risen to greater life as the city of Phoenix in the heart of a fertile empire.

I have risen from whatever race or color I might be; from whatever status in life I might have held; from the immaturity of girlhood.

I have risen to the full stature of the noblest profession given to womanhood — that of nursing.

God alone could tell where the ripples would reach from this stone thrown into the pool of humanity.

But the Provincial Council said I was a bad priest, that good, docile priests of Holy Mother Church were not so material. They were spiritual. They always wore the Roman collar. They ate meals on time. They were regular at morning meditation.

I had tried mentally to separate the " Church " from the " organization." My loyalty was to Christ, to God, to the Church — not to the Provincial Council that had just sat in judgment upon me. Since the beginning of my disillusionment, I had tried to think of the Church as a thing apart from the hierarchy, a " deposit of faith," a body of doctrine, suspended, in some fashion, in the air of time, unpolluted by greed, selfishness, and hypocrisy. It was dawning on me now that this separation was impossible. The water could no longer be pure if the pipes were corroded. The doctrine of Roman Catholicism could not be true if the hierarchy were false.

But what was I going to do? Submit to the Provincial Council or break away from the Roman Catholic Church? I felt that a time would come when I would be man enough to face the test. I prayed to God to give me the moral strength to leave the priesthood if the hierarchy should finally order me to leave Phoenix.

In a quiet restaurant, waiting for a plane — without benefit of formal prayers, statues, or rituals — I had experienced the most profound spiritual meditation of my life.

Back at our hospital a situation developed that proved that I did have the strength to stand up to authority.

A baby girl lay on our emergency-room table, twisting and shaking in agonizing convulsions. She had been stung by a scorpion. The attending physician injected a barbiturate and calcium gluconate and applied ice at the site of the sting. An intern from the University of Mexico stood in the background watching. The convulsions increased. The baby choked — and died.

The intern, Dr. Jorge Deyden, turned to me and said simply, " In Mexico that baby would not have died."

" Why not? " I asked.

" Because we have a serum made from the venom of scorpions. The Mexican government furnishes it free to all doctors as a public-health precaution, because there are so many scorpions in Mexico."

" Get me some," I demanded.

" I can get it," he replied, " when I visit Nogales, Sonora. But I cannot bring it across the border. It is not approved by the American government, and its use here is illegal."

" Get it," I told him. " Smuggle it across the border. We are dealing with lives — not laws."

In the southwestern section of the United States — in the interior of southern California, in New Mexico, Nevada, and particularly Arizona — there is a species of scorpion that is dangerous. It is a little yellow devil approximately two inches in length. The sting of its tail, injecting the venom, will throw an adult into prolonged, painful convulsions and may kill a child.

There was no secret to the Mexican serum. It is made by the Myn laboratories in Mexico City from the blood of horses which have been injected with repeated and increasing doses of scorpion venom. The method of manufacture is similar to that of tetanus antitoxin, rattlesnake serum, or any of the other horse serums we routinely stocked in our pharmacy. The only reason that scorpion serum was not manufactured commercially in this country was that the market was too limited to be profitable. But the United States Public Health Service and the United States Customs Bureau forbade the importation or use of any drugs or serum not approved by our government.

So we smuggled it in. Dr. Deyden got in touch with his schoolmates south of the border. Doctors, druggists, nurses, friends going to Nogales or Agua Prieta brought back a few vials of the contraband serum.

Dr. Deyden instructed our attending medical staff in its use. Its effect on a convulsing, choking child was miraculously dramatic. Within seconds the convulsions slowed and stopped. The child relaxed and dropped into a deep, calm sleep. Within an hour our doctors usually advised the parents that all danger was past. They could take the baby home.

We told all our two hundred attending doctors that we were smuggling the serum. We used it in our emergency room on scorpion cases as routinely as we used aminophylin for asthma, aspirin for headaches, or tetanus antitoxin for punctures from rusty nails.

Then occurred a dramatic incident that catapulted our life-saving underground into the headlines.

A two-year-old girl, Dahnell Parliament, was playing with her four-year-old brother when she was stung by a scorpion. Her mother was six miles away operating a cleaning shop. The baby-sitter telephoned to tell her that the child was ill. When the mother reached home, the little girl was unconscious. Mrs. Parliament stopped at the first doctor's office on the way into Phoenix. He recognized the scorpion-sting convulsions, forgot his office full of patients, put the mother and child in his own car, and broke all speed laws in reaching our hospital.

By that time the baby was almost choking to death. She could not breathe. While one doctor injected the serum, another cut into her windpipe and inserted a tracheotomy tube. Within a few minutes she was relaxed and asleep. The next morning the picture of the beautiful mother and child and the tale of the smuggled serum made up the most prominent story on the front page of the daily newspaper.

"Columbia World News" broadcast the story over the C.B.S. network. With a sense more dramatic than accurate, they told of my friends south of the border, and of thousands of peons stealing across the line at night to bring me live scorpions hidden in their serapes and huaraches. Huaraches — the Mexican sandals — would be a rather inconvenient hiding place for live scorpions.

The magazine *True Experiences* ran a story entitled "A Smuggled Drug Saved My Baby's Life," with a subcaption, "Breaking the law was easier for a gentle priest to do than watching a child's agony." Another magazine, *Saga*, entitled its version "Arizona's Mercy Smugglers."

The publicity had strange reactions. Government hospitals, especially on Indian reservations, asked us to supply them with the serum. The Arizona Highway Patrol and the United States Air Force assisted in rushing it to stricken children in far corners of the state.

The United States government slapped my wrist; I was openly defying a federal law. The Mexican laboratory must be approved before an import license could be granted. I agreed to encourage the Myn laboratories to seek approval but made it clear that we would continue to break the law until the importation was legalized or a source provided in the United States.

The medical director of the Mexican laboratory wanted no dealings with Washington. Too much red tape, he insisted. I secured the voluminous questionnaire from the National Institute of Health, had it translated into Spanish, and sent it to Mexico City. The Mexican consul in Phoenix wrote to the President of Mexico, urging co-operation on the ground that many of the children receiving the serum were of Mexican ancestry. The laboratory was finally inspected and found to be as clean, modern, and scientific as that of Parke-Davis, Lederle, or Squibb.

As the battle was being won, a long-distance call came about 2:30 P.M. from Albuquerque, New Mexico, five hundred miles away. A child had been stung at 1:30 P.M. No anti-scorpion serum could be found in New Mexico. We called the Air Force base at Williams Field, thirty miles away. Officials agreed to send a jet plane to the Phoenix Sky Harbor, the municipal airport, three miles from the hospital. A call to the Arizona Highway Patrol sent a car with a siren screaming across southern Phoenix. The jet pilot took the serum at 3:00 P.M. He covered the five hundred miles in one hour. The unconscious, convulsive child received the smuggled serum a few minutes later.

At 5:00 P.M., he was playing with the other children.

The battle of the serum and my public defiance of the United States government were in sharp contrast to my groveling, humble, servile reaction to the edict of the Provincial Council in the palace above Malibu Beach. I had not yet purged myself of the concept of the divine origin of the hierarchy and its power to strike down with the thunderbolts of hell, disgrace, and ostracism any who dared defy it.

I postponed the break as long as possible. The hierarchy was trying to force me out of the hospital, transfer me from Phoenix, then through isolation and enforced inactivity break my spirit. I had seen this process too many times not to recognize it.

A few months after my summons to Malibu Beach, I received this letter:

> Office of the Provincial
> Franciscan Province of St. Barbara
> 1500 Thirty-fourth Avenue
> Oakland 1, California
> May 26, 1947

Dear Padre:

The purpose of these few lines is to inform you once more of the Council Board's decision arrived at some months ago, and which was recalled recently at the Malibu sessions, that the material administration of St. Monica's Hospital is to be placed into the hands of the Trustee Board of Directors' jurisdiction.

I mention this decision on the part of the Definitors so that you will be duly prepared to accept any assignment as proposed and in accordance with the policy of the regular Franciscan routine in this regard.

The summer sessions will probably be held at the close of

June. Consequently you are requested to be responsive to the Definitorial Board's decision at that respective period.

With Fraternal and Prayerful wishes,

As ever in St. Francis:

Fr. Gregory, O.F.M.
(Provincial)

In my reply, I tried to stall:

St. Monica's Hospital
1200 South Fifth Avenue
Phoenix, Arizona
June 2, 1947

Very Reverend and Dear Father:

Since you first told me several months ago of the decision of the Definitorium, I have been seriously concerned about it and have been trying to work out a solution that would be satisfactory to the Council. It is not an easy task to develop a million-dollar institution which depends upon the collaboration of a multitude of people and then suddenly drop it into the laps of people who have relied on you to carry on.

In all my activities in connection with this hospital, I have never forgotten that I am a Franciscan. I have always tried to bring credit to the Order. Every article of praise that has appeared in the press, and there have been many, has always repeated that I am a Franciscan. We have been taught that the true Franciscan worked among the poor. I have known some Franciscans who forgot the poor and catered to the well-to-do in their parishes. This I have never done. I have worked consistently among the poorest of God's poor — the Negroes. As a result it is a confirmed fact that Negroes not only in Phoenix but throughout the west think of all priests as Franciscans. This attitude among them can certainly do the Order no harm.

I have now worked with, for, and among Negroes for twelve years. You will agree that I should know them and their problems better than any other member of our Province. Several years ago it became painfully evident that the intelligent Negroes were not entering the Church. Most of those becoming Catholics were doing so with the selfish purpose of trying to get something — generally food, clothing, or financial aid. I began reading every Negro publication I could find and talking to all Negroes who would speak frankly to me about their attitude. It didn't take long to find the sore spot. Thinking Negroes felt that the Church was not sincere in trying to convert them. Their papers claimed and still claim that the Church preaches Christianity and equality and the Mystical Body but does not practice them. As proof they point to the system of segregation in the Catholic schools and hospitals throughout the United States. There are a few exceptions among the schools. There are no exceptions among Catholic hospitals. Racial segregation and lack of economic opportunity are to Negroes the greatest evils in America. One has to be a Negro or work very closely with them to realize how deeply they feel this. The attitude of Notre Dame University in refusing to accept Negro students (they have changed in the last year or so) has done more harm to the Catholic cause than all the missionaries in the United States have done good. This has been admitted to me even by the Holy Cross Fathers themselves who are working among Negroes in South Bend, Indiana.

The Definitorium feels that the active administration of a hospital is not in conformity with the traditions of the priesthood and of Franciscanism. I respectfully beg to differ from the opinion. The corporal works of mercy are just as much a part of Christianity as the spiritual works of mercy. The history of the Church is filled with examples of this. Christ himself in speaking of the end of the world mentioned only the corporal works of mercy as a norm for the joining of the "blessed of my Father": "What you have done to one of these, my least brethren, you have done it also to me."

In 1946, St. Monica's Hospital took care of more than 20,000 in- and out-patients; 10,000 clinic patients and emergencies were cared for free of charge. Approximately $75,000 in hospitalization of in-patients was donated. I would venture to say that this is more than was done by all the St. Vincent de Paul societies in the western states.

As you probably know, our Corporation has bought and now owns St. Monica's Hospital. I have told a majority of the members of the board of directors of your wishes in my regard. They were very much upset. They joined the board to help me carry on this project but not to carry the load themselves. They know that I had the approval of my bishop and the Provincial and thought, as did I, that this approval would not be withdrawn.   They feel that it would be very unfair of the Church to throw the complexities of the institution on them. I, too, feel that I would be letting down these fine friends of all creeds and walks of life who have so generously assisted in carrying out my dreams.   They have been criticized just as viciously as I have for our racial attitude.

Very sincerely yours in Christ,
EMMETT McLOUGHLIN, O.F.M.

The Roman Catholic bishops of America, back in the early days of the Republic, met in the Council of Baltimore. They adopted a catechism — the question-and-answer form of teaching religion — and they prescribed the garb for priests.   It was to consist of a black suit with matching shoes and hat, black vest, and a reversed white collar.

Among the people of Arizona, informality in dress is an old and beloved tradition.   So long as the conventional anatomical area is covered, or nearly covered, everyone is on his own.   Especially before the days of universal air-conditioning, most men did not wear coats even at funerals, weddings, or in the awesome presence of the courts.   Men were and still are seen on downtown streets dressed only in shorts, and women frequently do their shopping in much less than a negligee.   This contempt of convention extended to the Roman Catholic clergy.   They came in from desert missions dressed in khaki and Indian shirts.   In the cities they wore slacks and sport shirts.

As the tempo of hierarchical correspondence increased, this and other minor items were added to the fuel of condemnation.   The Rev. Brendan Mitchell, a member of the Provincial Council, wrote me on June 10, 1947:

. . . There isn't the slightest doubt that your work in behalf of the social betterment of the Negro population of Phoenix has been a magnificent job. As a *job* it has been perhaps the most spectacular thing ever done by anybody in the Province ever, or by any priest west of Omaha. As a job done *in behalf of the colored*, I suppose it is one of the largest and most thorough efforts at social betterment and racial integration done by any one individual, certainly by any Catholic priest or layman.

It is fairly evident to anyone giving the matter attention, I think, that the Catholic Church has lagged scandalously in general in the United States in working to achieve the ends you are and have achieved. . . .

I am given to understand that the housing work and the hospital is almost purely social in its emphasis. I am not one of those who subscribe to the opinion that the kind of social work you are engaged in is un-Franciscan, or even less Franciscan than teaching algebra or physical education. But as I think any Franciscan educational program that would de-emphasize the Faith would be lop-sided and inadequate, so I think a social program conducted by the Church, or by a priest for the Church, should include a pretty strong and explicit shot of the integral Catholic Faith. What are the facts? . . .

This next one is touchy, but I'll tackle it. It's touchy because I have no right, being aware of my own public shortcomings, or most of them, and they are largely indefensible, to censure another guy's. But it's part of the job and enters into the question. The charge is made that you appear to be reluctant to appear as a Catholic priest in the hospital; that is the interpretation put upon alleged reluctance to wear the collar in your capacity as superintendent of the hospital, and that there is no reason for publicly and continuously disregarding the law in that matter which would be adequate in this case. What explanation should I render?

The next one isn't easy either. . . . There is an opinion current that your approach to the hospital work lacks priestliness and is too naturalistic, if that is the right way to try to characterize what is expressed otherwise in common talk. Very frequent references to unsavory anatomical matters, were doubtless meant, it is interpreted, to arouse a guffaw or to have some fun shocking the more susceptible, but after a while the observers rationalize, and have done so, that your approach to this social problem you are working at is coarse, natural, roughly humane, but lacking a supernatural element. . . . I am aware this begins to sound like an old woman. The application may sound so; the principle is definitely not, or else off goes my collar too. There was one thing I resolved to try to practice when this job was wished on me, and that was to keep my guts, even if it involved leading with my chin . . . but to go back to the subject: this is one of the reasons why you are supposed to be spoiling on the job and need salvaging from it lest the talents God gave you be dissipated. . . .

From my reply of June 23, 1947:

If the Definitorium objects to an "unbalanced social program," why didn't they object years ago? For many years I have devoted just as much time to this sort of thing as I do now. Ten years ago my program included a day nursery, a sewing program, full schedule of clinics, arts, crafts, dancing classes, and a complete recreational program with nine teams of various ages and sexes playing at the same time. I was chauffeur and general manager of the teams. Besides this I was on various boards and committees. I have always felt that the "priest in the sacristy" ideal had much to do with Catholic European countries being such easy victims to Fascism and now Communism.

The Roman collar. I do wear it whenever the occasion warrants it. The Council of Baltimore was not held in Arizona or the regulations would be different. If I am going to be condemned on this score then most of the clergy should be run out. Do you know that when Fr. Burkhard Kuksht was chosen Definitor he was finally located in the Fox Theater in Phoenix and had to borrow clerical clothes from the boys at St. Mary's so that he could appear properly attired? I do not try to hide the fact that I am a priest. Everyone in town knows me no matter how I am dressed.

The Provincial Council met. For the first time in my career I received a formal communication signed by all the members of the Provincial Council — including the one who had not bothered about clerical garb until the day he was elected to that body.

June 29, 1947

RESPONSE: To Rev. Emmett McLoughlin, O.F.M.

In response to your letter to the Very Rev. Provincial and the Definitorium of June 2, 1947, kindly be informed as follows:

1. We are concerned with the spiritual care and corporal works of mercy in behalf of the Negroes as much as that tendered to any other group, and wish to promote it properly in due proportion and within the limits of the resources of our Province.

2. The work you have done in behalf of the Negroes in Phoenix has been outstanding and in many things praiseworthy.

3. However, in the course we have here set down we have the concurrence of your Superior, the Pastor of St. Mary's, a large number of your confreres, and not a few well informed Catholic laymen.

4. In our judgement and by our decision, you may no longer serve in the capacity of superintendent of St. Monica's hospital, as we are convinced that it has led to the spiritual neglect of your Negro parishioners and to laxities in your manner as a Franciscan and a priest.

5. You may, and we hope you will, continue to direct the policies of St. Monica's hospital insofar as you can as chairman of its board.

6. We call your attention to the law of the Church with regard to clerical garb.

7. We are convinced that there has been a shift of the emphasis of your policy of handling your care of souls from the spiritual to the temporal, and direct you to reverse this policy and give your main attention to the spiritual development of St. Monica's parish.

8. We direct you to carry this out with as much prudence and absence of public disturbance as possible, lest your real work be impaired and damage be done to the spiritual welfare of the people you are proposing to help.

9. We do not wish to proceed with argumentation on these matters and consider such argumentation closed.

10. We await the immediate expression of your willingness to follow these directions, and to co-operate in a sensible plan to obtain these objectives.

FR. GREGORY WOOLER, O.F.M., Min. Prov.
FR. BURKHARD KUKSHT, O.F.M., Def.
FR. DAVID TEMPLE, O.F.M.
FR. BRENDAN MITCHELL, O.F.M.
FR. ALFRED BOEDDEKER, O.F.M., Def.
FR. AUGUSTINE HOBRECHT, O.F.M., Custos

There were many points in this letter that made me suspicious. The Provincial Council stated that my local Superior at St. Mary's rectory and the pastor of the parish concurred in their decision. Both those reverend gentlemen professed to be my friends and had repeatedly told me that the Provincial Council was persecuting me. Who was telling the truth? A " large number " of my confreres, or fellow priests, they also said, were helping to twist the knife in my back. Again I remembered the bishop's words shortly after our hospital opened: " This is a good work. But you cannot go on with it. You will be forced out . . ." And the " well informed Catholic laymen " — who could they be? Could a Catholic layman be " well informed " in these matters?

The Provincial Council had extended a gesture of conciliation. They would permit me to direct the destiny and policies of the hospital as chairman of its board of trustees. Was this a token of weakness on their part — or strategy?

The majority of my board of trustees had assured me of loyal backing in a showdown with the Roman Catholic Church. The Provincial Council knew this. They knew that thirteen of these sixteen trustees were Masons.

My backbone was finally stiffening. My ancestral Irish

temper was rising, and my American birthright was asserting itself. I answered the Provincial Council in a tone as discourteous as their " Response."

July 2, 1947

RESPONSE TO THE REVEREND DEFINITORIUM:

In previous correspondence I have tried to explain the impossibility of my withdrawing from the superintendency of St. Monica's Hospital. I have never wished to have any argumentation over the matter and am glad that it is now closed. I regret to inform you that I cannot accept your decision.

By " public disturbance " I presume you mean newspaper and radio publicity. Whether I wish to be or not I am somewhat of a public figure in Arizona. Whatever I might do would undoubtedly be publicized. If you gentlemen are so sure you are right, then why should you worry if your decree is shouted from the housetops? Personally, I have no fear of publicity because before God I feel I am doing the right thing.

REV. EMMETT McLOUGHLIN

The members of the Fourth Estate had always been very gracious to me. I had confided in newspaper reporters, and they had respected my confidences. Contrary to the policy of most hospitals, we have always given them all the information concerning the hospital and its patients, especially emergency cases, that our attorneys will permit without disclosing " privileged communication."

Several of the local reporters knew for more than a year that I was reaching an impasse with the Church officials. Some of the reporters were Roman Catholics. One, who had been trained by the Jesuits, told me that he had seen many Jesuit priests " persecuted " with the same tactics that the Franciscans were employing against me.

Honesty and frankness with reporters have always

seemed to me better "public relations" than attempts at concealment.

During this period, in addition to my other functions I was still a member and secretary of the Arizona State Board of Health. In spite of the hierarchy's displeasure at my "worldliness," it still wanted to use me when I could further its ends. The following letter from the bishop of my diocese might be of interest to those who have heard the Roman Catholic Church proclaim its belief in separation of church and state in America:

> Bishop's Residence
> Tucson, Arizona
> August 7, 1947

The Rev. Emmett McLoughlin, O.F.M.
231 North Third St.
Phoenix, Arizona

Dear Father: —
. . . I wish now to bring to your attention a matter that has to do with the welfare of the Church and the State. I have read of the retirement of Dr. Manning [the Arizona Director of Public Health]. I shall state now a few things which have been given to me by reliable authority. I have been advised that Dr. [Hilda] Kroeger, a member of your Welfare Board [State Board of Health] is not interested in succeeding Dr. Manning.

Mrs. [Margaret] Sanger, who is now touring Europe in the interest of cutting down the race, was reported to have said that no "fish eater" would ever occupy this position. The campaign is to pack the Welfare Board so that the Legislature will be compelled to pass a law legalizing all the clinics which her group is opening throughout the State not to speak of Phoenix and Tucson.

The result would be that a Catholic must either refer all his patients or clients to the clinic for proper fittings, etc., or resign his job.   It is a bloody shame that such people should be allowed to carry on without some protest.   Dr. Clarence R. Kroeger of Tucson now employed under Dr. Howard in the Welfare Office is still a "fish eater."   I say still for unfortunately he married a Catholic woman after his former Catholic partner left him.   Nevertheless, he comes from good stock and he has a conscience governed by right principles and he and his present wife go regularly to mass.

He has made application for the position and I would like to see him get it.   There may be the objection that he is not in welfare work five years yet.   In manus tuas commendo casum [I place the matter in your hands], and a notice of this should be brought to the other priests to head off any such legislation if it should come up.

See what can be done to have the proper doctor put in.

With sentiments of esteem in the union of prayer, I am

Devotedly yours in Christ,

† DANIEL J. GERCKE
Bishop of Tucson

The fact that his candidate did not meet the requirements of the state law did not seem to bother the bishop. When the Board of Health met, we unanimously chose an Episcopalian doctor who was a strong believer in Margaret Sanger and birth control.

The Roman Catholic prohibition of birth control has exploited women, bankrupted and disrupted families, and burdened the Catholic population with thousands of unwanted and uncared-for children.   It is the greatest cause of "leakage" from the Church.   It is the plague of "mixed" marriages, the cause of marital aberrations, and in the confessional the source of more trouble to priests than any other "sin."   By orders of the hierarchy, priests must preach against birth control as mortally sinful.   But they are closer to the people than the bishops are.   They know, on the one hand, that it is practiced by a very large percentage of their parishioners; and, on the other hand, many of those who don't practice it are either too old to need to, too young to care, or in the middle of mental and psychic conflicts. Many a priest I have heard utter in despair, "If only they wouldn't confess birth control, we wouldn't have to tell them it is wrong."

My beliefs regarding birth control, of course, were heretical. I believed in it and instructed our medical interns to give all the contraceptive advice necessary to the numerous mothers who crowded our clinics, spawning more offspring than they could feed. Our experience had shown that too large a percentage of unplanned waifs would be back later in our pediatric department, suffering from malnutrition, diarrhea, and simple neglect.

It was easy for the hierarchy from its ivory towers to issue edicts that men and women, to avoid children, should live as brothers and sisters, or sleep with a calendar on the bedpost. The Church condemns birth control as a frustration of nature — whereas the alternative they offer is, in actuality, far more unnatural and destructive, physically and emotionally.

During the summer of 1948 occurred a coincidence that further heightened the ecclesiastic wrath. St. Joseph's Hospital, run by the Sisters of Mercy, was fifty years old, most of its buildings outmoded, decrepit, and dangerous. The sisters, backed by the hierarchy and a large segment of the Phoenix population, embarked upon a drive for $1,500,-000. They already had the promise of another $1,500,000 from the federal Hill-Burton funds. The commercial fund-raising firm they employed, instead of pointing out that the existing buildings had outlived their usefulness, utilized the scare technique. They campaigned on the theme of a hospital-bed shortage; they implied that a person falling acutely ill would have to stay at home. Prospective mothers were terrorized at the thought that they might deliver on an ambulance cot. The radios screamed that surgery reservations must be made three weeks in advance.

But actually, at the time of the drive, there was no bed shortage at all. The summer slump was on. The winter visitors had gone east. Doctors were on vacation, and elective, non-emergency surgery was at the lowest ebb of the year.

At St. Monica's Hospital, we decided to do the economical thing. In the midst of St. Joseph's Hospital's public plaints, we closed down a forty-bed wing. The newspapers picked up the story. The nuns were frantic. Their drive slumped like a pricked balloon. I was immediately blamed. A leader in their fund drive — who was active in a construction firm which everyone said might get the new hospital construction contract regardless of bids, and a devout Roman Catholic — called me on the telephone. He berated me for thirty minutes in language unbecoming a Roman Catholic gentleman addressing a Roman Catholic priest. When I asked meekly if I might tell my side of the story, he hung up the phone. This incident, occurring when it did, did not help cement relationships between myself and the hierarchy. News of the affair was immediately sent to the Provincial Superior in Oakland, California.

The attempt to intimidate me continued. This time the effort was made by my own brother, also a priest of the Franciscan Order. I had sent him a copy of one of my letters to the Provincial Council. He now replied:

Franciscan Fathers
Old Mission
San Luis Rey, Calif.
Sept. 12, 1948

Dear Johnny: [1]

Frankly, your letter made me feel like hell. Somehow, I feel partly to blame. I've half way suspected for a long time that something like this might come up. And I did nothing about it. I thought a daily memento for you at mass was doing my part. Perhaps if I had been really fervent in my prayers and masses, and less self-centered — and really lived the life I've promised, God wouldn't have let this happen. Or maybe if I had taken a more active interest in your affairs and kept in closer contact with you — but you're a hard man to influence, Johnny. You're always right, and everyone else is a fool, except those who agree with you.

Forgive me, but are you sincere in your letter to the Provincial? Do you really believe it when you assign a *spiritual motive* for holding out, quoting the words of Christ in your defense? Doesn't the anomaly strike you? — alleging your loyalty to Christ as a justification for violating your solemn vow of obedience? Doesn't it strike you that *that*, in itself, is a rejection of Christ? that you are turning your back on Christ by this and going over to the devil's side? Or do you no longer believe in the doctrines of the Church?

You have always expressed a lot of contempt for most of the friars and things Franciscan. I've often wondered why you joined.

But you did join, and you promised solemnly before Christ, whom you now profess to serve, to observe the vow of obedience, and keep the rule all your life. Who is right and who is wrong in the various difficulties you have been involved in, I am in no position to judge. Only one thing stands out clear as judgment to me, and that is that the final norm for you and me before God is the obedience we have promised, and you are throwing that over.

Besides, from the viewpoint of your work at the hospital —

[1] My name before entering the seminary.

aren't you cutting your own throat? How long will your prestige hold up, once you are suspended, or an ex-priest? Besides the harm to others from the scandal that is bound to result, and which you could prevent, don't you think the stigma will undermine your standing? Not that your standing will be worth having in the position you will be in before God.

Please, come to your senses. Look ahead a few years — and into eternity. Give your soul a break.

This letter is strong. I realize that. But I hope it won't antagonize you. You wrote to me first, which indicated that you would give me a hearing. Surely it is not too late. You can still retract. And it's not public as yet, I hope. I would give my life, I swear, to see you saved from this. Please, in the name of Christ, don't go through with it.

Your anxious and loving brother,

CHARLIE [2]

His letter produced no reaction. Suddenly he appeared in Phoenix, wanting to enter our hospital for a complete heart check. He had been dismissed from the seminary at one time because his heart was so bad that the Order shied away from assuming a medical liability. He had been given a month to live by a famous San Francisco heart surgeon. When years went by without his demise, he was reaccepted but kept under the surveillance of one of the best heart specialists in California. It was obvious to me now that he did not need to come to Arizona for medical treatment. I knew that the hierarchy had sent him to make the last emotional appeal — at my expense. (I subsequently paid his hospital bill.) I avoided any opportunity of what might have been an acrimonious fraternal discussion. On leaving he put his thoughts in writing:

[2] Rev. Dermot McLoughlin, O.F.M.

St. Mary's Church
Franciscan Fathers
231 North Third Street
Phoenix, Arizona
November 22, 1948

Dear Emmett,

I wanted to thank you for all the trouble you went to for me, and for the fine care you and your staff gave me. I also wanted to mention a few more things I heard about you, which I think would interest you. They indicate what some of the doctors and people around town are thinking about the case.

Dr. Flinn was asking one of the Friars about your present status. (I got this straight and know it is true.) He then remarked that if you would try to continue as superintendent of St. Monica's as an "unfrocked priest" (expression his) you would be a damn fool — to put it mildly. Some lay person was asking Matt Curtin what in the world you are — a "minister without portfolio?" (You do dress more like a fop than a priest.) There is a dentist, part Negro, I think, who was a member of your parish and a good friend of yours. He, too, was asking about your present status, and told a Friar that he thought you ought to get out of the hospital before it is too late. He also mentioned, incidentally, that the St. Monica's parishioners had been rather spoiled for regular mass and sermon attendance because you had them out so fast always. He said you dashed out, raced through the mass in a few minutes, and dashed in again — and some of the Negroes have told Lucian that they were glad you got changed from the Church because you never preached any more. Many of them have asked if you still say mass. And some of them have told Lucian about others who are saying that you are leading a bad life and all your preaching was just talk and so they no longer try to live right, or practice their religion. They say, if you don't, why should they?

There is also a rumor going around that your hospital board is already casting about for a new superintendent. Perhaps it has no foundation.

But the fact that so much adverse talk *is* going on about you indicates, that the people feel that you are not in the right. I really don't think you are in a position to see your own position. You have lost your true perspective. You have gotten so used to looking only at *one side* of the question, that your vision is warped. You can see only the fact that you originally had the O.K. of the Provincial to go on with this project. But you don't realize how much you have changed in your outlook and manner since then. You can't realize how you appear to others and what others are thinking of you.

Also, regardless of what your original intention was, or that of Fr. Martin, judging from what I've seen and heard in Phoenix and at the hospital, I really believe that it would be better if you were out of the hospital now — better for you *and* better for the hospital and the people you are trying to help. I believe if you keep on as you are going, you will do those people more harm than good. Up to now you have gained a wonderful reputation in Phoenix and have accomplished great things. If you have sense enough to step out at the right time your work will live on and your reputation in Phoenix be secure. But you could easily spoil it all and ruin your reputation and your past work, and that is what you are headed for now.

You say that this is a matter between you and God. That implies that you are praying over it. I hope you are. God bless you and thanks again.

CHARLIE

I have always been sure that Dr. Robert S. Flinn had made no such statement. That very fine doctor was then — and for several years remained — chief of the medical staff of the hospital and a good friend. He is still my personal physician.

Meanwhile the Provincial Council had met again and issued the following orders:

September 3, 1948

Rev. Emmett McLoughlin, O.F.M.
St. Mary's, Phoenix, Ariz.
Dear Father Emmett:
In September, 1947, the Very Rev. Provincial and the Definitorium, in consultation with you concerning certain difficulties

of which you are aware, arrived at the decision that you were to adopt certain external proprieties, and were to sever your connection with St. Monica's Hospital as superintendent as soon as you could arrange certain details of finance and personnel.

Much more than ordinary forbearance, consideration and tolerance were extended to you in this matter than a Religious, living under obedience, would ordinarily expect.

By this time it was expected that you would try to co-operate at least by offering some factual evidence of the improvements of the financial and personnel situation to your Superior, and by voluntarily showing cause why your connection with St. Monica's Hospital need continue. Instead there are, among other things, newspaper reports of a controversy with civil officials; and also further newspaper publicity which needlessly injected controversy into the campaign of St. Joseph's Hospital, to the chagrin of the Catholic community of Phoenix. Such evidence of a lack, among other things, of prudence, have moved the Very Rev. Provincial and the Definitorium to the following decisions, which are hereby communicated to you.

1. You have been removed as pastor and administrator of St. Monica's Parish, and you are kindly asked to turn over to your successor, as soon as he is publicly named, the records, etc., which are confided to the custody of a parochial administrator.

2. You are to arrange the matters of your connection with St. Monica's Hospital so that by January 1, 1949, if not before, you will no longer be superintendent of the hospital, and that you will be in a position to resign from its board, should the Very Rev. Provincial and the Definitorium decide at that time to assign you to a new post in the Province.

3. In the meantime, your work at St. Monica's Hospital is to be confined to office hours from 8 A.M. to 5 P.M. Your absence from the Friary at other times is to be accounted for each time to the local Superior, just as any other Friar is obligated.

4. Moreover, you are to grant no interviews to the press, nor to make statements for publication without the previous, individual and express permission of your Local Superior, and with due regard to the regulations of Canon Law regarding the rights of the Ordinary in this matter. Regardless of technical considerations of who originated such publication, or how,

your Provincial Superior will judge of your good or bad faith in this matter.

5. To apologize to the Sisters of St. Joseph's Hospital, if you have not already done so, for the injury needlessly given their financial campaign, would be the gentlemanly and sportsmanlike thing; however, that is left to your judgement. But under no condition will any further open or apparent controversy between yourself and any other religious community of the Church be permitted to occur without your immediate removal. And if there is any public criticism or controversy with civic officials to be indulged in, you are to submit the matter first to your Provincial Superior.

6. You are appointed " cooperator " to St. Mary's parish and the Fr. Guardian and the Rev. Pastor will be instructed to assign certain work to you in that capacity.

It is the sincere hope of the Very Rev. Provincial and the Definitorium that this clearer definition of your present status will materially assist in solving the difficulties discussed with you in the past two years, and it is their confident hope that you will do your best to comply.

> Sincerely yours in Christ,
> Fr. Gregory Wooler, O.F.M.
>   Provincial Minister
> Fr. Alfred Boeddeker, O.F.M. Definitor
> Fr. Augustine Hobrecht, O.F.M. Custos
> Fr. David Temple, O.F.M. Definitor
> Fr. Brendan Mitchell, O.F.M. Definitor
> Fr. Burkhard Kuksht, O.F.M. Definitor

The showdown was approaching. I answered:

September 6, 1948

Dear Fr. Provincial:

Your letters of September 3 received and their contents noted with care.

You refer to a controversy with civil officials. I assume you mean the dispute of this hospital with the Maricopa County Board of Supervisors concerning the care of indigent patients. I have been involved in two other controversies, but they have occurred since your June meeting. One was with the Public Housing Administration. The other is current with the United States Customs Department. The newspaper story appeared yesterday and is enclosed.

Regarding the controversy with the Board of Supervisors, it strikes me that the Franciscan Order and the Catholic Church have struck a new low when they condemn a priest for doing what Christ taught us to do in the story of the Good Samaritan. Or should it still hold true that " a certain priest was going down the same way; and when he saw him, he passed by "?

It is quite evident that St. Joseph's Hospital and the Sisters of Mercy are still " hitting below the belt " as they have always done as far as this hospital and myself are concerned. Apparently the guidance of the Holy Ghost over the decisions of the Reverend Definitorium eliminates the necessity of that honorable body trying to discover the facts before handing down arbitrary decrees. If the Sisters of Mercy had conducted their financial campaign on a basis of truth they would not have been hurt when we closed a forty-bed wing. That wing was closed for reasons of economy — not spite — and it is still closed. The newspaper reporters visit this institution daily and news of anything that transpires is available to them.

I am as tired of this wrangling as you undoubtedly are and therefore will very plainly record my decisions in response to yours — in the same order as they appear in your letter.

1. All documents are ready for my successor. I gave my farewell talk to the congregation yesterday and squelched, I believe, all attempts at circulating petitions, etc. I told the people only about item No. 1 in your letter. You will have to buy an automobile for the new pastor since the one I have been using does not belong to the parish and will not stay.

2. I reject your decision regarding St. Monica's Hospital. I have no intention of giving up the superintendency of the hospital on January 1, 1949, or at any other time. Nor do I intend to resign from the board of the hospital, the Phoenix Housing Authority, or the Arizona Board of Health.

3. This item is ridiculous.

4. I shall naturally be cautious in what I tell the press but if necessary I intend to defend myself. I believe in the God-given American right of free speech and do not intend to surrender it to anyone. We live in America — not Russia.

5. I certainly shall not apologize to the Sisters of St. Joseph's Hospital. I have done nothing to apologize for. Regarding controversies with religious communities or civil officials, I believe I am old enough to use my own judgment without having recourse to my Provincial Superior.

6. My duties at the hospital preclude the possibility of taking on the work of a " co-operator " at St. Mary's Parish.

In conclusion, I propose to work to expand our services to the sick and the poor. I still believe Christ meant what he said in the words, " Amen, I say to you, as long as you did it for one of these, the least of my brethren, you did it for me."

Sincerely yours in Christ,
FR. EMMETT MCLOUGHLIN, O.F.M.

I had sent a copy of this letter to the bishop of the diocese. He had known for more than a year of my clash with the Franciscan Order. In the light of this fact, his answer sounded a bit amnesiac:

September 8, 1948

Dear Father:

This is to acknowledge the receipt of your reply to the Very Rev. Father Provincial. This is the first intimation that I have had of the difficulty between you and the Provincial or of the controversies mentioned in your letter. In fact, I had thought that the difficulties had been ironed out.

In reply, I wish to advise you as your friend to reconsider what you have written in the above mentioned letter to your Provincial. As I have told you before, in all sincerity, I have admired you and the work you have done. However, there is liable to come into the life of every man, particularly into that of a priest, when he will be tried and when he must stand at the parting of the ways.

I ask you then, before it is too late, to reconsider and write to the Provincial that unconditionally you give strict obedience to all the six points mentioned in his letter. You know as well as I do that Obedience is the greatest of all the virtues and the hardest one to practice. Put yourself now in the place of the Provincial and, if you had put certain conditions in a letter to a subject, and if he refused to obey, you would have to do something about it.

Then the climax is liable to occur that may mar or spoil your remaining days in the priesthood. I can almost hear your reaction to this appeal. There should be no reaction. You have only one duty: that of obedience. Then you will be happy and safe. I have seen controversies of this kind make for great evil. Even if your obedience would result in the undoing of all that has been accomplished it were better that it should be so. . . .

Any amount of controversy couldn't convince me to the contrary and you know that this is the proper advice for me as a bishop and as your friend to give. I pray God then that you may have the courage to admit you are wrong and submit in toto to the will of your Superior. I am not denying you the right to talk things over, but I deny that your present stand may be defended coram Deo [before God].

> Devotedly yours in Christ,
> † Daniel J. Gercke
> Bishop of Tucson

On September 18, 1948, the ultimatum arrived from the Provincial Council:

September 18th, 1948

Rev. and dear Father:

After having read your letter as of September the sixth, and after having corresponded with His Excellency, the Most Rev. Daniel Gercke, Bishop of Tucson, the members of the Definitorium unanimously decided that you are to sever all connections with St. Monica's Hospital by January the first, 1949.

On or before the first of the year you will receive an obedience to leave Phoenix.

The Definitorium is convinced that you have openly and seriously violated your vow of obedience.

> Very sincerely yours in Christ,
> Fr. Gregory Wooler, O.F.M.

This was it. Melodramatic as it may sound, the hour of decision had come. No one could help me. No one can help anyone in the time of crisis. Friends can only stand mutely by. Man must go through his agony alone. He must climb the mountain of thought and there above and beyond the noise of humanity, with the prayerful help only of God, he must make the choice.

An old spiritual expresses that loneliness so simply:

> You've got to cross that lonesome valley.
> You've got to cross it for yourself.
> There ain't no one gonna cross it for you.
> You've got to cross it for yourself.

The choice was clear. On the one hand, if I submitted, there was the certain knowledge that because of disobedience I would be withdrawn from the active ministry. I would be forced to do penance. I would be isolated in a monastery. I would be crushed in spirit. But if I took the other course, I would face the certain wrath of the powerful and unforgiving hierarchy. I would face the condemnation of relatives and Roman Catholic friends. I would face all those promised curses of God and man — in addition to economic insecurity.

For two months, in the quiet of my own mind, I prayed and pondered and reached my decision. I would not obey. I would leave the priesthood. But I determined also that I would not sneak away into the oblivion of a large city. I would stay in Phoenix and face the storm.

The formal "obedience" ordering me out of Phoenix was to come on January 1, 1949. My plan was to await it, ignore it, and allow the mechanism of hierarchical excommunication and suspension to expel me from the Church. This was the passive and the easier course.

Two doctors persuaded me to change my plan. One was Dr. Maurice Rosenthal, our hospital pathologist. The other was his friend, Dr. Victor Donnet. His family, as Huguenots, had been chased out of France by Roman Catholics after the St. Bartholomew's Massacre three centuries ago. In my defiance of the hierarchy, he was achieving vicarious revenge. Both doctors felt that I should take the initiative and resign, not be expelled. To carry on in the hospital, I must have the sympathy, co-operation, and respect of the general, non-Catholic public. That public would respect me more, the doctors advised, if I had the courage and dignity to defy the hierarchy, rather than let them throw me out like a disobedient dog.

Their counsel seemed good, and I prepared my final statement. At 9:00 P.M. on November 30, 1948, I stood at the door of St. Mary's rectory in Phoenix. I must step out of my past life's work with as much assurance, calmness, and dignity as if I were merely resigning from a university faculty because I disagreed with the policies of its trustees. I felt like a coward, but I forced myself to enter the monastery where I had lived for fourteen years. I called the priests together — men I had studied with, lived with, prayed with. I told them I was leaving the priesthood and the Roman Catholic Church. When I offered my hand in parting friendship, some wept, some blessed me, and others openly cursed me.

As I stepped back out into the fateful insecurity of that night, my letter of decision was being delivered to the Provincial Superior.

November 29, 1948

The Very Reverend Gregory Wooler, O.F.M.
1500 34th Avenue
Oakland, California

Very Reverend and Dear Father:

For a period of more than a year, correspondence has taken place between the Fathers of the Provincial Council and myself regarding my position in this hospital and my work in Phoenix.

You have insisted that I give up the superintendency of St. Monica's Hospital, the presidency of its board of directors, and finally that I prepare to leave Phoenix. This, you insist, I must do if I am to remain in good standing as a priest of the Catholic Church and a member of the Franciscan Order. As a reason for your demand you have contended that my activities are too material in nature and do not conform to the spiritual duties of the priesthood.

I have prayed that no irreconcilable difference might arise between myself and the officials of the Church. However, my ideals are such that I have never been nor can I ever be content with the mere preachings of the tenets of Christianity. I have striven to transform these teachings into buildings, schools, and living realities in the hearts and minds of man. This has not been an idle dream. The record speaks for itself.

With the assistance of other individuals and organizations, things were done that aided thousands of people. During the depression the distressed were clothed, fed, and given employment through Father Emmett's Mission. Recreation was organized. Day nurseries were started. Venereal clinics were established, and mothers were given scientific care when their babies were born in shacks, tents, and under bridges.

The United States Congressional Record attests the success of our Phoenix slum-clearance program. Four thousand people are living in decent homes with an opportunity of bringing up their children in sanitary, wholesome surroundings. Almost 100,000 people have been treated in St. Monica's Hospital — thousands without charge. For years I have taken an active part in the Arizona State Board of Health and have served with the Urban League and various other civic groups. Racial barriers are being broken down. St. Monica's Hospital is a throbbing, living proof that people of all races, creeds, and backgrounds can study, live, and serve humanity together and in harmony.

These are some of the things which have been done, but much remains to be done. If my activities have conflicted with the interests of a few, their antagonism will not swerve me from my appointed task. To its accomplishment I have dedicated my life and I shall remain in Phoenix and work toward this goal.

Since apparently there can be no reconciliation between your decision that I give up my work in Phoenix and my resolve to continue it, I can reach only one conclusion: I respectfully submit to you my resignation from the Franciscan Order and from the active ministry in the priesthood of the Roman Catholic Church, as of December 1, 1948.

I make this decision with the full and prayerful consciousness that God will be my judge.

Very sincerely yours,

REV. EMMETT McLOUGHLIN, O.F.M.

Superintendent

CHAPTER FIVE

"Founded Upon a Rock"

The die was cast. That night I was frightened, mentally naked, and alone. I had stripped my mind of the robe that throughout my youth had protected me from the cold questions of life. I knew that I could not and never would go back.

I had rejected the only security I had ever known. It had been the mental security of intellectual inertia. It had been the physical security of a big institution, of big buildings, of big churches. I felt like a convict who had escaped from the security of a life sentence in a penitentiary, who knew that the guards would be after him and that he must build his new life while protecting himself from their attacks.

I felt like the Jews of the days of Nehemiah as they faced the Arabians, the Ammonites, and the Ashdodites. "They which builded on the wall, and they that bare burdens, with those that laded, everyone with one of his hands wrought in the work, and with the other hand held a weapon. For the builders, every one had his sword girded by his side."

True, I had a position and I had friends. But the position depended on those friends. All my life I had been taught that if I turned back those friends would despise and desert me. I expected neither sympathy nor assistance from Roman Catholics.

When I reached the hospital the next morning, the switchboard was jammed with calls. Some people were congratulating me, some were expressing sincere regret, many were cursing obscenely and anonymously.

In the early afternoon my secretary told me that a gentleman wished to see me. His name was Dudley Field Malone. Every priest in the United States knew of Dudley Field Malone. He was considered the most famous Roman Catholic lawyer in America. He had been an associate of Clarence Darrow and had helped him confound William Jennings Bryan in the famous " monkey trial " in Tennessee. Any Catholic club, organization, or convention would boast loudly if it were privileged to hear the flowing English of Dudley Field Malone. He had been chosen to play Winston Churchill in the moving picture *Mission to Moscow* because of his resemblance to the British prime minister and because of his parallel powers in the use of language. This man, I felt, was surely coming to try to persuade me to change my decision.

He shook hands cordially and then with his magnificent, expansive gestures, he said, " As a lifetime Irish-American Roman Catholic, and one who is still a daily attendant at mass and communion, I wish to extend to you my appreciation, my congratulations, and my humble blessing. If every priest in the United States would only do what you have done, it might bring the hierarchy to its senses."

By the next morning, December 2, 1948, the mail had started. On top of a bundle of several hundred letters was the one that broke the tension:

Dear Father Emmett:

You gave up so much and we want you to know we are grateful. Most of us are working here because we believe in your
ideals and in what you are trying to do for the common people.
Many of us have heard of your work and have come across
the country to help further your cause.

Your hospital and clinics give all classes and races of people
real service. We also believe strongly in your very-much-
American School of Nursing which trains young women who
represent a cross section of all races and denominations. We
NEED you as our leader to guide us in the work which was inspired by your ideals. Thank you for staying with us.

Sincerely,

The Nursing Personnel of
St. Monica's Hospital

It was signed by eighty-nine nurses, attendants, and or-
derlies. Twenty of them were Roman Catholic. Many of
them are still in the hospital, five years later. With loyalty
like this within the hospital, what need had I to fear the
curses from without?

Time magazine carried the story in its issue of December 13, 1948. Thousands upon thousands of letters reached
me from all of the forty-eight states, from Europe, from
China, India, and South America.

Bishop Gercke of Tucson, who had previously written
that he knew nothing of my differences with the Order
although the Provincial Council was in constant contact
with him by correspondence, now tried to coax me back
through fear:

. . . In this appeal I am concerned only with the supernatural
aspect, your soul. From a natural point of view, you are never
going to make a go of your venture if you stay in the hospital.
That is common sense. I have been praying for you. I shall
always do so, while hating your line of action I shall always try
to love you in the hope that some day you will come back. . . .

So forget the past and start over. I heard only yesterday that there is going to be a demand that you quit the presidency or certain people are going to quit the hospital. Then you see this will bring you into an altercation with the government. . . .

Bishop Noll of Indiana, the founder of *Our Sunday Visitor*, struck the same note:

Boyd Barrett, in his recent article in *America*, noted that the priest who " strays " is usually approached by Protestants who want to use him, but he warns even the ex-priest against yielding to their pressure because "they are not only not sincere but actually distrust the one who violated his vows."
. . . from my long experience — over a period of fifty years — I have learned that ninety-five per cent of them have deeply regretted the action they took, and have heartily wished that they had patched it up earlier.

The abbot of the Trappist monks in Kentucky threw me into the same category with the many priests, mostly alcoholics, who are sent to them for penance:

. . . The same thing happened. They began to cut corners on their supernatural life and gradually stepped down to live on a mere natural plane. Then, when a big trial came, they had nothing to stand on and the poor fellows collapsed spiritually.
But almost in every case we have succeeded in getting them back on their feet. Of course, with the help of our Sweet Mother Mary and Jesus.
Dear Emmett, Jesus never turns a man down.

The feeling of many of these people, both priests and the laity, was that in rejecting the hierarchy I had rejected *God*. Their letters show how successfully the Roman Catholic Church has indoctrinated its people with the illusion that it alone is the voice of the Almighty on earth. These are excerpts:

. . . Father Wooler's action may have been unjust. I have had conflicts with unpleasant clerical types and I have known religious whose talents were despised and who were frustrated by spiteful superiors. Yet two wrongs do not make a right. By taking the very human (and Irish) path of rebellion you have allowed yourself to be cut off from the most precious thing in life.

. . . the mental anguish resulting from your public denial of God and Christ certainly will not be conducive toward making this a very happy Christmas.

Your energies spent all these years in the furthering of aid to the unfortunate is dashed to atoms. How do you ever expect to retain the confidence or respect of your associates and followers?

. . . Do you in your Materialistic Shroud not realize that His work must be carried on to others in this poor miserable chaotic world and that maybe He had future laurels for your worldly crown — if that is your aim?

. . . What tides of worldly materialism have so engulfed the real greatness that is yours and blotted out your real vision of the Landing Place?

Will not the God Who gave you the intellect, courage, foresight and stamina to carry out this wonderful work in His Great Love continue to provide for your Good in His Great Omnipotence? How can you thumb your nose at him and say "From here on get out! Don't you know I am The Father, Emmett McLoughlin."

Of one thing you must be certain, nevertheless, Father, and that is this: You just can't resign from the priesthood. You may cease to be an active priest; you may refuse to follow orders of superiors (just or unjust — harsh or otherwise — it is not for me to say); but you know as well as I that we, once ordained, are *sacerdotes in aeternum* [priests forever].

We have given ourselves to God, Father. When we try to resign, we are only trying to take back our gift to God.

. . . Life is too short and eternity too long, Father, for us to think that the humiliation of obedience is too much for any of

us. Superiors are not always the better men; any more than we
priests are better men than some of the laity whom we serve.
God didn't call us because we were better; but rather only because of His unfathomable love. Let us not disappoint Him,
by loving ourselves more than Him and His Holy Will.

From Canada came a warning of unhappiness from one
who might have faced the same decision as I — but never
did.

Dec. 11, 1948

Dear Father,
  It was old Bill first told me of you two years ago. He spent
a winter in your town. He used to rave to me about you.
Told me we were so much alike — free lancers, antiformalists,
anticlericals (in full orthodox extension).
  And now I read of you in " Time."
  It affected me deeply. It was just such a thing I might have
pulled myself some ten years back. You see I ran a college —
on non-sectarian, co-ed lines — out in the clear wide and open.
Today it has proved itself — our system is valid and its product
human " pure gold " — and it runs like a river of oil. Church
authorities are now " all for it." It wasn't always quite that
way. I knew we were right — on the right course — but I never
knew when some ecclesiastical rigorist might clamp down on
us, cover us with the odium of heresy, etc., etc. Often and
often I speculated what I would do; would I give in and give up
— or do what you have done?
  God's grace, the issue never came to a head. Thank God
for that. And thank God too for His grace in making the
work prove itself for all the world to see. . . .
  How often I have brooded over the contingency you have
launched into — the very real aspects of order, of authority
and their relation to final course. As Plato so well said: Man
is both individual and social — The " Res publica " is *man*.
  And somehow we must fit ourselves into that scheme of
things — *with* its implications of order and its moral postulates
of authority.
  I am 57 today. I have seen many men kick the traces as you
are kicking them — as Paul, too, kicked them. They " reached

the conclusion " you reached for. The following years showed they were wrong — even the big guns, Abelard, Rabelais, Erasmus, Luther, Lamennais, Loisy were never happy. It just didn't work out. Don't be bull-headed, Emmett McLoughlin — there is still time. Don't waste your life work. Get back into line.

God bless you —

Again a reminder of the age-old control of the clergy by identifying the will of the hierarchy with that of God:

December 10, 1948

Dear Father McLoughlin:
  It was with real regret that I read in the December 13th issue of Time magazine of your decision to give up your greatest privilege, the active ministry of the Catholic priesthood. Such an incident makes one think and shudder at the sad histories of other priests who have placed their individual wills against the legitimate authority of Christ's Church. Even granting the unreasonableness of your superior's attitude, one cannot set aside the warning of Christ that the branch that is cut off from the vine will wither and die. And how can you have Christ without the Church? It was the spiritual value of your priesthood that gave real meaning to all your material accomplishments. We need competent hospital administrators, it is true, but far more desperately we need PRIESTS, men who are privileged to share in the priesthood of Christ Who always did the will of His Father. . . .

Fraternally yours in
the priesthood,

The laity too had its say:

. . . The indelible character of the priesthood is impressed on a priest's soul and for all *eternity* he shall be a priest according to the order of Melchisedech.
 "Dearly beloved son, you are about to be ordained to the order of the priesthood. Strive to receive it worthily, and

having received it, to discharge its duties in a praiseworthy manner. The office of the priest is to *offer sacrifice, to bless, to preach and to Baptize.*"

. . . Nowhere is slum clearance and building hospitals mentioned — an oversight no doubt — or did the writers of the ordination ceremony know their stuff?

" Go therefore and make disciples of all nations, *baptizing* them in the name of the Father, Son and Holy Ghost, *teaching* them to observe all that I have commanded, and behold I am with you all days, even to the consummation of the world." And not a word of organized recreation, venereal clinics, housing projects or hospitals, not to mention Boards of Health.

You can never baptize again or forgive sins, or say Mass or give communion, but you can build another playground or hospital. The poor you will have always with you — and no matter what you do, its trying to empty the ocean with a teaspoon.

. . . There are two things apparent in your action. You are abandoning *your* responsibility to God and His (and your) religion, and you cease to acknowledge the divine intelligence and infinite wisdom of the God Who created all things, including the universe, human nature, and the sanctity of vows made to Himself.

When in Holy Orders you assumed the Catholic priesthood, you voluntarily established a personal and permanent relationship between yourself and God — one much like marriage. In your resignation from the priesthood you would break this relationship, an act corresponding in seriousness to an adultery against God.

Your material accomplishments in Phoenix are good things, and are the result of your putting your God-given gifts to good use. But your decision now is a declaration that there are no other slums to clear and no other hospitals and churches to build in His name. In the *infinite wisdom of God which speaks to you through the instructions of your Franciscan superiors*, it would seem that He has other, even more important work for you to do elsewhere.

Think of how you scandalize your Church before the world, and of the damaging effect your act will have upon many who are weak in their faith. Think too, of how you will be degraded in the eyes, minds and hearts of your Catholic peers and many of your non-Catholic associates. May you realize before it is too late, how this will make hollow triumphs of your material accomplishments there in Phoenix. . . .

The hold of the Roman Catholic Church on children is shown in the following letter:

Dear Father:
  I am a girl 13 years old, seventh grade. I read the paper the other day and was very disappointed in it. I am writing you this letter to remind you if you know what you are doing by quitting the priesthood, it is a great gift from God to be able to have become a priest being able to hold the host which is God himself. I have gone to mass and communion for you asking God to forgive you for your sin. In order to have eternal happiness in heaven or to have a chance to try to get there you should try to ask God to help you. You think it over why you are quitting? You may think you are not a priest anymore but in God you are still one of his helpers to teach his religion, he is depending on you to do your part. Do you think youre giving a good example to those who are not Catholics? Another thing do you remember when you were made a priest, remember the oath you took; your hands were blessed, why don't you go back to help God? Some day I hope that I may give my life to God by becoming a nun, a Loretto nun, it is a great priviledge to be able to help God. That Mr. instead of Father does not fit you. Father you watch out because that devil is always around trying to tempt everybody. Please think it over. I will keep on praying.
                                          Yours truly in Christ,
                                                from Dolores A.

  The attitude that men exist merely for the next world, that the Roman Catholic Church is divine, that ecclesiastical superiors speak with the full and exclusive authority of God, that the formalities of Rome are the portal to heaven and that compared to these concepts all social freedom, economic stability, and human progress in the fields of health, welfare, and race relations are useless, undesirable, and even morally dangerous — this theme resounded like a bitter gong through thousands of letters. It gave a depressing but accurate picture of the *sententia Ecclesiae* — the " sentiment of the Church." It pointed up the reason for the poverty, disease, and backwardness of countries where the Roman Catholic " mind " prevails in education and in politics. It pointed up also the danger of retrogression in human progress that might take place if the hierarchy's drive to " make America Catholic " should succeed.

The difference between the Roman Catholic and the American viewpoint was expressed in several editorials. The first is from the *Central California Register* of December 26, 1948:

Strayed Shepherds

It was a chastening coincidence if ever there be such. Almost to the moment when any number of Catholic editors were rhapsodizing over the public and moving confession of faith by E. Boyd Barrett, author of note, who had returned to the Church after years as a strayed priest, the readers of Time were told of the public renunciation of both religious vows and priestly practice by Father Emmett McLoughlin of Phoenix, Arizona.

There is a long standing tendency on the part of many Catholic papers to assume the lofty pretense that there is no such problem as defection from the Catholic priesthood. Perhaps it is assumed that no good end is served by referring to such tragedies. Thank God that such acts of weakness are comparatively rare. But face the fact that from the time of the Apostles (you remember Judas, of course) there have been those few who for one reason or another fail to live up to the high ideals of their priestly calling. . . .

When he habitually ignored both common prayers and com-

mon life, then he was guilty not only of grave carelessness;
what is worse, he gambled — and in this case lost — on his independence of the means of grace assigned him. . . .

No one, as they say, is indispensable; to believe otherwise is
the first long step toward doom.

Father McLoughlin took that step. For when his Franciscan
Provincial thought it best for the man, and for the work as
well, that he go elsewhere, the answer was one of rebellion.
He would *not* go; in short, rather than obey he was prepared
to gamble with his religious life, with his priesthood, and with
the most precious possession of all — his soul.

Whether or not a change in duties was justified is a question
of no great importance; whether Father McLoughlin had been
doing exemplary work, whether he was or was not the best
available man for the job is equally pointless. It was on this
fundamental virtue that a man, once so successful — if not so
prudent — floundered and apparently damned himself.

The American Protestant viewpoint, however, was contained in a weekend editorial in the *Long Beach Press Telegram*, December 20, 1948.

THE MATERIAL VS. THE SPIRITUAL

There seems to be an irreconcilable clash between the material and the spiritual. The most common, and if true, the
severest criticism made of the United States is that the nation
is materialistic. When India's great poet, Rabindranath Tagore,
visited America he was unsparing in his condemnation of the
materialism of our civilization. The favorite subject of preachers and moralists in attacking the evils of America is the materialism of American culture. . . .

There is a lot of fuzzy thinking about the materialistic and
the spiritual. What is the materialism so roundly denounced?
It is making wealth and power for which money stands, an end
in itself. When the getting and the use of things becomes our
chief purpose or objective in life, we are debased to the level
of things. On the other hand, when things are sought and
used primarily to serve the higher uses of the mind and spirit,
character becomes elevated, spiritual. It is not the amount
which one possesses that makes him a materialist. Nor is it the
occupation or daily rounds in which one engages that make

him spiritual.   A spiritually minded person may engage in secular business.   And a servant of the church repeating rituals of worship and celebrating holy sacraments of religion may be thoroughly worldly in purpose and character.

The distinction which I am trying to make clear is brought out vividly in a story in Time magazine of a Roman Catholic priest.   The year following his ordination to the priesthood he was assigned to Phoenix, Arizona.   He soon became well known through his interest in slum clearance, better living projects and leading a crusade for a hospital for the poor. . . .

The priest was completely absorbed in his ministry to people through church and hospital.   On becoming a member of the Franciscan Order, Emmett McLoughlin had taken vows subordinating his own will to the wisdom and spiritual judgment of his Superior.   The Superior decided the time had come for the 41 year old priest to move and to devote his entire time to the spiritual duties of the priesthood.   The Superior contended that the priest's duties were too material and must be given up if he wished to remain as a priest of the Roman Catholic Church and a member of the Franciscan Order.   McLoughlin answered: "I can reach only one conclusion," and resigned as a priest.

The irreconcilable clash between the church Superior and the priest was in their judgment of what is material and what is spiritual.   According to Emmett McLoughlin, ministering to the poor through a modern hospital was a spiritual service worthy of a priest of the church.   According to the Superior it was too material.

The test of the spiritual is not the garb one wears or the round of duties performed, but in the purpose and the objective.   Repeating prayers for the dying and celebrating the holy sacraments is no more spiritual than the duties of hospital or home, office or factory.   Spirituality takes material things and transforms them into the higher uses of character and the soul.

The *Register* editorial had claimed that few priests cut their ecclesiastical ties: "Thank God that such acts of weakness are comparatively rare."   The hierarchy preserves this illusion by concealing, if at all possible, the news of any priest who sheds his frock. The faithful are always told that he has been transferred to another parish in a different state. Ex-priests themselves help perpetuate this myth by quietly folding their tents and secretly stealing away. They do this not out of love of "Holy Mother Church" but out of fear of ecclesiastical reprisal, family disapproval, and the persecution of the Catholic laity. I have known of ex-priests who, torn between the fear of discovery and their desire to let their parents know they were alive and well, have sent letters through a distant friend, so that their correspondence bore a postmark of a city thousands of miles away from that in which they lived.

The Roman Catholic hierarchy acclaim with extravagant publicity any public figure who joins the Church, or any "fallen" priest who returns to the fold. The hierarchy ignores completely, except in its "intramural" trade publications such as the *Ecclesiastical Review* and the *Homiletic Review*, the disastrous "leakage" from the Church and the constant, though numerically unknown, stream of priests who look back from the plow. Of the more than one hundred Roman Catholic priests whom I know to have made the break, only three have gone back.

Father Boyd Barrett is one of the three. He was a young Jesuit who broke with his superiors at about the time I entered the seminary. He rebelled against the discipline and hierarchy of Roman Catholicism. But he had obviously retained his belief in the doctrines of Roman Catholicism. His story was printed in the Jesuit magazine *America* and was reproduced in pamphlet form. I received copies from hundreds of solicitous Catholics. Since he was referred to in so many letters, I reproduce his letter to me. (He even got my name wrong.)

Soquel, California
Jan 14, '49

Dear Father O'Loughlin

This is "Boyd Barrett" who is writing to you. You may
have heard of me — 25 years ago — the "brilliant" (?) young
Jesuit who wanted to force his superiors to accept his ideas on
psycho-analysis and who resigned from his order because they
thought otherwise.

This is the "Boyd Barrett" who made the headlines then —
who was raised to the edition of "Who's Who in America"
and who wrote the smart, well-selling books, "The Jesuit
Enigma," "While Peter Sleeps," etc. He made money too,
and finally came to settle in a nice ranch here in California.

Well that "Boyd Barrett" knows only too well the right
you have to tell him: "Go to Hell! Mind your own business!" In reply all he can say is: "Please hear me! Father
O'Loughlin, I know I'm interfering. I'm sorry. I never,
never did the like before!" God knows I have no right or
wish to blame you. I'm not worthy to polish your boots. But
I just have to write to you. . . .

Fr. O'Loughlin, one thing I know — God it should bring
tears to your eyes! At the present moment ten thousand
nuns are weeping, imploring, praying *for you* to the Sacred
Heart and Our Lady. They love you in and through Christ's
love!

Fr. O'Loughlin, I know this too. There are today a thousand
masses offered *for you*. Poor priests, many of them far from
being saints, are begging their Christ and Savior for you.

And, here I come in, Father. There are poor "Stray Shep-
herds" like me begging our Lady to reach out her lovely
blessed hand to touch your heart. . . .

I tell Christ and my tears fill my eyes. I had broken their
hearts.

Fr. O'Loughlin, I "Boyd Barrett" got all the kind of publicity you are getting, as in "Time" Dec. 13. Now I see what
it means as I look back. They ran special articles about me in
"Newsweek," etc., and "The American Mercury" (H. L.
Mencken) who was glad to take my articles. They paid me
well and praised me. But in their hearts they despised me as
an "escapee" and "ex-priest," a man who broke his vows!

No! the boys who cheer when a priest disobeys his Bishop or Superior — however harsh and unfair the latter may be — are not in love with the priest but they hate the Church — and they hate Christ. Those boys are playing their own game and don't care a damn for us!

Dear Father, no one has asked me to write to you or even suggested it. No one, at least, *in this world*. One of your dear ones, perhaps, from heaven. Our Lady, maybe remembering the great things you did in her honor. I don't know . . .

I look back now to 1925. I was then in a spot in which I think you are — and so my heart does go out to you.

A Jesuit, a nice fellow, came to me with my " dismissal " papers in his pocket, but he was empowered to make a last appeal to me. He begged me, poor fellow, to think it over. All could still be settled, he promised, and no one would ever refer to what was past.

But I was too proud. I was " rotten with pride." I was cold. My mind was made up. I had persuaded myself I was justified in my rebellion. I cherished dreams of freedom and success. I was " nice " to the young Jesuit but said " no." . . .

Father Emmett — and to every Dublin man that name of yours means *selfless honor* — everyone knows the splendid work you have accomplished — and everyone looks forward to the further groundwork you will do in God's honor. But let the work have Mary's blessing on it — otherwise what comfort will it bring you?

She loves you — every priest of Irish blood is very dear to her. Most of all she loves her daring rebel priests in trouble — but she whispers to them that they must obey.

That big hospital you have done so much for will be blessed by her and helped and watched over by her *for your sake*. If only, dear Father O'Loughlin, you have the big heart to say to Mary just two words, " You win! " . . .

I offered Holy Communion for you today and Holy Mass and three rosaries. I sent burning words of prayer to Christ's Heart for Fr. Emmett O'Loughlin. I thought of all the thousands of people praying for you today. And then tears filled my eyes for Mary's lovely, blessed hand was reaching out to touch the heart of a priest she loves.

Sincerely in Christ

E. Boyd Barrett

The priests, bishops, and laity who urged me to go back spoke of the "greater work in the vineyard of the Lord," "future projects," "conversion of sinners." Father Boyd Barrett's letter inadvertently disclosed the fate of broken ex-priests who try to "go home again." In his own words, "I offered Holy Communion for you today." Ordinarily an ex-priest is not permitted to perform the mass itself, to hear confessions, to preach the teachings of Roman Catholicism. Or in the words of a former Unitarian clergyman, J. C. Petrie, "He is back in the Roman *obedience* — stripped of all faculties of Orders; a layman for the rest of his days."

It is a wholesome sign that some of the Roman Catholic clergy and laity are thinking for themselves and breaking away from the rigid mental control of the hierarchy. One anonymous note said simply, "Congratulations. So many of us Roman Catholic priests would like to shake off the 'Black Robe Curse.' Good luck." Another priest, who signed his name (omitted here for obvious reasons), was far more vehement:

Dear Emmett,
  Got a hair-raising thrill out of your tremendous act of courage. All will turn out well. Down at Yuma, Bonny hinted that all was not peaceful in Phoenix. I hit the table with my fist and yelled, "Hands off Emmett!" Bonny threw up his hands and protested, "I'm not against Emmett. It is just that there is talk going around." Too material, be damned! The priests-doctors in China are delivering babies. . . . What do they care if your institution passed from Catholic and moral supervision! You are still a priest, Emmett, and a true apostle. The clouds will lift in due time.
                    Your sincere friend,

                    _____

From a lifetime Roman Catholic layman in San Francisco:

Greetings —

The San Francisco papers report that you have decided to stay in Phoenix and work with the little people.

So I thought I would drop you a line, just to say " Good Luck " in your new adventure.

May your strength be that of 1000 men, and your wisdom exceed that of Socrates and Solomon.

Your friend,

_____

A young Catholic used my departure from Catholicism as an occasion to deplore the backwardness of the Church:

San Diego, California

Dear Father McLoughlin:

I should like to congratulate you on the stand you have taken in this particular instance. As a life-long Catholic, and one who has had a completely Catholic education through high school and college, I appreciate, perhaps more deeply than the casual observer the moral fiber that was required to place yourself in a very poor public light in order to remain true to your own convictions. The less publicized and private estrangements, family and otherwise, which will no doubt be your lot in some quarters are enough to make the average man effect some compromise to maintain the good graces of his clerical superiors.

Lest I sound like a complete rebel, I should like you to know that I am a staunch Catholic and have yet to find any other religion which surpasses my own. However, this does not prevent me from seeing and getting excited over what I consider archaic and autonomic rule in some cases. It has long been my belief that our Catholic faith would be strengthened and made better by more liberal interpretation of Church law and a streamlining of some of our " Chain of Command." I am 28 years of age, young enough to look around me and realize that in many ways other religions are making sensible appeals to the youth among their adherents, whereas we go along on our old horse and buggy theory that younger people are merely intended to follow along with no particular ideas of their own. Unless we come to the realization that we, too, have to make capital of the abilities of our younger and more open minded members, then the Catholic faith is guilty of short-sightedness almost beyond belief.

My sincere good wishes for the success of your hospital and your work, and my unbounded admiration for what I consider to be an outstanding display of personal courage and fortitude.

A Negro schoolteacher must have felt the same frustration toward the well-known racial discrimination of the hierarchy when she attended Christmas mass at my former church. She wrote:

You know I have thought about you considerably. At Christmas, Midnight Mass, I looked over the audience and saw Negroes, Mexicans, Chinese, Filipinos, Hawaiian and white, and as I looked upon the Cross over the altar I thought that: This is the kind of gathering Jesus would like. I thought *about you*. I do not know what *they* have done to you, but I for one wish you God's mercy.

If you scale the highest attainment please accept my best wishes, or if you fall to the lowest ebb, please accept a meal from my humble table.

An encouragingly large group of Negroes expressed themselves:

National Ass'n of Colored Women Inc.
1008 City Park Ave.
Toledo 2, Ohio

Mrs. Ella P. Stewart
President
January 11, 1949

Rev. Emmett McLoughlin
St. Monica's Hospital
Phoenix, Arizona
Dear Sir:

I have just recently picked up a Time Magazine on the train and read the article material.

This comes to say that the membership of the National Association, of Colored Women comprising 53,000 women in 42 states wishes to commend you on your stand.

It will be our prayers that you will continue to render service to mankind, and be a messenger in His name.

Yours most sincerely,

ELLA P. STEWART

I had expected the wrath of the bishops, the clergy, and the bulk of the laity. I remembered that scorn had been predicted from the non-Catholic public. Their disapproval would mean my failure, both in my hospital position and in my future confidence in myself. The first strong, warm word of encouragement came, within twenty-four hours of the first press dispatches, from a Unitarian minister, the author of *Days of Our Years:*

I have heard a good deal in these regions of your activities in the interest of the real Gospel of Christ and the establishment of the Kingdom of God on earth and in our time. I greet you, therefore, as a brother and fellow believer. And I want to assure you that there are many unseen brothers, like myself, who extend their hands to you in the dark hour through which you are passing. Be of good cheer, always, in resisting " this world," which our Lord overcame in principle. The Spirit of St. Francis be with you.

Yours fraternally,

PIERRE VAN PAASSEN

And from a doctor who had worked with me as a resident physician in our hospital and who had left for further studies in the East, came this beautiful message:

December 10, 1948

Dear Father Emmett:

I have just been informed of the article about you in Time Magazine.

Not one, but several have called my attention to it; for ever since I have left Phoenix, the name of Emmett McLoughlin has traveled wherever I have gone. To all who would listen, I have told your story . . . It is my profound conviction that you are the most Christ-like man I have ever encountered. This opinion is not unique. It is shared by those who know you personally as well as those to whom I have spoken about you.

To imply that materialism touches you is as fantastic as painting a portrait of Hitler with a halo about his head. How a man can serve Him better than by following His precepts and principles in deed and thought, I cannot imagine. No man can have done more than this which you have wrought.

This is a very tiny community — far removed from Phoenix. Yet in this village there is a group who send you their greetings, their congratulations for an act which must have required great courage, their cheers and encouragement for your great work.

I do feel, I know, that you are a great man with the greatest, most generous soul I have ever had the great fortune to meet. If it is not true that you are one of God's chosen people, then nothing is true.

Whenever, wherever, however, I can aid and abet any project or plan which you may have, I am — and always have been — your man. For I agree that you do not have to be a priest of the Catholic Church, for you are a priest of God.

Since the opening of our hospital, I had been working with the labor unions. In my crisis one of their members, a carpenter, spoke up:

Phoenix 12–2–48

Fellow citizen and brother:

I find it impossible to resist the urge to express my admiration for what you have done — I am sure it was not the easiest of your many tasks.

You must be a pretty bad fellow — the news this morning reports your excommunication, and we hope that isn't true — I've looked for many years for Adolph Hitler's excommunication without success.

If you are in need of a *church* — and if a building constitutes a church — why I'll be glad to help you build one. If you need a place to put it — my wife and I would like to consider giving a site for one.

Frankly — I get confused when it happens that I work on two buildings which are very similar and they label one a *church* and the other *barn* and I see more human blessings come from the barn than from the church — I feel the labels should be interchanged, but, of course, that would be ridiculous. Anyway, the word on a building doesn't convince me — I'll settle for the work you have been doing — as a church.

With very best wishes,

———————

The warm encouragement of these and hundreds of similar touching letters convinced me that the general public did not condemn me, that the man on the street did not consider me a traitor to God, and, more important personally, that my hospital board of trustees would stand behind me.

Whenever a priest is known by the laity to have left the priesthood and inquiries are made at the rectory concerning him, an inevitable threefold series of rumors emanates from the hierarchy. Its pattern is too similar and too consistent to be coincidental. The rumors always begin with dramatic stories of his ill health, followed by lurid tales of his drunkenness and immorality, and ending with solemn assurances to the faithful that " poor good Father So-and-So has come to his senses, has appealed to Rome for forgiveness, and is now doing penance in some distant monastery."

A very popular priest, Father Kilian Pryor, mentioned earlier in this narrative, was transferred out of Arizona by orders of the bishop at the alleged request of some of the wealthier laity because of his collaboration with labor unions. His departure from the priesthood was widely known in Phoenix. Within a few months he was said to be suffering, according to conflicting rumors, from alcoholism, leukemia, anemia, and arthritis. He was married to a girl from Phoenix, well known to many of the local parishioners. The inevitable conclusion was carefully planted in the minds of people who would circulate it most widely; they said that he had appealed to the Order and to Rome for forgiveness, that he had an incurable disease, that he had rejected his wife who was now destitute, and that through the magnanimous charity of the hierarchy he was spending his last days in an unnamed hospital in southern California.

I determined to find him. The local labor unions were anxious to help him. An ex-priest found Kilian Pryor for me. He had never been sick at all. He had not been in a hospital. He had not asked the Franciscan Order for forgiveness. He was not doing penance.

I have been in touch with him throughout the intervening years. In contradiction to the rumor that he was unhappy, that his marriage was about to break up, and that he was " beating his wife " (the exact words of a priest who sneaked a call to me in July 1952), he is happy, has an important position with a manufacturing firm, and is the father of two healthy children.

The most vigorous denunciations of the Roman Catholic Church came from ex-Catholics. From an Ann Arbor, Michigan, couple came the following:

Dear Mr. McLoughlin:
    We have just read about your case in *Time* magazine.
    Your case is of personal interest with us, because we left the

Church 20 years ago from the same causes of narrowness and selfishness which caused you to resign your membership in the Order of Franciscans and your priesthood.

We can see several cases parallel to yours. . . .

You, too, have been doing a job, and it seems that you have done it too well. And, because you, too, were dealing with a dictatorship, you found friction because there was jealousy there. . . .

On the part of the parishioner, the worker and the scholar, we find faith, sincerity and great personal effort and sacrifice; but in the administrative part of the Church and the Orders we find too much of the kind of thing you are so dramatically dealing with. We can't help thinking of the billions and billions of dollars worth of property that has been given, *or taken,* for the ostensible purpose of effecting the very kind of service you have been doing. Then, when someone, anyone, really demonstrates some actual outside-the-wall help to mankind, he is told, in so many words, to "lay off." Yes, we understand the whole structure, and we congratulate you.

From Toledo, Ohio:

Dear Sir:

I have read in *Time* magazine this week with much interest of your "Declaration of Independence" from Roman Catholic authorities, and beg the liberty of telling you with what deep admiration my husband and I have read of your action. I have lived quite a while, most of the time in the Church with which you have just severed relations, and have seen so much wickedness, envy, spite, malice, greed among priests, bishops, and even nuns, that it has sickened me. So many of them are materialists, while hypocritically preaching against it. So many are opportunists, gluttons, drinkers, socially ambitious, etc.

It must come as a shock to non-Catholics to realize the possessiveness of even the lay Catholics toward their clergy. It is accepted practice among Protestant, Mormon, and Jewish groups to recognize a clergyman's right to change his vocation. Rabbis become merchants, Mormon bishops enter politics, and ministers in unknown number exchange the pulpit for farming, law, mining, teaching, trade, or just plain loafing. They are not ostracized, persecuted, or gossiped about. But not so a former Roman Catholic priest.

Paul Blanshard in his two very accurate documents on the Roman Catholic Church, *American Freedom and Catholic Power* and *Communism, Democracy, and Catholic Power*, tells the various forms of controls the hierarchy exercises to further its aims and to control its subjects. Particularly in Chapter 8 of the second book, "Discipline and Devotion," he tells the steps taken to control priests. What I went through is a factual counterpart of his chapter.

First, there were the usual rumors: I was supposed to be spending most of my time and all of my money in bars. . . . I was so sexually promiscuous that I was being kept by four wealthy country-club women at the same time. . . . I was having affairs with dozens of our eighty graduate nurses, and our nursing school of seventy girls was my own personal harem.

While in San Francisco attending a regional hospital convention in 1949, I telephoned my sister in Sacramento. She said the local Roman Catholic clergy had told her that I had come back into the Church and that I was doing penance in the Franciscan monastery in Santa Barbara. A few weeks later I heard that I was repenting in the ecclesiastic " jail " at Jemes Springs, New Mexico.

My health has been constantly rumored to be so bad that members of the clergy have surreptitiously called to inquire about it — perhaps so that they might time their visits correctly, catch me unconscious, and give me the last rites before I died. Then the faithful and the public could be triumphantly informed that I had returned to Holy Mother

Church before I died. Even now, five years after my leaving the priesthood, Catholics who wish to be friendly or who seek business from the hospital reveal the indoctrination of their clergy by asking about my health. When I tell them I have never felt better, they are embarrassed and admit that " the priest " told them I was critically ill.

An order went out from the hierarchy that the clergy were not to speak to me. Some called me secretly to express their good wishes. But others were hostile. My successor in the little church I had built was the Rev. Lucian Pargett, O.F.M., who had started in the seminary with me in September 1922. After eleven years of study, work, and play, we lay prostrate side by side on the floor of the sanctuary of the ancient Santa Barbara Mission, in token of obedience, while Archbishop Cantwell of Los Angeles prepared to pronounce the solemn words of ordination. We had been priests together in St. Mary's Church in Phoenix. At the time of my break with the hierarchy, we had known each other intimately for twenty-six years.

Since December 1, 1948, when I left the priesthood, I have seen him a hundred times in the corridors of the hospital, functioning as its Catholic chaplain, visiting his parishioners, and giving the last rites to the dying of his faith. Never once in these five years has he spoken to me. When he has seen me approaching in the corridors, he has turned and hastily ducked into a room or gone in another direction. When he has been cornered and I have addressed him, he has murmured " Hello " and moved away.

In San Francisco, I telephoned a priest who had been an official of the Franciscan seminary when I entered in 1922. I had known him through the intervening years. He had been my Superior and pastor in Phoenix, and my friend.

He told me that the clergy were forbidden to speak to me. We held a secret rendezvous in the Palace Hotel — a meeting of old friends.

As recently as June of 1952, an old schoolmate called secretly to ask if it were true that I was critically ill. Again he informed me that the priests were forbidden to have anything to do with me.

The first step of the hierarchy, besides the rumor mill, was to attempt to oust me from the hospital. A Catholic member of the board of directors proposed that a survey be made among the doctors of Phoenix to determine whether they felt that the hospital was being efficiently administered. He argued that while I had been a priest the " dignity of the cloth " cloaked my " inefficiency " and gave the board an excuse for not actively scrutinizing my administration. Now that I was a mere layman, however, the board had an obligation to the people of Phoenix to see that the most competent administrator was hired.

The strategy was obvious. The Catholic physicians and others whose staff privileges had had to be withdrawn would naturally vote against me. This would create a doubt as to my ability and would split the board. The strategy was so obvious, however, that at the next meeting this Catholic member was himself dropped, a non-Catholic was elected in his place, and a unanimous vote of confidence was given me by the board of directors.

In January 1949, my second five-year term as a member of the Arizona State Board of Health expired. The governor was a Roman Catholic. A month went by. I was not reappointed. Finally, an influential friend of mine insisted on an interview with a high official of the state administration. Was I going to be reappointed? If not, why not? And why the delay? The official told him they did not dare make the appointment without informing the Roman Catholic bishop. My friend threatened to make public the fact that the administration was a figurehead and that the sovereign state of Arizona was actually being ruled by the Roman Catholic hierarchy. I was forthwith reappointed to the Arizona State Board of Health for another five-year term.

The clerics were more successful in removing me from the Phoenix housing authority, which I had fathered.

As my third term of membership and chairmanship on the housing authority drew near its end, rumors began to circulate that ecclesiastical pressure was being exerted on the city administration. A close friend of mine, who was also a member of the authority and a former mayor, went to the city hall and asked if I were to be sacrificed. They admitted the pressure was too great. I could not be reappointed. Within a few days I was replaced with the Catholic who, as a member of the board of directors of our hospital, had tried to oust me from that institution.

The action of the administration in a city that I had served, without recompense, for more than a decade hurt me deeply. I wondered whether the mayor, a well-known Mormon, really believed in the freedom of religion, of speech, and of thought professed by his denomination.

Two years later, on July 31, 1952, I received the following document from the mayor:

CERTIFICATE OF APPRECIATION

In acknowledgment of outstanding cooperation and service to the citizens of the City of Phoenix as a member of Housing

Authority, This Testimonial is Gratefully presented to Emmett McLoughlin. Much of the success of City Government is the result of the unselfish contribution of time and effort by citizens who serve on boards and commissions with little or no recompense.

As one of those who has served, your efforts have been an inspiration to all others in City Government and to the many persons who have come to you for help in solving their problems. Your fair and impartial consideration of these many problems has played an important part in giving to the Citizens of Phoenix the kind of government to which they are entitled. Resolution passed by the Council of the City of Phoenix, Arizona, this 15th day of July 1952.

NICHOLAS UDALL
Mayor

Attest:
TOM SULLIVAN JR.
City Clerk

Mayor Udall was resigning as mayor to run for a Superior Court judgeship. It was rumored that I could deliver the vote "south of the tracks" to the candidate of my choosing. All past members of the Phoenix housing authority had received belated certificates of appreciation — could it be that the mayor wanted to heal old wounds?

The months passed. I was now an ordinary American citizen. I worked hard at the tremendously complex administrative job of managing a hospital. Business experts are right in their contention that hospital administration is among the most difficult executive work that a person can choose. The product for sale — hospitalization — is something no man wants. Every man resents being sick. He has not planned for it. It interrupts his life, his business, and his pleasure. He does not want to pay for an unwanted purchase, and often he can't.

The hospital administrator deals, on the one hand, with the miracle of life and the tragedy of death, and, on the other, with cold, commercial firms and utilities which regularly demand payment for food, drugs, dressings, linens, lumber, pipe, wire, gas, water, and electricity.

He must be also a school superintendent. Our hospital operates six training courses: for registered nurses, for practical nurses, for laboratory technicians, for X-ray technicians, for medical interns, and for medical residents. We must conform to the educational requirements and the periodic supervision of the State Board of Health, the State Board of Nurse Examiners, the American Medical Association, the American College of Surgeons, the National League of Nursing Education, and the United States Department of Education.

These problems were all part of a day's work. I was kept busy trying to solve them — far too busy at the time to worry about the Catholic Church's rumors and schemes to hurt me. But the problems did leave time for a free and normal life. The open antagonism of the Roman Catholic Church began to subside — until a reporter discovered that I was contemplating matrimony.

CHAPTER SIX

A New Contract

"And the Lord God said, It is not good that man should be alone" (Genesis 2:18).

The night that I walked out of St. Mary's rectory I was still a semi-Catholic and a semi-priest. I had torn off the robe, but I had worn it so long that the material had decayed and fragments still clung to my skin. Most of my "faith" in Romanism was gone. But I was confused.

My doubts were not whether the teachings of the hierarchy were wrong; I *knew* that many doctrines and practices were morally wrong and therefore untrue. I had discarded as the superstitious accretions of the centuries — or as the clever devices of a hierarchy grasping for control, power, and money — all the formalism of Roman practice and power, relics, indulgences, medals, rosaries, blessings, novenas, fasting, saints, miracles, the authority of bishops, the prohibition of divorce, the condemnation of birth control, the "imprisonment" of nuns, the index of forbidden books, and the morally enervating, infinite multiplicity of sins.

I still believed in God. I believed in prayer. I believed

in the Bible. I believed in Christ. I believed in a " church."
I signed myself " Reverend." I considered myself a priest
— of what, I knew not.

Once I went to mass. It was within two weeks after I
had made the break. Away from the altar and at the back
of the church, I had a new perspective. The priest rattled
off the Epistle, the Gospel, the Gloria, the Credo — all in
monotonous, unintelligible Latin, as I had done so many
thousands of times. The children herded into the front
pews fidgeted as another priest, in an unkempt cassock,
patrolled the aisles and in a harsh whisper barked at the
little boys who were teasing the little girls. The adults
pulled the beads of their rosaries or, with their minds
on the fun of the night before, stared blankly at the expres-
sionless faces of the statues clustered around the altar.
They were in church because it was a mortal sin not
to be.

The worship of God! Where was the worship and where
was the God? Certainly not here. For all those years I
had been a party to this mockery of religion.

A half-year passed. I felt no guilt, no qualms, no consciousness of sin regarding what I had done. I still believed
in a promise, a vow, a man's word. But I believed in it
when it was given honestly.

Many letters from Roman Catholics had lamented that I
had broken my solemn vows, my word to God. But I felt
no guilt. I had entered sincerely into a contract, a bilateral
contract, when I solemnly vowed poverty, chastity, and
obedience. I was one party to the agreement. The Provincial Superior claimed to represent God. My indoctrination trained me to believe that he did. I knew now that he
did not. The contract was null and void.

In November 1946, a young woman named Mary Davis came to work in our hospital because she had a revolutionary idea that the other Phoenix hospitals would not accept. A registered medical record librarian (one of the key personnel of any approved hospital), she offered to serve without salary if she could also handle all of the hospital medical stenography, paid on a " per word " basis. I did not think it possible for one person to transcribe all dictation from the laboratory, surgery, and X-ray department. But financially the plan was so attractive that I accepted.

The medical record librarian is a hospital watchdog — daily checking the completeness of medical reports on physical examinations, treatments, operations, X-rays, laboratory tests, and in general watching for indications of good or bad medical care. It is she who must note the difference, if any, between the doctor's written diagnosis on the admission of a patient and the proven diagnosis upon the patient's discharge. She must catch any " commercial " surgery, any " ghost " surgery, any malpractice and report it to the hospital's medical staff.

On one occasion, the American College of Surgeons inspector found a number of incomplete medical records in our files. The doctors of Phoenix were surprised by the pleasant firmness of this arresting blue-eyed brunette who, with a knowledge of medical terminology fully equal to their own, calmly informed them that if their records were not completed within so many days they would be suspended from the staff and their patients would be asked to choose other doctors. And in stubborn cases she recommended such suspension. The medical staff officers backed her up and suspended several doctors. At the next annual inspection, Dr. Southard of the American Medical Association told me that the only record department he knew of comparable efficiency was in Harper Hospital in Detroit.

Mary Davis had a background that was the complete antithesis of mine. Her family had been Americans so long that no one knew when they had arrived. The symbol of her family history is a flax-wheel which her forebears used more than a century ago. Her parents with their four daughters came to New Mexico from Kentucky because her father was dying of tuberculosis. After his death, her mother served for fifteen years as a dietitian in the Veterans' Administration Hospital near Silver City, and during the shallow years of the depression Mary worked her way through four terms as a premedical student in Baylor University. When it became clear that she must sacrifice her plan to study medicine if she wanted to eat, she transferred into medical stenography. As a medical secretary in La Jolla, California, Mary worked through the early years of the Second World War, while her doctor-fiancé in the South Pacific was lost and finally declared dead in the battle of the Java Sea. She taught medical stenography and records for the United States Army; after the war, she came to Phoenix and in 1946 to our hospital.

During 1947 and 1948, when I was corresponding with the officials of the Franciscan Order, I dared not trust my devout Catholic secretary. I turned to Mary Davis, for I knew that she was professionally trained to be completely trustworthy, to respect every confidence.

After I left the priesthood, I shared frequently in the social events of the medical staff and the hospital personnel. Their favorite picnic rendezvous was the favorite of all Phoenicians — South Mountain Park, the largest city park in America, created through the efforts of two members of our hospital board, both former Phoenix mayors. The *ramadas* — large roofed-over concrete picnic tables, served by batteries of barbecue pits — are scattered among 100,000 acres of huge, tumbled rocks, mesquite, and giant saguaro cactus. One evening, as a group of us were sitting by the fire waiting for the coals to burn down for broiling steaks, a quartet of youngsters began to sing in a nearby *ramada*. Mary Davis and I wandered toward them. I took her hand to help her over the rocks, and, as we watched the children, we both realized that our mutual respect and confidence had flowered into love.

The story of my coming marriage hit the local newspapers on June 15, 1949. From the newspaper " morgue " a picture of me in a Roman collar was disinterred and, with a photograph of the bride-to-be, sent over the newswires. The news story emphasized her two previous marriages, which had ended in divorce.

The story seemed to rub salt into ecclesiastical wounds. It mentioned that the marriage would be held at the home of the Potentate of the Shrine and that a Jewish judge, who was also a Shriner, would perform the ceremony.

It was to be expected that the reaction of Roman Catholics to the announcement of my forthcoming marriage would be more violent than their reaction to my leaving the priesthood. In leaving the priesthood I had been merely disobedient. I had, of course, committed a mortal sin and incurred an excommunication; unless I repented I would spend eternity in hell. I could at that time have gone back to the Church. But I could not marry. Any marriage by an ex-priest is called *matrimonium attentatum* — " attempted marriage." To the hierarchy it is no marriage at all. It is merely a civil, legal sanction for concubinage. It is punished by immediate, automatic excommunication.

This punishment means a cutting off from the Roman Catholic Church. Theoretically an excommunicated person still must fulfill all the obligations of the Church, but he is ostracized in his performance of them. He must still attend mass on Sunday. But he must, according to the letter of the law and medieval traditions, sit in the rear seats of the church with " lepers and lunatics." He may not receive the sacraments of the Church. A priest who has been excommunicated will never again be admitted to full fellowship with the clergy. If he returns, like Father E. Boyd Barrett, he must spend his days as a penitent layman, unable to live as a normal citizen, and yet forbidden to function as a Christian clergyman.

I know one ex-priest who deliberately planned to marry so that he would be excommunicated. If then he were tempted to return to the Roman Catholic Church, the obstacles would discourage him. He planned this before he met the girl he wanted to marry. The day after he left the priesthood, he married the girl and wrote a letter to the bishop resigning his position. He now has four children and is a successful college professor in the middle west.

Excommunication is one of the " censures " that the Roman Church uses to reinforce the penalties for sin. Protestants and other non-Catholics try to guide their steps through life and toward eternity by the Ten Commandments. It is not so simple in Roman Catholicism. The Code of Canon Law itself has 2414 sections covering 762 pages. Many of these Canons cover the multitudinous penalties (besides hell) which either automatically are, or by proper authorities can be, inflicted upon erring members. The three principal censures are interdict, suspension, and excommunication.

The interdict deprives an individual or a group of certain spiritual functions of the Church — for instance, the prohibition of mass and the other sacraments in the church of a rebellious parish.

This rebellion has frequently occurred in America in "national" parishes (those composed predominantly of European immigrants) which refuse to permit bishops to transfer local priests. In 1952 a small parish of Mexican Catholics in New Mexico was placed under the interdict and the individuals under excommunication when its members refused to deed the church property over to the Bishop of El Paso. Trusteeship — the control of church finances and property by lay trustees of individual congregations, such as everywhere still prevails in Protestant churches — was crushed in the American Catholic Church in the last century by means of the interdict. Now the titles to all parish properties within a diocese are vested in the bishop alone — legally a "corporation sole." He can mortgage or sell them at will without consulting the Catholics of the diocese.

Suspension is inflicted only on the clergy. It suspends their right to perform clerical functions, such as saying mass, hearing confessions, baptizing, burying, or preaching.

Excommunication is the most common Church censure. There are forty-five different "crimes" which incur automatic excommunication. They fall into five groups according to their heinousness and to the hierarchical heights that must be reached to obtain forgiveness. Three categories are reserved to the Pope himself, some in a "most

special " manner, some in a " special " manner, and others
in a " simple " way. Among the " most special " crimes
are tampering with the consecrated bread and wine or as-
saulting the person of the Pope. Laying hands on a cardinal,
archbishop, or bishop is a " special " offense. This degree
of the penalty is incurred also by those who join " false "
(any non-Catholic) churches, or who restrict the " liberties " of the hierarchy — for instance, by bringing them
to trial in an American civil court.

The ban of excommunication automatically affects those
who procure abortions, marry before a Protestant minister,
manufacture false relics, educate their children in a non-
Catholic denomination, assault a parish priest, print the
Bible without permission, or steal Church property. Likewise excommunicated and bound to appeal to the Holy
See for forgiveness are Catholics who join the Masons,
nuns who leave their convents, and priests who marry.

My marriage announcement brought a new growth of
correspondence:

I'm aware of all the good work you have accomplished in
Phoenix, Arizona, and when I was there a few years ago everyone spoke highly of you. What must they think now? Whatever your trouble with your superiors, Father, forget it and
come back with the humility of St. Francis and St. Anthony
and pray for true humility — that is what we all need in this
Godless age. . . .
So I'm asking you again, Father, to please come back and in
some measure try to make up for the awful scandal you have
and are still causing. You may be assured many are praying
for your return — a return with humility.
. . . if you persist in your intentions with this woman, I wish
to you all possible happiness. As long as you are willing to
forego happiness in the " hereafter " for the uncertain joys of
the " here," I trust *you'll* get some satisfaction from it. But

one last chance to test the courage of your convictions — why don't you go for a walk, Mac, in the lovely gardens of Santa Barbara Mission — reflect on what an utter fool you're being — you've lost the respect of all worthwhile men. . . .

A CHRISTOPHER

Many nuns felt moved to save me. One letter came from a nun who had been married and now wanted to mother me:

Already true to Motherhood, I have shed many tears for you, and even if it were to cost me my life, I shall not abandon you, until I have broken the influence that satan holds over you. . . .

You are my prodigal son, and I shall always keep you close to me in my prayers. May God forgive you and may He hold you close to His Sacred Heart.

Sincerely, Yours in Christ,

———————

Another nun used a more common approach, appealing to the Virgin Mary:

Your name was on every lip in praise of your Christlike charity, of your saintly forgetfulness of self, of your heroic generosity in laboring to ameliorate the condition of the poor. You were spoken of as a true son of St. Francis, and we prayed for your success. News of what has happened during the past year has penetrated even to the middle west and you have been the object of many prayers and sacrifices, Rev. Father.

There are hearts which are grieving because of your sorrow, Father! Do not lose it all by turning from God to human love as the Kansas City *Star* has announced. Would I could describe what is known to me. There is a soul who suffers each week on Thursday and Friday for the sins of priests. She is intimately known to me, and her soul endures the agony of Gethsemani, in union with the Divine Sufferer, because of the infidelity of God's love, most beloved ones — His priests! As the Image of the Suffering Heart of Jesus, as though pierced with a sword is perceived by her in interior vision, she seems to hear the pleading voice of our Saviour: " See — the Heart of

thy Jesus, crushed by the sins of My priests! " She is praying
for YOU, suffering for YOU, and would beg you, through the
Wounded Heart of Jesus to give him JOY, to do what will
bring peace to your sacrificial soul now, and union with God
in eternity. I cannot think that August 13th, a day near our
Heavenly Mother's feast, will ever see you, once her loved and
beloved son, turn from your noble, sacred priestly calling and
lower yourself to espouse a bride of the earth. Never was it
known that anyone who fled to Mary's arms was left unaided.
Throw yourself into her maternal arms, upon her maternal
breast this moment, and beg her to strengthen the weakness
which doubtless a misunderstanding has enervated still more.
Only the STRONG can be humble and obedient Father, and the
whole clinic and plant of St. Monica's isn't worth bartering
your soul for eternity, much less the passing subtle charms of
an enticer.

Prayerfully in His Wounded Heart,
MOTHER M.

" Never was it known that anyone who fled to Mary's
arms was left unaided." The Roman Catholic Church has
constantly denied the overemphasis of the " cult " of Mary.
Thousands of letters received bear out the fact that, regardless of the subtleties of definition, the faithful do consider
Mary divine. With nuns there seems to be the additional
touch of Mariolatry, even though their wedding bands
proclaim their " marriage " to Christ.

Officially, the Catholic doctrine has gradually placed
more emphasis on the cult of Mary. The doctrine of the
Immaculate Conception was proclaimed by Pius IX in 1854
and ratified (reluctantly, according to some historians) by
the docile Vatican Council in 1870. In 1952 the bodily
Assumption of Mary into heaven was declared an essential
dogma of faith by Pius XII. As the next step it has become a common teaching, which will probably be papally
defined, that Mary, though not technically divine, is the

" mediatrix of grace " — that all blessings and graces from God to men must pass through her hands and are obtainable through her intercession.

" In view of these truths," writes Rev. Robert Kekeisen in the *Arizona Register*, March 6, 1953, " it is safe to say that, though it is *possible* for one to attain heaven by praying directly to God without reference to Mary, the actual attainment of salvation without her help is *most difficult.*"

In actual practice the laity and the clergy are taking no chances. Regardless of theological distinctions, Roman Catholics actually do worship Mary. Devotion to her is undoubtedly the most spontaneous characteristic of Roman Catholic worship. Attendance at Sunday mass is obligatory, but priests and people by the thousands voluntarily attend novenas to the " Sorrowful Mother," cross the world to Mary's shrines, and fill football stadiums for the " Family Rosary Crusade."

Every religious order dedicates itself to the Virgin and promises its candidates and members easier entrance to heaven because of her " protecting mantle." The rosary itself, including the fifty-three " Hail Marys," is by far the most popular Catholic routine of prayer. About the year 1200, St. Dominic alleged that the Virgin Mary appeared to him and promised that the saying of the rosary would defeat the Turk and confound the heretic. The popular current appeal is that Mary is said to have promised that the rosary will convert Russia.

National shrines to Mary, usually built on the site of an alleged apparition of the Virgin to a child or to an illiterate peasant, vie with one another like rival carnivals for the patronage of devout Catholics. For years Lourdes in France attracted millions in Europe, while the basilica of

Guadalupe in Mexico was the favorite in the Americas. The comparatively recent vision of Mary at Fatima in Portugal has attracted hierarchy and laity — with their money — and inspired a conducted tour by a statue of " Our Lady of Fatima " throughout the United States.   The French rallied and appealed in 1953 to American Catholics with a new favor from Mary — a rosary with beads filled with the miraculous water of the fountain of Lourdes.   Catholic newspapers, such as *Our Sunday Visitor* and the *Register,* printed full-page and three-quarter-page illustrated advertisements offering money-back spiritual satisfaction:

IMAGINE PRAYING TO OUR BLESSED MOTHER AND ACTUALLY TOUCHING BEADS CONTAINING WATER FROM THE MIRACULOUS SPRING GIVEN BY HOLY MARY!

Imagine — actually holding in your hand, touching with your fingers, beads containing water from the Miraculous Fountain at Lourdes, France — the exact place where St. Bernadette saw the Vision of Our Blessed Mother. . . .

Now YOU can say this special Rosary, with three beads filled with Lourdes water, to help you gain special favors, graces, blessings, to deepen your understanding of the Rosary and bring you closer to OUR BLESSED MOTHER. . . .

NEVER — NEVER BEFORE A ROSARY LIKE THIS!

The special water filled beads are made of clear, transparent polystyrene plastic, so that you not only FEEL the beads but actually SEE the water inside. . . .

You must see, feel, examine, OWN this magnificent " Lourdes " Rosary.   Only a limited supply of precious Lourdes water is available so we urge you to act quickly.   Send no money now. Simply mail the coupon, stating color of beads you desire. On arrival, pay only $4.98 for each Rosary, plus small C.O.D. and handling charges. Or, to save delivery charges send remittance with the coupon.   You must be completely delighted or return it within 10 days for full refund.

The Roman Catholic Church in America explains superstition among its members as a remnant of immigrant days or as a consequence of ignorance. However, the building of a bigger and better shrine to promote the cult of Mary in the United States is sponsored by Cardinal Spellman, Cardinal Mooney, Cardinal Stritch, Cardinal McIntyre, and an array of archbishops and bishops. The release, in the *Arizona Register*, datelined Washington, September 18, 1953, stated:

The national temple in honor of the Mother of God will be the equal when completed, of any similar shrine to Mary, including the famous Basilica at Lourdes. . . .

The year 1954 will see the start of a project here that will give the United States a monument to the Blessed Mother to rival the Shrine of Our Lady of Guadalupe in Mexico or the Shrine of Our Lady of the Cape (Cap de la Madeleine) in Canada.

Even Pope Pius XII in his encyclical *Fulgens Corona Gloriae* (" The Radiant Crown of Glory "), issued at the Vatican on September 8, 1953, strongly encouraged this worship of Mary:

But where — as is the case in almost all dioceses — there exists a church in which the Virgin Mother of God is *worshipped* with more intense devotion, thither on stated days let pilgrims flock together in great numbers and publicly and in the open give glorious expression to their common faith and their common love toward the Virgin Most Holy.

The announcement of my marriage brought out another facet of the Roman Catholic mind, both clerical and lay — its preoccupation with sex. Of the thousands of letters that I received, the majority, even from married Catholics, spoke of matrimony as if physical gratification were its only purpose. And they wrote of natural love as a deplorable, filthy, unnatural thing. Many drew obscene cartoons.

Others wrote such obscene letters that I burned hundreds rather than let my fiancée see them.

The following note was enclosed with a Sunday bulletin from the home parish of a " Catolic " girls' club:

Sunday June 19, 1949

Fathers' Day
Mr. Emmett McLoughlin:
  On Fathers' Day. I wonder if your father and Mother, if they are living, TODAY. What their THOUGHTS, are about their TURNCOAT SON, EMMETT, in your going to marry such a GIRL, where is your WILL POWER, what do your FOLKS, think about your actions, leaving the Church, and your ACTIONS with that Davis girl, well you are not dead YET, and maybe, GOD will GIVE you Emmett something to think about, as CANCER or Polio, of the MOUTH, and you die, a very HARD DEATH. You are a DIS-GRACE to any CREED, Emmett.

From a Catolic [*sic*] Girls Club
in New York City.

The details of the hierarchy's denunciations of the sins of sex would lead one to wonder if there might not be, at least in the subconscious minds of the moral theologians, something deeper than a war against sin. (The newspapers, in their stories of *Sexual Behavior in the Human Female*, quoted Dr. Alfred C. Kinsey as stating that the largest collection of books in the world on the subject of sex is in the Vatican library.)

A compendium of Roman Catholic moral theology, merely a summary of the several volumes studied in the seminary, devoted thirty-two pages of fine print to the infinitesimal details of the multiplicity of sexual sins. In a mere twelve pages it disposes of the hierarchy's teachings on assault, suicide, murder, dueling, capital punishment, the relations among nations, and the morality of war from the stone age to the atomic era.

The sins of sex are described as " internal " and " external," " complete " and " incomplete," " natural " and " unnatural," " single " or " double." Infinite detail describes whether they are mortal or venial. There is an analysis of sins ranging from thoughts and conversations to such categories as abduction and adultery.

Kisses are divided into paternal, fraternal, customary, affectionate, ardent, prolonged, and soul. The morality of each is described, with the last three being censured:

236. Kissing and embracing.

a) Decent kissing and embracing as customarily done as a sign of politeness, friendship, relationship of honorable love, is lawful even between persons of the opposite sex, but always on the condition that these actions are not done to excite sexual pleasure and that one does not consent to it or to pollution should these result. One should not readily consider young people guilty of grave sin when they kiss and embrace in their games and merrymaking.

b) Ardent, prolonged and repeated kissing is often a mortal sin. Not so, however, would be such kissing and embracing between parents and children.

c) . . . . So also is tongue-kissing (or soul-kissing) usually seriously sinful.[1]

Adultery can be " single," " double," or " multiple," depending on whether one party or both are married, and whether the non-participating spouses of the respective parties have given their consent to the act.

Rape is " single " or " double " depending on whether or not the woman is a virgin. The vaginal douche is sinful except in case of rape, since in that instance the spermatozoa

[1] Jone, Heribert, *Moral Theology* (Newman Press, 1952), p. 155.

are considered an "unjust aggressor" and can be legitimately expelled from the household as a robber, assailant, or
common trespasser.[2]

There are compoundings of sin by "co-operation."
Textbooks go into details in discussing burlesque shows,
pinpointing the varying degrees of immorality attributable
to all persons involved. The girls, promoters, directors,
and musicians commit mortal sins. So does the owner, if
no other theater is available. If plenty of showhouses are
handy, he sins only venially because the performance would
be staged anyhow. The carpenters and maintenance crew
sin venially if they could obtain other work. The cop on
duty does not sin at all because the chief ordered him there:

151. Co-operation in immoral shows and dances.

He sins mortally who takes part in, arranges, conducts, finances or invites others to mortally sinful shows and dances.
If the same are only slightly indecent there would only be a
venial sin in so doing. Musicians who play for immoral dances
sin gravely unless excused by some weighty reason.

Policemen or watchmen who must be present on duty are
excused. Those that keep the theater or hall in repair, etc.,
co-operate only remotely and are, therefore, excused for a less
weighty reason. A very serious reason is necessary to rent
one's place for such purposes, when his refusal to do so would
prevent their taking place. Less reason suffices if other locations are easily available.[3]

The most common sexual sin in the eyes of the hierarchy,
judging by sermons, treatises, and ecclesiastical lobbying, is
birth control.

It is not only the users of contraceptives who sin seriously, but also the manufacturers, jobbers, salesmen, druggists, and hired pharmacists. A druggist sins mortally when

[2] Jone, pp. 148, 541.
[3] Jone, pp. 89–90.

he sells an antiseptic if he knows it will be used to prevent conception; venially if he merely suspects it; and not at all if he thinks it will end up as a gargle. Unless a seamstress is starving, she goes to hell for making a strapless dress with a plunging neckline, because the gown may tempt a susceptible male to " morose delectation " and a " fall from grace." However:

Taxi drivers may give their services to those who ask to be conveyed to houses of ill-repute because on the one hand, they cannot hinder sin anyway, and, on the other, their refusal would mean considerable loss to themselves.[4]

Ribald songs are analyzed according to the age and sensual propensity of the listener:

238. Conversation and Songs.
a) Unchaste speech and songs are gravely or venially sinful according to the influence they exert in arousing carnal pleasure. Among adults of the same sex who have become somewhat cold in matters of the sixth commandment they are often only venially sinful. It is generally a grievous sin if young people engage in such conversation, or if adults do so with persons of the opposite sex, especially if they have an inordinate affection for each other. Besides, such conversation or songs may be gravely sinful on account of the evil intention or scandal or because of the sinful joy one derives from recalling past mortal sins. If scandal is given one need not, according to a probable opinion, indicate the number of listeners when confessing the sin.
b) Voluntarily listening to evil talk and songs is gravely sinful if it greatly influences the arousing of sexual pleasure, or if doing so gives another occasion to indulge in such conversation or if one derives impure delight from listening to it. — It is only venially sinful if the matter has little influence in stimulating sexual pleasure and one listens out of curiosity or laughs with others out of human respect or perhaps even adds a word himself or laughs at the manner in which an off-color story or

[4] Jone, p. 90.

joke is told and not at the story or joke itself, provided, of course, no scandal ensues.[5]

All this may sound ludicrous. It is ludicrous. But these are only a few samples of the dividing and subdividing, of the accumulating and multiplying, of the dissecting and analyzing of human behavior, as taught in Roman Catholic moral theology. They may be found in the textbooks and in the *casus*, or "cases," presented for conference study in the required meetings of the clergy.

The avalanche of letters that I received, berating me for my sins, and blaming me for the sins of those who would be led to sin because of the example of my marriage, showed me with clarity the intricate, contradictory, and amusing pattern of Roman Catholic moral teaching.

This ecclesiastical accounting of the high moral relationship between man and his God destroyed for me my remnants of faith in the Roman Catholic system of morality.

As August 13, 1949, the date of our marriage, drew near, the feeling among many Roman Catholics became intense. One devout woman felt commissioned by God to prevent this disgraceful thing. She tried to kill my fiancée — but she broke into the wrong house.

The director of nurses at our hospital was a Roman Catholic. She had remained silent when I left the priesthood, but the thought of the marriage of an ex-priest threw her into a panic. She stormed into the medical-record department and in the presence of doctors and clerks berated Mary as a thief who was stealing a priest from the Church and who would make it impossible for him ever to go back.

[5] Jone, p. 156.

Someone discovered that my bride-to-be had, during her first marriage, lived in Santa Barbara, within a mile of the seminary where I studied. The story swept through town like a prairie fire that we had had an affair while I was a student and that this marriage was merely the culmination. The rumor-mongers failed to learn or to reveal that I had left Santa Barbara in 1934 and that Mary Davis had arrived there in 1944.

When I had left the priesthood, my relatives had expressed regret but friendship; they hoped something could be worked out. But the news of my marriage convinced them that I would never be reconciled with the hierarchy or return to the Church.

Those who believe that blood is thicker than water — or religion — do not know the indoctrination of devout Roman Catholics. One of my father's sisters would rather have seen me dead than married:

. . . It was with the utmost shock and sorrow we read in the daily paper of your proposed marriage. Fr. Emmett, whatever came over you for you to even conceive such an idea. You know the McLoughlins have always been the pillars of the Church and to think that you, who reached heights never to my knowledge reached by any of them, who could and can change bread and wine into the body and blood of our Dear Lord, contemplate sinking to the depths of degradation, such as you will sink to if you go through with this horrible thing. . . .

I am sure that if your father could have foreseen that you would be considering such a step as you are now taking, he would have prayed to God to take you in your infancy when your soul would be safe. . . .

For God's sake, Fr. Emmett and for the sake of your soul give up this mad idea. You know the minute you enter into this unholy alliance your life will be hell on earth, but I still can't believe it is true. You are always in my mind. I dream of

you at night and I think of you all day and pray for you to
be dead in the State of Grace than that you should go through
with this.

Her condemnation did not surprise me. My father had
been the only one of her family to venture west. The rest
of the family had virtually established a branch of County
Sligo in the provincial seclusion of Staten Island. They
lived for the Roman Catholic Church and in the memory of Ireland. They insisted that all their children
marry Catholics, preferably Irish. They had apologized
to me earlier because one of my many cousins had married
an Italian boy; but they mitigated the disgrace with the
assurance that he attended mass every Sunday. They carefully guided their sons into the police force and the fire
department and violently deplored the fact that, under
Mayor LaGuardia, Jews were beginning to " infiltrate "
into those two fine Roman Catholic institutions.

I did not expect to hear again from my brother who had
followed me into the priesthood. My sisters would not
approve my step, I knew, but I did not think they would
openly condemn me. In this I was mistaken:

I don't imagine that you really expect me to come to the
" wedding." I won't insult your intelligence by telling you
what I think of it. Of course, your big announcement makes
it look like another bid for publicity. I can't help thinking
you seem to be trying awfully hard to be shocking. Maybe
you don't realize it just comes out disgusting.
As you say, it's your life, and you're not concerned with our
feelings. That's obvious from the way you choose to encourage publicity regardless of how much it hurts your family.
I don't suppose a letter like this will do any good, but I
thought I'd better let you know where I stand. Perhaps my
unhappiness is partly due to disillusionment. I guess I had been
clinging to the hope that, in spite of your press releases last

November, you might be sincere in the reasons you gave for your actions.

Your loving sister

Kathleen

Those words hurt, though they should not have surprised me. At one time I might and probably would have written them myself. I could recall the stultifying suppression of the freedom of thought; I remembered the constant repetition of the doctrine of the identification of the will of the hierarchy with that of God; I knew full well that allegiance to the Pope was taught to be above love of parents, children, brothers, sisters, friends, and country.

It was with a feeling more of pity and of sorrow than of anger or resentment that I wrote my sisters a letter. It was two days before our wedding:

Dear Marie and Kathleen:

This is probably the last letter I shall ever write to you. You have indicated by your letters that you too have " written me off the books." One of you has called me a cheap publicity hound. The other has said I am insane. But before the book is closed I wish to make a final statement, calmly, dispassionately, and bluntly; I hope you will have the sisterly affection to at least read it before you close me out of your lives forever.

We have received almost a thousand letters, most of them vicious, damning, and not a few threatening. I wouldn't cheapen myself by answering them. You are the only ones to whom I am writing, because I would like to have you two believe, if not in my sanity, at least in my mental integrity and sincerity.

My action of last December was not a childish, petulant, defiant act of temporary disobedience. It was to me a definite, final, and irrevocable break with the Catholic Church. Mary Davis had absolutely nothing to do with it. Eventual marriage was not its motive nor its occasion.

You should both remember that over a period of years I had been growing more and more critical of the financial antics of the Church and the completely inconsistent attitude of bishops, priests, and especially nuns toward God's poor, particularly the racial minority groups. I discussed these matters with you both many times during vacations. The ramifications went deeper. It gradually dawned on me years ago that the Church did not exist for the benefit of the people but the people for the benefit of the hierarchy. To me the proof of this was evident everywhere in the world where the Church was in numerical majority and controlled the countries' politics. Witness: Spain, Italy, Mexico, South America, and the Quebec area of Canada. The Church accused the Communists of unfair tactics in Italy in the last general election when they put Communist candidates on the ballots under the names of St. Joseph, St. Anthony, and other saints. The significant thing to me was that the Church has been the dominant force in Italy for two thousand years — yet the people were so ignorant that they thought they were voting for the saints.

To me, regardless of the niceties of dogma, ritual, ceremony, and moral code, and the close logical reasoning which attempts to establish them, the tree that does not bring forth good fruit is not a good tree and is not of God. It would take too long to go into all the details of thought and study that brought me to the conclusion that I was an unsuspecting pawn or tool in the greatest swindle of all history. One of the final proofs to me of the crass political nature of the papacy was its failure to excommunicate Hitler and Mussolini.

I fully realized, when I left the priesthood and when our marriage was announced, the torrent of vilification and abuse that would ensue. I had determined to make the break openly. There have been nine other priests who have left the Church from St. Mary's here in Phoenix since I have been here. They all sneaked out and lost themselves in other cities. Hundreds of priests quit the Church every year. Hundreds more would if they had the means of earning a living. Several of them have contacted me. My great crime in the eyes of the Church is that I have not become anonymous.

I am now a simple American citizen with no church affiliations. I have a right to do anything the law permits. One of those things is marriage. I intend to live a normal, American life. That generally includes marriage.

You have indicated that now even the non-Catholics will have no respect for me. There is no sign of it yet. We have had to insure our wedding presents for $3000. A great many of them have come from Catholics. Among them are complete sets of china, crystal and silver, barbecue sets, an R.C.A. console combination, a dishwashing machine, linens, etc. Mary has already sent notes of thanks to 150 people and the gifts are still pouring in. There are apparently a great many people, including Catholics, whose attitude is broader than yours. They don't have the additional tie of blood relationships.

As to my own attitude, I have absolutely no regrets over the step I have taken. I know I shall have none over the step I am taking Saturday. I feel closer to God than I have ever felt in my life. I have not defied God — I have rejected an organization that has usurped the prerogatives of God and claims an exclusive right of speaking in His name. My only regret is that it took me so many years to come to my senses.

In conclusion — you probably agree with very little of what I have written. I know what indoctrination is. Our family has been steeped in it. You may finally break away, too; I sincerely hope so. But if not, Marie and Kathleen, and if you wish to continue your present attitude, we shall meet in Eternity. There, where our own dear parents have gone, there when time shall be no more, there when all human institutions, including the Roman Catholic Church, shall have passed away, in the brilliant, all-encompassing light of God's truth itself, we shall learn who is right and who is wrong.

Your still loving brother,

EMMETT

In the ensuing years one of my sisters has resumed correspondence with me.

We had planned our wedding as a quiet, private, intimate occasion. But we were determined that it must not be secret or cowardly. The marriage license must appear in the vital statistics; therefore we would marry within the county. A close friend, Ralph Watkins, a member of the hospital board of trustees, lived in the town of Buckeye, thirty miles from Phoenix; we would marry at his home. Another member of the hospital board, Charles Bernstein, was a judge. He would perform the rite. We planned to have not more than eight people at the wedding, including Mary's mother and stepfather (a lifetime Mason).

But people began to telephone, asking to come to our wedding. Some were displaying friendship. Others were registering approval of an act of defiance toward the Roman Catholic hierarchy. Some were merely curious. We finally decided to invite everybody we knew — Jews and Gentiles, Protestants and Catholics, doctors and nurses, Negroes, whites, Latin-Americans, Chinese, Japanese, and Indians.

As the tension in the community increased, a lawyer friend sent a short message: " It appears that you may be shot by your former brethren before the week is out. A last resting place may be worrying you. With all your excommunications they wouldn't want you dead in a Catholic cemetery. Cease worrying and examine the enclosed. If you do survive the coming ordeal it will serve as a valuable wedding present." The enclosure was a properly executed deed to two cemetery plots.

The day before the wedding, we heard from our Catholic friend Dudley Field Malone, who had moved to Los Angeles. He had been assaulted in an attack which later resulted in his death. But in spite of injuries he remembered us. He telegraphed from Hollywood: " Dear Emmett. Because of the beating by hoodlums I received a month ago I have not been able to return to Phoenix or I would be with you both tomorrow. Love and blessings always. Dudley Field Malone."

The wedding was scheduled for eight in the evening. In the morning, special services were held in Roman Catholic churches asking God in some way to prevent this "scandalous" demonstration of sinfulness. Throughout the day, local radio stations announced that in spite of written and telephone threats the McLoughlin wedding would take place.

The locale had necessarily been moved from the Watkins living room in Buckeye to a vacant lot next door. The power company had without charge installed poles around the property, mounted huge floodlights, and focused spots upon the altar. Yes, there was an altar, the gift of a Phoenix florist, made from a truckload of white gladioli, carnations, and stock. A high canvas wall surrounded the area, apparently designed to keep out straggling children but actually intended to protect us. Everyone knew of the tension and the threats.

An interracial, interdenominational choir sang the devotional and traditional wedding hymns as a thousand people gathered from the heat and sultriness of the desert. Then the ceremony proceeded in intense silence. As we turned back from the altar into the spotlight, someone shouted across the crowd, "Bravo! They did it!"

The solemnity and dignity of the occasion were forgotten. A spontaneous burst of applause broke out. People don't usually applaud at weddings. Those people were applauding a "declaration of independence," an act of two people asserting their right to seek their own happiness regardless of the laws of ecclesiastical tyranny.

CHAPTER SEVEN

Speaking the Truth in Love

Now that I was married and apparently determined to remain in Phoenix, hierarchical orders went out that I must be disgraced, that I must become a failure, that I must be forced to leave Phoenix.

Nuns in the local parochial schools told impressionable children that I was a bad man. They told the children of Catholic nurses working at our hospital to tell their mothers that it was sinful to work for me. They told the devout Catholics that they should never come to our hospital as patients.

One of the Roman Catholic clergy in the neighborhood demanded that I routinely call him when any Mexican or Latin-American was brought to our emergency room. I told him that we would call if the patient asked for a priest. He insisted that all Mexicans were Roman Catholics, or should be, and that he must be called. I refused. " I shall denounce you from my pulpit next Sunday," he said, " and tell all my people to stay away from that hospital." I threatened to take action if he did. I had Catholic friends attend all his masses the next Sunday; but he said nothing.

A Hollywood agency had been interested in producing

a motion picture of my work in the housing authority and in the hospital. I had told them that the hierarchy would never permit it. Finally they rather naively approached the Production Code office. The agent's experience bears out the findings of Paul Blanshard in respect to Roman Catholic pressure on Hollywood:

Hollywood 46, California

Dear Mr. McLoughlin:

Well, a house fell on us when the Johnson office learned we were contemplating a motion picture based on your work in Phoenix. A monsignor, who is advisor to the Johnson office, gave a flat refusal and forbade any producer to make such a picture.

This to me is the most unfair attitude imaginable and I heartily disagree with it. I further resent being dictated to. . . .

We are going to pursue the matter further after hearing your reaction and advice in the matter.

With all good wishes,

Sincerely,

_____

After our wedding, a representative of a Catholic hospital proposed that my wife be expelled from the Arizona Association of Medical Record Librarians on the grounds of immorality. When the representative of a Protestant hospital pointed out that a successful lawsuit for libel would be the only result, the Catholic hospital representative withdrew her recommendation.

A few months after our marriage, I received a telephone call. "This is Police Chief O'Brien of San Mateo, California," the voice said.

"Yes, chief," I answered, expecting an inquiry about a patient.

He proceeded to tell me that a woman, a Roman

Catholic, had just sworn to a bastardy complaint against me. The Irish county attorney had consulted the Irish judge, who had insisted that I fly to San Francisco immediately to answer charges. The woman had furthermore sworn that I had been in San Mateo the previous evening and had visited her. After telling the police chief that it was all malicious nonsense and that I had no intention of going to California to satisfy him, the judge, or the county attorney, I forgot the incident and left the hospital to help choose housing-project sites.

My secretary informed me, upon my return, that the Phoenix police department was searching for me. I called, to find that San Mateo's Chief O'Brien had telephoned to demand proof that I had been in Phoenix the night before. If I could furnish no proof, he was prepared to demand my extradition to stand trial. Affidavits had to be produced at once. The previous evening we had dined late with friends. Two of them were now in northern Arizona. I found the third, secured her sworn statement, and added that of my wife and myself.

The case was dropped.

The attacks on us were not confined to accusations of immorality. A war of nerves began. The telephone would ring. My wife or I would answer. After a long pause the receiver would drop at the other end. Several times anonymous voices threatened my life if I didn't quit the hospital and leave Phoenix.

We were invited to the birthday party of a prominent Catholic businessman. We felt that he was probably ashamed of the tactics of his ignorant or vicious co-religionists and was offering the hand of friendship. It seemed ungracious to refuse.

His house was crowded with people we knew. While I was chatting with a candidate for the gubernatorial election, a stranger tapped me on the shoulder and asked to speak to me. Since the room was crowded and noisy, he suggested that we step out on the lawn. Unsuspectingly I agreed.

There he began to curse me with a violent stream of invective. When he stopped for breath, I asked him in amazement who he was.

"I am a devout Roman Catholic," he hissed; "that's enough for you to know. And you are a disgrace to the faith, a traitor, a scandal to our people."

I was becoming accustomed to such charges and was not too much perturbed. But I was completely off guard when he grabbed me by the throat and suddenly choked me so violently that I could not cry out. He swore he would kill me and avenge the hierarchy. He was well on his way toward doing just that when I finally broke his hold, pushed him away, and frightened and disheveled dashed into the house.

My wife and I made a hurried departure. On the way home, we recalled that the hostess had telephoned us separately, telling each that she knew the other well and that the other was anxious to come to the party. We had each accepted in deference to the supposed desire of the other.

The prayer barrage continued. At the time of this book, five years after my farewell to my fellow clergymen in St. Mary's rectory, letters of supplication, generally anonymous, still come to me. They are most frequent during the Church holidays. One such letter is a sad testimonial to the power of the hierarchy over its subjects and the willingness of some to destroy their own marriages and families in their blind devotion to Roman Catholicism:

Los Angeles, Calif.
Nov. 25, 1951

You will recall Joseph and Mary Smith — who paid their first visit just about a year ago — inquiring about the scholarships for colored nurse students. Well here we are again — THIS TIME APPROACHING YOU AS WE SHOULD HAVE THE FIRST TIME — with all the cards on the table. . . .

Mr. McLoughlin, Joe and I have been married most happily eight years plus two months and have a wonderful adopted daughter, Patti Ann, now in the first grade of school. We adopted Patti when she was only seven months of age and no family has ever been closer than the three of us. Everything is enjoyed together and we are so proud of Patti Ann. Joe was a convert to Catholicism before we married. Our love is for the active type of life and we have certainly been living that. Many are the friends we so enjoy — both back east (Ohio) and out here in the west — Phoenix, Cactus, Monrovia and now Los Angeles. . . .

I am not going to ask any of the questions which curiosity would have me ask of you; nor am I going to lecture on why we want to help you to return to " where you belong and can find happiness and peace of soul and mind " — but, please believe me when I assure you that our reasons are of sufficient importance to make worthwhile our GIVING EVERYTHING LEFT TO US NOW — EACH OTHER, PATTI ANN, A LIFE IN THE WORLD OF ACTIVITY WE SO LOVE.

JOSEPH AND I THROUGH PROPER ECCLESIASTICAL CHANNELS ARE SEEKING ADMISSION INTO CONTEMPLATIVE RELIGIOUS ORDERS AND ARE GOING TO PLACE PATTI ANN WITH SOMEONE ELSE FOR ADOPTION — with our prayer and intention — that long existing SPECIAL INTENTION of ours — YOUR RETURN REGARDLESS OF THE HUMILITY IT WILL REQUIRE TO THE LIFE SO RIGHTFULLY YOURS UNDER THAT INDELIBLE MARK OF THE PRIESTHOOD. You, and we, alone — need know of our intention — but we wanted you to know.

Sincerest prayers and best wishes. May God give you peace! Truly your friends always —

The clergy themselves avoided me. I was supposed to be an evil influence. If I talked to them as old friends, they might be corrupted. Though I had been excommunicated for several years, I had not yet turned into a drunkard, become an impoverished failure, or been smitten with the wrathful thunderbolts of God. A friend contended that I had been excommunicated so often that I was no longer eligible for hell and that the hierarchy was designing a deeper, hotter section for more appropriate torment.

In August 1951 occurred an incident which gave the Catholic Church hope of a deathbed conversion. While pursuing my hobby of gardening, I was bitten by ants. I was apparently allergic to ant venom. Within five minutes I was unconscious, a victim of the choking asphyxiation called " anaphylactic shock." I was rushed to our hospital, met at the door by the chief of our medical service, injected with adrenalin, and put under oxygen and helium. As I regained consciousness I saw the tracheotomy set at the bedside ready to cut into my throat to preserve breathing. I had seen it often enough to know what it meant — that I was in danger of choking to death.

My wife was at my side. I had told her many times before that if I were dying I wanted her to keep all Roman Catholic priests away from me. I told her I still felt the same way. She obtained special-duty nurses with explicit instructions that no priest or nun was to be admitted. When the story hit the front pages that I was critically ill, priests who had refused to speak to me for three years suddenly called the hospital to express their sympathy, to offer their assistance, and to ask if they might visit me. The nuns of St. Joseph's Hospital also called, feeling that they, in spite of my doctor's order of " no visitors," would, as hospital officials, be permitted to cross the line. Some of the Catholic nurses working in Memorial Hospital asked that the nuns and the clergy be admitted and were informed that if they attempted to come near me the sheriff would be there to stop them.   The hierarchy contends that every ex-priest when dying wants to be reconciled with the Roman Catholic Church.   I had passed this spiritual crisis.

After my recovery, two priests tried to woo me back. One had been a friend of many years, my teacher and parish Superior.   He was visiting Phoenix friends and telephoned anonymously.   I recognized his voice.   He asked me to visit him and agreed to my suggestion that I should bring my wife.   (Earlier he had told me and another ex-priest that age and lack of ability to readjust were the only reasons he remained in the priesthood.)

We were ushered into the library of his friend's house. It was five in the afternoon.   His Reverence was asleep. When his host aroused him we realized why he was asleep — he was drunk.   When we were left alone the priest leered at my wife.   "What a cute trick," he said.   "How were you lucky enough to get that?   Better than I expected."

"You know," I interrupted, embarrassed, "D. M. is also married."   (I was referring to another ex-priest.)

"Yes, I know all about that," he stammered, "he went out on the desert, got hot for a woman, and married an Indian squaw."   Actually, however, D. M. had married a very charming schoolteacher from Missouri and is now very successful in a professional career.

My former Superior poured himself a drink of whisky and began berating himself for having been too lax in his discipline over me.   Between his self-accusations and his urgings that I return to the Church, he kept appraising my wife.   Ten minutes of this was enough.   We walked out in disgust, leaving him still muttering to himself.

Within a month of this unpleasant episode a former class-mate telephoned. He wanted to visit me. I agreed, on condition that religion should not be a topic for discussion. We had grown up together in Sacramento, California, had attended the same grammar school, and had both entered the seminary in 1922. As I closed my office door, he began the old refrain: "What are your dear parents in heaven thinking of you now? Think of all the good you have done and now you have fallen from grace!" The years in the priesthood had fattened him. He had become the ultra-pious type of priest and had developed a habit of cocking his head sanctimoniously. After I tried, with no success, to change the subject, I asked him to leave.

But the next morning he came again, rudely walked into my office, held out a religious medallion, and asked me to touch it and pray with him to save my soul from hell. Again I was forced to order him out. He left with his head bowed as though his great mission for God had failed.

Within thirty days I received a secret call from a priest who was friendly to me. He said that my determined visitor had left the Franciscan Order and the priesthood.

Perhaps this is why the clergy are forbidden to talk to me.

Another priest, a schoolmate, had returned from a fruit-less mission to the Indians of the upper Andes, in South America. He spoke to me of our seminary days, of the Arizona Indian missions, and of the sacrifices he had made for the "faith." I asked him if he could give me any rational arguments for the divine nature of Roman Catholicism. "Oh, no," he answered, "I must merely teach the cate-chism. It is easier to believe than to disbelieve."

Among all the thousands of letters that I had received

from saddened or belligerent Catholics, not one gave an intellectual reason for my return to the Church. Even those from bishops and priests and lawyers and doctors contained the same emotional arguments. I filled my wastebasket with medals, " spiritual bouquets," pious doggerel, Sacred Heart badges, " third-class " relics, and gaudy prints of the saints, Jesus, Mary, and Joseph.

Most Roman Catholic seminaries are empowered to grant collegiate degrees. But a Bachelor of Arts and especially a Master of Arts degree would be valuable to any priest leaving the Roman Catholic Church. Many seminaries therefore withhold the documents proving the degree unless it is necessary for some particular clerical assignment — such as teaching in a Roman Catholic high school in a state requiring all secondary-school teachers to have degrees.

I knew an ex-priest who had aroused the ire of his midwestern bishop and had been sent to the hierarchy's " prison " in Oshkosh, Wisconsin. He rebelled and escaped to Arizona. There he tried to get the degree to which he was entitled from an eastern Catholic university; but he was refused. He spent his stay in Phoenix working as a bus boy in the Westward Ho Hotel.

Another friend of mine, a Franciscan priest, was more shrewd. He planned his departure from the priesthood for a year. He enrolled in a state college for a special course and wrote the officials in the Santa Barbara seminary, telling them that the bishop desired him to take the particular course and that he would need a master's degree to pursue it. He received it immediately.

I had not been so foresighted. I had left the priesthood before thinking of a degree. It was obvious that a mere letter would secure me neither the degree or even a transcript of my credits. A Phoenix firm of attorneys, at my request, retained a Santa Barbara firm to investigate the legal possibility of forcing the hierarchy's hand.

The first reaction was a refusal, based on the statement that it was illegal to grant degrees to priests who had graduated prior to the receipt of the seminary's charter from the state of California in 1942.

Our attorney responded:

December 27, 1950

Prefect of Studies
St. Anthony Seminary
Garden at Pueblo Street
Santa Barbara, California

. . . At the time of our conversation, you advised me that it was your impression that some time during the war years, 1941–5, San Luis Rey College was first enfranchised by the State of California and that since Emmett McLoughlin had completed his studies prior to that time there was a question in your mind as to whether you could legally now award him such a degree nunc pro tunc, and I told you that I would investigate the law and attempt to answer the question. . . .

Hence, the first question to be resolved is whether or not San Luis Rey College complies with the statutory provisions above referred to. The Secretary of State of the State of California, in response to my request, informs me that they have no record in their office of a corporation named SAN LUIS REY COLLEGE and I conclude, therefore, that I have not been correctly informed as to the name of the institution operated by the Order of Friars Minor in this area, or that that institution is not located, as I assumed, in California. I would appreciate it if you would advise me on this point. . . .

If we assume that the Order of Friars Minor, or some institution operated by them, has authority in the State of California to award a degree such as that here involved, I can see no reason under the law of the State of California, why such a degree should not now be awarded to Emmett McLoughlin. . . .

In conclusion, it follows that if the Order of Friars Minor, or any institution operated by them, is now authorized to award such a degree as is here involved, it is authorized to award the same to Emmett McLoughlin as of date or as of any date subsequent to the date of its enfranchisements, and the fact that he completed his course of studies prior to the time that such institution was so authorized would not militate against the award of such a degree at this time.

This letter sent the ecclesiastical authorities scurrying for another answer. They consulted the priest who had set up their collegiate program, and this was his reply:

I know of no instance in which a Bachelor of Arts degree was conferred on any student who had completed his college course in San Luis Rey before the Charter was received. We would have looked on such a procedure as both *unethical and illegal*. . . .

The files containing the transcripts, and other data regarding the scholastic status of Emmett McLoughlin are now in Santa Barbara. The only information before me is that contained in the letter of [my attorneys]. If that information is correct, and I know no grounds for questioning it, I cannot see how the Franciscan Fathers can confer any degree on Emmett McLoughlin without departing from *precedent*. . . .

The seminary authorities sent this letter on to my lawyer, with a final jelling of their decision. It was no longer "illegal" for them to grant me a degree; it was "inadvisable":

. . . Since I have been prefect of studies for only a comparatively short time, I took the liberty of forwarding your letter to Father F., who, until this past summer, was officially connected with San Luis Rey Seminary for many years. I asked him to advise me as to the possibility of granting the requested degree to Mr. McLoughlin. I am enclosing his letter of reply. It would seem from the contents of Fr. F.'s letter that it would be *inadvisable* for us to grant Mr. McLoughlin's request for a degree.

As in our conversation of a few weeks ago, I wish to repeat that we would not be adverse to granting your client's request for a degree if his claim were legitimate. In fact, only this morning I spoke to our Father Provincial about this matter, and his attitude is the same. Our reluctance is caused by the fact that the granting of such a degree would be a *departure from our policy and standards*. . . .

The Santa Barbara attorney informed my Phoenix attorney:

. . . While it would appear that there is small reason for feeling that such a discussion will result in any startling success, I think there is some possibility that we might be able to effect a change of heart for the reason that the ground upon which Father P. now relies in his refusal to award a degree to Mr. McLoughlin are administrative and internal to the Franciscan Order, and the position which he originally took in his discussion with me was that the only thing that would bar such an award was the limitations imposed by external regulations, i.e., the statutes of the State of California.

My attorneys advised me to give up the fight. Although the hierarchy could legally give me a degree, and although I was morally entitled to it after twelve years of the same courses given in Roman Catholic seminaries all over the world, they could not be forced. My attorneys could, however, secure a transcript of my high-school and college credits. So for considerable legal fees I secured a record of my own credits — a record which most students can secure for a three-cent stamp, but which a student for the Franciscan priesthood will never see without the threat of a lawsuit.

Seventeen years after completing the courses, I learned

my grades. In the high-school courses I had received A-plus in forty-one subjects and A in fifteen. In the six years of the " upper " college division, I earned A thirty-five times and B twice.

But I had not earned a degree.

Some years ago, when hospitals were shedding the pest-house and almshouse stigma and striving to become centers of the scientific practice of medicine, a group of leaders in the field organized the American College of Hospital Administrators. It was intended to give hospital administration standing comparable to the American College of Surgeons and the American College of Physicians. To this end it conducts intensive " institutes " in many cities of the United States. It encourages university courses in the complexity of hospital stewardship. And it also publicizes itself to the subtle effect that, when administrative openings occur, boards of hospital trustees cast a more confident eye toward an applicant who can boast of membership in the American College of Hospital Administrators. The whole movement has been a delicate and refined approach toward union membership and the administrative " closed shop."

Requirements for admission to the " College " are the usual good character, recommendations by five members, and either a college degree in hospital administration or three years of superintendency of an approved hospital. In the fall of 1950 I applied for admission.

I had had not just three years of superintendency but seven and a half in a hospital which the American College of Surgeons approved as having " excellent " administration.

For references I gave the names of five of the best-known

administrators in the country. One, the former president of the Baptist Hospital Association, wrote:

> Concerning Emmett McLoughlin, he has really done a monu-
> mental work at Phoenix in building that hospital out of nothing
> to one of the finest in the country. . . .
> I know that it is impossible to take in everybody but this
> man, having done such outstanding work and having achieved
> so much, ought to have this recognition for a good job well
> done.

The executive secretary of the American College of Hospital Administrators is Mr. Dean Conley, a devout Roman Catholic. And as months went by I heard nothing. Finally I wrote and asked the status of my application. This was Mr. Conley's answer:

> The Credential Committee in meeting recently considered
> your request for admission.
> After careful consideration of your application, the com-
> mittee was unable to recommend you for admission at this time.

I received no word of explanation, only vague messages that the credentials committee was composed of honorable men who certainly would not stoop to the influence of religious prejudice.

In a gentler manner the same freeze has been exercised toward me by the local Arizona Hospital Association. Our hospital is, of course, a member, one of the five major hospitals in Arizona.[1] Two of these are Roman Catholic institutions. I have not been proposed for any administrative position within the organization. They do not know that it has always been my policy to refuse titular offices and that their strategy merely entertains me.

[1] The name was changed from St. Monica's Hospital to Memorial Hospital in 1951.

In the hospital field — one of the largest industries in the nation — the Roman Catholic Church has quietly assumed a dominant role. It owns 772 hospitals and in 1951 treated 5,177,094 patients. Some 12,490,844 people were entered in all the nation's non-governmental general hospitals. The hierarchy controlled more than 40 per cent of those admissions.

There are 1170 state-approved nursing schools in America. Of these 366 are Roman Catholic, and they train almost one-third of the country's nurses. More than half of these are non-Catholic girls but all of them are trained in the Roman Catholic code of hospital ethics. They are taught that every unborn fetus must be baptized into the Catholic Church; that no means of contraception, regardless of family finance or circumstance, mental or physical health, must ever be explained; that a wife and mother must be permitted to die on the operating table rather than have a therapeutic abortion, even when it is authorized by the laws of the state.

In 772 hospitals, the Canon Law of the Roman Catholic hierarchy supersedes the laws of the forty-eight states of the Union. And American women die. And American doctors say nothing. And the American Medical Association says nothing. (And the United States government gives millions upon millions of dollars of non-Catholic taxpayers' money to Roman Catholic hospitals under the Hill-Burton Act to build more Catholic hospitals, to defy the laws of the land and permit more women to die, because to save their lives would be against the laws of the Roman Catholic Church.) And the United States Public Health Service permits this to happen because it is afraid of the hierarchy's pressure and the " Catholic vote." And the state boards of

health are submissive because they, too, are afraid of local
Roman Catholic pressure. I know that all of this is true
because, at this writing, I am still secretary of the Arizona
State Board of Health. This tremendous power over the
very lives of Americans is held by a religious minority
group that in its most exaggerated statistics does not claim
more than 20 per cent of the population.

This defiance of the non-Catholic American taxpayer is
evident in other attitudes of nuns after Hill-Burton hospitals
are built. In Phoenix, the Sisters of Mercy refused, in spite
of the local need, to open their psychiatric wing until they
could secure a " good " Catholic psychiatrist to supervise it.

One need merely glance at the program of the annual
convention of the American Hospital Association or any of
its regional conventions to be impressed with the deference
given to the Catholic hospital group. The day before the
official convention starts, the Roman Catholic section begins with a special mass by the local bishop. The adver-
tisers and the trade groups serving hospitals sponsor expensive dinners for the attending nuns. Throughout the
convention, the nuns are fawned upon by convention officials, hospital executives, and surgical-supply salesmen.

Graduating medical students, however, do not share this
adulation of Catholic hospitals. The report of the choice
of hospitals by student doctors, published in March 1953,
is revealing. Of the 772 Catholic hospitals, only 194 are
even listed as being approved to train interns. Only sixteen
of those (or 8 per cent) received their quotas of the young
doctors. Seventy-nine of the sisters' institutions received
no interns at all. Of the total quota of 1718 positions offered by Catholic hospitals, only 572 were filled by men

who chose to complete their training there. That is less than 10 per cent of the doctors placed throughout the country for the year 1953–1954.

The support and friendliness of the general public have become more pronounced as the years have passed since I left the priesthood. The hospital has operated at normal capacity. Our women's auxiliary, composed of socially minded and important women of the community, after its Catholic members dropped out took a much more active interest in our nursing school, clinics, and other hospital functions. Its annual ball is an outstanding social event of the year.

The hospital's medical attending staff has increased to more than three hundred doctors. Every Catholic doctor in Phoenix has applied for membership, has been carefully screened by the twenty doctors of the executive committee, and has been accepted.

The local medical society continued to be friendly to our hospital. In 1953 the president of the group asked permission to attend our medical executive committee meeting and after a flattering speech presented a plaque which was reassuring in the light of rumored attacks by some of the doctors. The plaque read:

AWARD

For Distinguished Public Service

Presented To

EMMETT McLOUGHLIN
By the Maricopa County Medical Society

In recognition of his assistance in the establishment and continuance of the Intern Service at the Maricopa County General

Hospital, which aided in the accreditation of the hospital by
the American Medical Association.

Kent H. Thayer
President
Wallace A. Reed
Secretary

(Seal)

May 20, 1953

All Catholic doctors belong to the county society. The
vote for the award had been unanimous.

The award was the result of a plan, first suggested by our
hospital, for affiliating our medical interns with the county
hospital. The plan gave our interns experience in charity
cases and gave the county an intern service.

The nursing shortage has affected us less than other
Phoenix hospitals. Our executive nurses and department
supervisors, some of them Roman Catholics, have stayed
with us since I left the priesthood. While St. Joseph's
Hospital advertised even in Canadian papers and magazines
in 1953, and the county hospital advertised in the eastern
United States, we have been able to meet our regular needs
without recourse to newspaper appeals.

In the fall of 1953 the American Medical Association,
without warning, canceled the internship program of the
Good Samaritan Hospital (Methodist) in Phoenix. Such a
spirit of co-operation had been built up between the Good
Samaritan and Memorial Hospital that the immediate reaction of their officials was to turn to us for aid. Our response, with the approval of the chief of staff and the chairman of the board, was to offer to give our approval to their
interns and combine the teaching programs of the two hospitals. The Memorial Hospital board in its October 1953
meeting, by unanimous resolution, offered its complete

co-operation to the board of trustees of the Good Samaritan Hospital.

Associations and luncheon clubs invite me to speak on public health and on hospitals, just as they did in the past. Non-Catholic churches schedule my talks, the Phoenix Ministerial Association has given me a standing invitation to its meetings, and the Arizona Council of Churches has chosen me as chairman of its committee to plan a Protestant social-service agency. When a Protestant chaplain was appointed for our hospital to work with all churches, letters of endorsement came from Episcopalians, Mormons, Baptists, Methodists, and many other denominations.

Individual lay Catholics have become more friendly as the years have passed. They have seen that the curses and thunderbolts have not struck me down. Catholic salesmen have never stopped calling at the hospital. At election time, Catholic politicians, even the graduates of Notre Dame's law school, have assured me that my rift with Roman Catholicism could never affect their personal friendship for me — and that any good word passed on to the Negroes and Mexicans about the " right man " for county attorney would be appreciated.

But my family, both immediate and remote, have, with the exception of one sister, " disinherited " me.

After I left the priesthood, there developed a program of co-operation between our hospital and Phoenix labor unions which is almost unique in the country. It began with a suggestion by a board member, a former mayor of Phoenix, Ray Busey, that three labor executives be elected to the board. They were the secretary of the district council of carpenters, the executive secretary of the operating en-

gineers' union, and the editor of the *Arizona Labor Journal*.
The latter served as vice-chairman of the board in 1952 and
as chairman in 1953.

Our first step was a plan whereby paid-up union cards
served as " credit cards " in the hospital. The unions in
turn agreed to assist in the collection of slow accounts of
their members. After four years this plan is still in effect.

The second project was the reframing and reroofing of
the entire hospital. Sixty carpenters and thirty laborers laid
100,000 square feet of sheathing on a Saturday and a Sunday. In lieu of cash they received hospitalization credit
applicable to anyone they wished. Some gave theirs to
C.I.O. friends who needed it during a strike at the local
aluminum plant. During any strike or threatened walk-out,
we routinely extend credit to the striking employees.

This same " credit instead of cash " plan was followed in
the construction of a new X-ray department, central supply,
and pharmacy. It has become a year-round arrangement
with the local painters' union, which assumes complete
painting maintenance of the institution.

We asked the hotel and restaurant employees' union to
recommend improvements in our dietary department. A
year's study resulted in the employment of a union steward
of forty years' experience, an entire union crew of chefs,
assistants, and counter girls, increased wages, excellent food,
and an unusual saving in the department of more than
$30,000 in raw food costs within one year.

The gifts of hospital equipment presented by individual
unions led me to get in touch with other voluntary associations, and I found them equally interested in helping and

equally indifferent to my background in the priesthood.

The multitude of free associations in our nation — from Elks to Chambers of Commerce, from Rotary to the National Real Estate Board, from the National Education Association to the eleven million members of the American Federation of Women's Clubs — are taken for granted by the average American. But an ex-priest is not an average American. The associations I had known were Catholic societies, sponsored by the Church and strictly supervised by priests. The result is that in Catholic countries, societies are few in number, sterile of initiative, and oriented always toward the welfare and preservation of Catholics and of the Church. I marveled at the spontaneity of origin and democracy of rule of the many groups that I approached for help.

The occasion for most of these contacts was our assumption of the responsibility for the care of infantile-paralysis patients from most of Arizona and the bordering areas of surrounding states. Organizations whose primary purpose was fun, or "brotherhood," or luncheon acquaintanceship, or political pressure bought iron lungs, hot-pack machines, suction equipment, rocking beds, and ventilation meters. They were simply neighbors, together doing stupendous things that in other countries must be done by government or — as is usually the case — not done at all.

This co-operation that I observed between clubs and the polio foundation and our hospital made me conscious of the great but largely unnoticed role of these voluntary groups. They furnish eyeglasses for youngsters, outfit school safety patrols, buy wheel chairs for crippled children, and — to me most important of all — provide innumerable scholarships so that ambitious youngsters may receive the education they deserve. I drew additional comfort from the fact that none of them cared a whit that I had been a Roman Catholic priest.

Although the feeling of the Roman Catholic laity has mellowed toward me as the years have passed, that of the hierarchy has not. It has become less violent, but it has never ceased. Friends inform me that their devout Roman Catholic friends, when my name is mentioned, quote the clergy: " He must still go; he cannot remain in Phoenix; he must be forced out of that hospital. We Catholics will never give up."

And they have not given up. They have constantly forced our board of trustees to face this question: " Is Emmett McLoughlin good for this hospital? Would it be more successful without him? " The implied threat has been that of a boycott by Catholics — backed by the power of their supposedly great numerical strength.

It can easily be shown that their claimed strength is fictitious. The 1953 *Official Catholic Directory*, as quoted in the *Arizona Catholic Register* of May 29, 1953, listed 30,425,015 members. This figure, at first glance, to a politician, would constitute a terrifying block of votes; to a manufacturer, a salesman's dream of customers; to a timid soul, an overwhelming force of enemies to defy. But the figure is completely false. It can be proved false by an insight into the manner in which it is compiled and also by a little simple arithmetic.

Once a year the bishop's office of each diocese in America sends a questionnaire to each pastor asking the statistics for the *Official Catholic Directory*. The pastor must list the number of baptisms, converts, marriages, and the total number of Catholics — infants, children, adults — in his parish. No parish that I have ever known, or heard of, keeps an actual count of its parishioners. Roman Catholics do not have to register with local churches as some Protestants do. They merely have to attend mass. It makes no difference in which church they attend the ceremony. The pastor makes a guess as to the number of his flock, always making sure that it is higher than the previous year. If it were lower he would incur the episcopal wrath for laziness and inefficiency.

Furthermore, the hierarchy in its computations never admits that a Catholic has left the fold. The letters quoted in this book amply demonstrate that I, for one, am still considered a Catholic.

The hierarchy, in publishing its annual gain in membership — and there is always a gain — gives the impression that its members are reasonably good members. Its minimum requirement for good standing in the Roman Catholic Church is attendance at Sunday mass. Failure to attend mass, unless excused by sickness, even on one Sunday is a mortal sin and punishable by the eternal torments of hell.

The church page of the Saturday newspapers, in most cities, lists the Catholic churches and the hours of masses. If one assumes that all these masses are attended at capacity — a more than generous tribute to their drawing power — and if one multiplies the number of Sunday masses by the average church capacity and then compares the result with the supposed number of Roman Catholics in the city, an interesting total will be realized.

Let us take Phoenix as an example. A 1952 survey informed the Phoenix Union High School Board that the population of the area it served comprised 225,000 people. This same area is served by thirteen Roman Catholic churches averaging four hundred in capacity. Sixty Sunday masses are recited in these churches, according to the listing in the daily papers. This gives a total capacity of attendance of 24,000 faithful. The claims to Roman Catholic membership in this area, used for pressure upon press, radio, and the movies, varies from 20 to 40 per cent of the total population. Twenty per cent of 225,000 would be 45,000 people; forty per cent would mean 90,000 Roman Catholics. But their churches at all their masses will hold only 24,000.

Are the other 21,000 to 66,000 Roman Catholics non-existent or merely " bad " Catholics? If " bad " Catholics who violate the commandment of attendance at mass every Sunday — a mortal sin — they certainly do not heed the hierarchy's denunciation of a book, a motion picture, or a political candidate.

A survey conducted by the chaplaincy committee of our hospital showed that one-fourth of our patients are nominal Catholics but that less than 1 in 50 will permit a priest to visit them.

The hierarchy certainly does nothing to discourage exaggerated estimates of its membership and power.

In accordance with the plans we had worked out, the medical interns of all the Phoenix private hospitals spend part of the year in the Maricopa County General Hospital, a fine institution of 350 beds. In a discussion I had with its medical director, a non-Catholic, concerning its obstetrical service, he told me that he had appointed a Roman Catholic doctor as chief of that service. I asked him if this choice might not cause difficulty when the necessity arose for a therapeutic abortion or some other surgical procedure forbidden by the Roman Catholic Church. He assured me that no difficulty could arise because he was operating the county hospital according to the Catholic code of medical ethics. He said he was doing so for two reasons. He didn't want to risk losing his own staff membership at the St. Joseph's Hospital, run by the Sisters of Mercy. In addition, he could not risk the political antagonism of the Roman Catholic populace, which he said came to 65 per cent of the total public. (The 65 per cent that had been quoted to him would mean 146,000 Catholics. And this in an area whose maximum church capacity of Sunday mass is only 24,000!)

And so in a county hospital, built and maintained by taxpayers' money, women may die, children may be orphaned, and birth-control information may be withheld because at the command of Rome the laws of the Catholic Church are above the laws of a sovereign state of the United States of America. And free Americans cringe because of the falsified Catholic membership and strength.

The same kind of pressure has even been exerted on members of the board of trustees of our hospital. Some of them have been told that no financial drive could ever be successful so long as an ex-priest was the administrator — that the Roman Catholic public would not contribute. What the informants failed to point out was that no appreciable amount of Catholic funds would have been contributed anyway to a non-Catholic hospital in a city where there is a hospital of the Sisters of Mercy.

Whenever a problem has arisen regarding a medical contract, a departmental change, or the disciplining of a doctor, rumors have spread throughout the city. Problems of this nature arise constantly in every hospital with a medical staff of three hundred doctors. But when we have faced up to them, board members have been told that the existence of these problems has been due to my administrative inefficiency. I have been accused of fraud, of giving the board false statistics, of failure to co-operate with the medical staff, of being too tolerant of medical carelessness, of persecuting doctors, of permitting laxness, carelessness, and immorality among nurses, of being so strict with nurses that none wished to work for me, and even of being so mentally deranged as a result of my conflict with the Roman Catholic Church that I was psychologically incompetent to operate the institution.

In November of 1952 it seemed that the clerical strategy might be successful. A member of the board of trustees felt the situation to be so precarious that he told me he would fight for a renewal of my contract even if the Church's revenge meant the destruction of his own business. He did fight and defied the Catholic hierarchy, and its " representative " on our board; with the help of the other sympathetic, liberal members he succeeded in having my contract reapproved and making it automatically renewable.

On hundreds of occasions since, I have been invited to speak before Protestant groups. At times the assigned subject has been public housing, or public health, or some aspect of hospitalization. I have accepted many of the invitations. In the inevitable question period, queries have gradually veered toward the real reason I had been invited — my relationship with the Roman Catholic Church. I have been frank in my answers, filled with my new-found freedom of speech regarding church, state, and politics.

On one occasion, a Methodist church in its Sunday bulletin stated: " Come tonight and hear Emmett McLoughlin tell why he left the Roman Church." Catholics were apparently " planted " in the audience. Word spread to the clergy and to the faithful laity. Hospital trustees were immediately informed. A Catholic friend of one swore that I must be chased out of town because I had spoken in public against the Roman Catholic Church.

" But," he was told, " you have often spoken against the Protestant Church."

" That's different," he replied. " Protestant churches are all false. The Catholic Church is the only true Church and we will not tolerate any ex-priest criticizing it."

I was warned by board members to " lay off " and stay away from Protestant churches, or my position in the hospital would be jeopardized. " But," I asked, " don't I, as an American citizen, have a right to attend any church and express my opinions on religion? "

" This situation is difficult," I was told; " Catholics are too numerous. We can't afford to offend them. They may boycott us."

In 1953, with the opening of the new St. Joseph's Hospital, the majority of our board of trustees realized that appeasement or silence was impossible. They encouraged me to speak about our hospital and my background whenever I could. They themselves made the advance arrangements for my talks in Protestant churches. After several lectures had been held in churches, I discovered that the sheriff had stationed plain-clothes deputies in each audience to make certain that the threats I had received were not carried out.

Some might feel that I have been struggling with a persecution complex. It might be well to point out that my experiences as a result of leaving the priesthood are not unique.

One ex-priest applied to the United States Civil Service Commission for a rating so that he might teach in the Indian Service. After a year he had still received no rating. The manager of one of the Arizona reservations needed a teacher with his qualifications but could not hire him without civil-service approval. I telephoned the district office in San Francisco; when the director stated that the application had never been received, I called again and asked an assistant the status of this man's application. The assistant said the papers were on the director's desk. Then I telephoned the director once more and told him that if the civil-service rating did not come through within twenty-four hours, I would call Washington and refer the case to the two Senators from Arizona. The rating was approved.

The ex-priest assumed his teaching position, did well, and married one of his fellow teachers. But one day he called me frantically. He had just received a letter from the San Francisco Civil Service office notifying him that he had been accused of homosexuality. He was given ten days to disprove the allegation or his Civil Service status would be cancelled. Summer storms had closed desert roads and downed telephone lines and it had taken five days for the letter to reach him. When he came back to Phoenix, I took him to the city's best attorney. He asked, " How can you disprove homosexuality — and how can you disprove it in five days? " He couldn't, of course. My friend lost his rating and his position.

He was later able to determine that the accusation had

come from the Roman Catholic hierarchy in the diocese in which he had been serving and had been accepted, without proof, by the United States Civil Service Commission. I had lived with this man for many years, knew him as intimately as one fireman knows another in the dormitory of the same firehouse, and knew that he was completely normal. He is at the present time very happily living with his charming wife. For a time, in spite of the influence of church over state, he successfully pursued his career on the faculty of one of America's universities; and today he is an Episcopal minister.

Another priest wrote from China:

. . . I am a Maryknoll missioner who has been in the China missions for eight years. Last year I returned home to the states for a year's furlough. While there I fell deeply and irrevocably in love with a woman, so deeply that after several months of careful and sincere consideration have come to the conclusion that I would be better off in the lay state. Even before love came my way this decision was in the back of my mind. So now I'm looking forward to some position whereby I might make my livelihood in the lay state. Having come to a knowledge of the same step that you have accomplished I wonder if you could help me. I realize only too well that you know nothing about me, that you have no idea of my abilities. But looking at it objectively and dispassionately I may say that I have a personable approach, am friendly with everyone and have the knack of getting on with almost everyone. It's true that because of my seminary training I possess no college degrees. Could you use me in your hospital or exert your influence to assist me in obtaining some position? I guarantee that once I got " placed," once I was started in some position, I could go on from there on my own merits. Would you take a chance on me, would you give me an opportunity to get started again in the lay state? That's all I ask of you.

It may seem odd that I left the States to return to the missions in China, if as I say, I wish to return to the lay state. The

reason for this seeming irrelevancy is that my decision had not
" jelled " until after much meditation on the ship across the
Pacific. Now my decision is final and irrevocable. To prove
my determination I have written to several people I know as I
have you. But I am very doubtful they will aid me because of
the shock and surprise occasioned by my desire to return to the
lay state. But you would be more capable of understanding the
reason. That is why I am appealing to you. May I restate that
I am not a " crackpot " and that my decision has become final
after much cogitation. So can you, would you " place " me in
some position. If you are willing or require further details
would you please write me.

Hoping to hear a favorable reply from you soon,

I remain,
Determinedly yours,

_____

I placed him in touch with people I hoped might help
him.

Another who had already left the priesthood was unable
to escape his past:

Seattle, Wash.
August 19, 1949

Dear Sir:

The enclosed clipping appeared in the Seattle Times a few
days ago and prompted me to write to you. I hope you do not
feel this is an imposition. I thought perhaps you might understand my position and be able to sympathize with me better
than anyone else.

I, too, am an ex-priest of ten years' duration. I had a difference with my Bishop in eastern Canada and came to the west
coast in 1938. Since that time I have been employed continu-
ally in hospitals by a community of sisters. I have held positions as Personnel Director and Business Manager.

Needless to say they knew nothing of my past. However,
a few months ago the knowledge reached them in some way
and the Superior terminated my services at once. Since that

time, as you will well realize, it has been impossible for me to find another suitable position.

Each time I make application for a position I must supply the names of places of previous employment for the past several years. That Superior undoubtedly sees to it that I do not get a good reference.

I am married, no children, and have been in the U.S.A. for the past four years.

My work record is excellent and I feel that I am well qualified in the hospital field. I can supply the names of people well known in the hospital field who can vouch for both my character and work record.

I thought you might have something suitable for me in your hospital. If not, do you know of a hospital where it might be possible for me to get located?

I would deeply appreciate hearing from you.

Very truly yours,

———————

I referred him to a Masonic friend in the northwest who is the administrator of a large non-Catholic hospital.

As for myself: I felt like a cross-country runner who had passed many obstacles and had covered a great distance. I stopped and looked back, and my pursuers were far behind.

I was emotionally, mentally, and matrimonially at peace. I had not dreamed that a person could be so happy. I felt that God had doubled for me the joy of marriage when I finally reached it after twenty years of loneliness.

I now had a home. It was a very simple dwelling, located in a modest subdivision in south Phoenix. Its furnishings and conveniences were much less luxurious than those of the monastery I had left.

At the age of forty-two I began to learn mentally and physically to live as a human being and a normal American citizen. The one who helped me most and made the transition possible was the woman I had married.

I had been used to doing big things for people, building houses, getting jobs, saving lives. My wife repeatedly and patiently pointed out the little things that brought happiness to people who did not need the big things. Priests are so idolized by their people and in every material way supported by them that often they do not realize the need or the value of the thoughtful, common courtesies of good manners.

My wife showed me that no longer should I be entertained without entertaining, receive a wedding invitation without sending a gift, hear of the death of a friend or acquaintance without expressing sympathy to the family of the deceased.

She always listened calmly when I lost my temper in the face of unreasonable cruelty by the Church I had left. Then she would hand me her stepfather's huge Masonic Bible. "Read to me from the Book of Job," she would say. "It is so beautiful and it will help us, because nobody ever had more trouble than he."

I had become embittered by the attempts to disgrace me and displace me at the hospital. My wife helped me rise above that bitterness by planning for our home. We built a ranch-type porch and a redwood fence, added a patio, and with crude, home-made masonry constructed a barbecue fireplace. In the balmy Arizona evenings we charcoal-broiled steaks, entertained friends, talked politics, condemned Communism, planned neighborhood improvements, and listened to the stirring words and music of her favorite song — "The Battle Hymn of the Republic."

She talked of her days in Baylor University and of the

intellectual freedom encouraged in that school built and financed by the Southern Baptists. The authors she re-called were mere names to me, Robert Ingersoll, Thomas Paine, Dostoevski, Thomas Wolfe, Omar Khayyám, and many others.

Unlike Roman Catholics, Baptists do not fear the chal-lenge of freedom of thought and expression. They do not need any "index of forbidden books" to guarantee the fidelity of their members.

I began to read with the avidity of a college freshman entering for the first time the vast library of the world's great minds. I read *Look Homeward, Angel*, the Rubáiyát, *The Hills Beyond*, the lectures of Robert Ingersoll, the tracts of Tom Paine, and a host of others.

I read and thought and discussed and gradually came to several disturbing, humiliating, and frightening conclusions. The first was that the Roman Catholic Church preserves its hold, over those it does hold, not only through fear but also through calculated ignorance — ignorance accomplished by the prohibition of certain reading and by mental isola-tion or separatism. The second was that Catholic "educa-tion," whether in a seminary or in a college, is not education at all and that I, for one, had not been educated. The third was that the Roman Catholic Church actually does want to make America Catholic and thinks it will succeed. The fourth conclusion is that if America becomes Catholic or to the extent that it becomes Catholic the freedom of thought, of initiative, and of progress in America will be destroyed.

The *Index of Forbidden Books*, as devised by the Council of Trent in the sixteenth century and still enforced by the

Code of Canon Law, is an effective weapon for keeping the laity and the clergy in obedient submission. It is a guarantee that the faithful shall not think and therefore shall not rebel. The penalties for disregarding its proscriptions prevent millions of free Americans, who would fight and die to protect their right to vote, from exercising their equally sacred right to think — without which the right to vote is meaningless.

The Catholic who prints, sells, keeps, or reads all or part of a book forbidden by the *Index* not only commits a mortal sin but is also automatically excommunicated.

Books forbidden by name constitute only a fraction of those covered by the *Index*. Whole general categories of books are prohibited, and a volume under one of these categories goes under the ban the moment it is printed.

The following are the regulations of the *Index*:

Books forbidden by the common law of the Church are:

1. Editions of the original text of the Sacred Scripture published by non-Catholics; likewise, translations of the same made or published by them.

2. Books that in any way defend heresy or schism or that tend to undermine the foundations of religion.

3. Books which, of set purpose, attack religion or morals.

4. Books of non-Catholics which professedly treat of religion unless it is clear that they contain nothing contrary to Catholic faith.

5. Books published without the ecclesiastical approval which treat of Sacred Scripture, or contain annotations and commentaries thereon or translations thereof into the vernacular; books containing new apparitions, revelations, visions, prophecies or miracles or which seek to introduce new devotions.

6. Books which attack or ridicule any Catholic dogma, or defend errors proscribed by the Holy See; books which disparage divine worship, or seek to undermine ecclesiastical discipline, or avowedly defame the ecclesiastical hierarchy, the clerical or religious state.

7. Books which teach or approve of superstition, fortune telling, divination, magic, spiritism and other such practices.

8. Books which declare duels, suicide and divorce to be lawful; furthermore, books that treat of freemasonry and similar secret societies, maintaining that they are useful or that they are harmless to the Church and civil society.

9. Books which, with avowed intentions, treat of, describe or teach, lewd or obscene matters, such as the methods of birth control.

10. Liturgical books containing unauthorized changes so that they no longer agree with the authentic editions approved by the Holy See.

11. Books which contain apocryphal indulgences, or such as have been condemned or revoked by the Holy See.

12. Also forbidden are all images, however reproduced, of Christ, the Blessed Virgin, the Angels, Saints or other Servants of God that are not in keeping with the sentiment and decrees of the Church.

N.B. Besides those named there are other books proscribed by the special decrees of competent authorities.[2]

The various functions of collaboration in the production and distribution not only of forbidden books but also of comparably objectionable magazines and newspapers are called " co-operation " and are considered as varying degrees of sinfulness:

Printing, publishing or editing such literature is never allowed. Linotyping or proofreading the same is considered proximate co-operation, hence, permissible only for an extremely grave reason, e.g., if one cannot otherwise make a living. Preparing and handling the paper, mixing the ink, servicing the presses, etc., is lawful for a time for a moderately grave reason. Selling ink, paper, machinery, etc., to such printing establishments is only remote co-operation and is lawful for the sake of profit. To write a good article for an objectionable publication is to promote (although to a small extent) the interests of the magazine and is allowed only for a just and reasonable cause recognized as such by the bishop (C. [Canon] 1386).

[2] Jone, *Moral Theology*, pp. 272–273.

In an urgent case the bishop's permission may be presumed. To contribute good articles regularly as an associate editor of an evil publication is to promote the same considerably and is lawful only for an extremely grave reason, e.g., if one cannot otherwise support himself or his family. Advertising in a disreputable newspaper is generally not a great aid to its publication and, therefore, lawful for any reasonable cause. Extensive advertising of an individual business man or a company may imply considerable assistance and is justifiable only for much more important reasons. One needs special faculties from the Holy See to sell irreligious literature; even then he may sell only to those who he has reason to think have faculties to reach such literature. . . .

To others than these one may sell only to avoid an unusually great detriment, e.g., complete loss of trade. Professedly immoral literature may not be sold (C.1404). Distribution of bad papers is considered proximate co-operation and is, therefore, justified only to avert great harm. Subscribing to such papers likewise requires a grave reason, e.g., great advantage to one's business. Merely to see what one's competitors have to say or sell is not a sufficient reason to receive such papers. To buy a copy now and then would be very remote co-operation and would be justified for an unimportant reason, provided no scandal would ensue. In the reading of such literature the Church's laws on the prohibition of books must be observed.[3]

The Roman Catholic Church is not satisfied to isolate its members from the written, intellectual opposition of the past and the present. It tries to separate them from current contacts that might lead them into the " danger " of thinking for themselves.

It is obvious that Roman Catholics, to a large extent, are a people apart in America. Their clergy will not associate with other clergymen. Their laity may not visit non-Catholic churches. They have their own schools, clubs, societies, and lodges. They have a feeling almost of pity for those not " blessed with the faith." I can remember

[3] Jone, p. 89.

my sister's remark about a Protestant: " She's a nice person even though she is not a Catholic."

To some extent this separatism can be explained as a result of the self-consciousness of the Catholic immigrants of my parents' generation, particularly the Irish immigrants. They were proud, and Catholicism gave to them and especially to their clergy a circle of circumscribed social prominence that they could not have attained by their background and attainments in broad American society. Priests, bishops, and cardinals — whose parents were not even the " lace curtain " but, like mine, the " shanty " Irish — could feel superior to their parishioners in their handsome rectories, luxurious vestments, and beautiful automobiles.

On many a St. Patrick's Day I have heard the boastful graduates of Maynooth, the famous Irish seminary, with a brogue too thick even for me, one generation removed from the peat bogs, reminding Americans that the Irish were in truth God's chosen people. If God's providence had not sent them across the seas, they said, the Italians, the Germans, the French, and the Polish Catholics would all have lost the faith in the pagan wastes of the United States.

Thomas Sugrue, in his provocative meditation *A Catholic Speaks His Mind*, is inclined to attribute Catholic separatism almost entirely to the ambitions of the Irish:

This was the Church into which I was baptized in 1907. The Irish clergy ran it: they dominated its organization, its hierarchy, and its point of view; they set the pattern which oriented newcomers first to Americanism, then to American Catholicism. They were disliked and resented — quietly — by priests of the other immigrant groups, who came from countries in which the aristocracy and the intelligentsia traditionally stood guard over the natural inclination of the clergy to exploit its relationship with the peasant classes, and who therefore were accustomed to performing their religious duties and to leaving well enough alone otherwise.

The old feeling among American Catholics of not belonging and of not being wanted has developed now into a separatist tendency which displays itself in an increasing number of organizations, institutions and committees whose title begins with the word " Catholic." The habit among Irish clergy of acting as aristocrats and intelligentsia for their congregations has developed into a system of supervision and censorship for literature, the arts and entertainment. . . .

Their clergy will not join with the clergy of other faiths in any endeavor, however nonreligious. . . . A Catholic convert of any prominence is welcomed into the Church with the discreet tumult of a gangster's funeral; if he can write or talk he is then put to work as a propagandist, and if his life story ends as a best seller everyone is happy. He has been thoroughly converted to the " we." [4]

But Sugrue overlooked the fact that Irish separatism was backed by the Canon Law and the moral theology of the Roman Catholic Church.

Catholics, even under the latest regulations, are forbidden to co-operate actively in non-Catholic worship. " To sing or pray along in non-Catholic services is wrong because it is participation in an illicit form of worship." However, " A Catholic architect may design churches for Protestants and synagogues for Jews for some very good reason. . . . It is lawful to sell pews, tables, carpets, lights, etc., to non-Catholics for their churches if otherwise one [the Catholic] would lose the profit." [5]

Special circumstances may sometimes justify attendance at Protestant worship: " Soldiers and prisoners may attend such services [non-Catholic] if commanded to do so for the

[4] Sugrue, Thomas, *A Catholic Speaks His Mind on America's Religious Conflict* (New York: Harper, 1951, 1952), pp. 52, 56.

[5] Jone, p. 88.

sake of order. . . . Attending the sermons of non-Catholic ministers may often be forbidden because of scandal or danger to faith; this latter holds also for listening to such sermons on the radio, especially if done often." [6]

" Sisters in a hospital may not summon a non-Catholic minister for a dying person to assist him in death." [7]

Separatism is found also in the Catholic attitude toward public schools. The Catholic parochial-school system in America, enrolling 2,800,000 children, has grown largely because the Vatican through its Code of Canon Laws has forbidden attendance at public schools under the penalty of mortal sin: " Catholic children must not attend non-Catholic, neutral or mixed schools, that is, such as are also open to non-Catholics." [8]

The ecclesiastical laws on marriage, with their prohibitions, promises, " impediments," and dispensations, emphasize in a personal and practical way the Vatican's determination to wall off Catholics from other people. The basic law forbids marriage with non-Catholics. As shown in Chapter 3, canonical reasons must be presented to the bishop for dispensation. The non-Catholic must submit to at least six one-hour instruction classes in Catholicism and must promise in writing to rear all children as Catholics even if the Catholic spouse dies. The Catholic must also give a written promise of his sincere effort to convert the non-Catholic. Both must promise that there will be no Protestant or Jewish marriage ceremony either before or after the Catholic rite.

However, with an eye to producing further Catholics,

[6] Jone, pp. 70–71.
[7] Jone, p. 88.
[8] *Codex Juris Canonici*, Canon 1374.

the Church would rather take the chance of having its lay members marry non-Catholics than not marry at all.

This is shown by some of the reasons considered canonical or sufficient to dispense with the "impediment" of "mixed religion." Lack of prospects, or a community with less than 1500 Catholic inhabitants, justifies a girl in looking elsewhere. Advancing age is another good reason: "Her super-marriageable age (aetas superadulta) i.e., if the bride has not been married before and has completed her *twenty-fourth* year." Other reasons would seem to encourage the woman to marry an unwary Protestant: "The poverty of a [Catholic] widow burdened with numerous small children . . . the evil repute of the [Catholic] woman . . . the presence of infirmity or deformity . . . the fact that the girl has been deflowered by another man." [9]

The Church does not encourage its members to associate with non-Catholics even in ordinary business and social activities, but it does *permit* such association if the Catholic remains on guard against temptation:

Association with non-Catholics in civil affairs is allowed as long as this does not constitute a danger to one's faith. Because of the danger to faith it may be forbidden to *work for* those not of our faith, to join certain societies or attend non-Catholic schools. Since *debates* and *controversies* on religious subjects with those not of our faith are fraught with many dangers, especially if they are public, they are forbidden without permission of the Holy See, or in urgent cases of the local Ordinary [the Bishop]. [10]

Separatism is also the rule for public meetings with non-Catholics. Perhaps the Vatican fears that Catholic teach-

[9] Jone, p. 483.
[10] Jone, p. 69.

ings can only with difficulty be defended in open debate and that both layman and priest might succumb to the arguments of non-Catholics.

The regulations for public debates issued by the Congregation of the Holy Office on December 20, 1949, under the heading "Interdenominational Conferences," resemble the detailed reports said to be required of Communist party members. Among them are the following:

#9. Where there is hope of good results from mixed conferences, priests must be designated for taking part in them who are entirely fitted for the exposition and defense of Catholic doctrine. Others of the faithful may not attend these conferences without special permission.

#10. As to debates between Catholic and non-Catholic theologians, those priests only may be appointed who have proved themselves truly fitted by their theological knowledge and firm adherence to the principles and norms laid down by the Church.

#14. In regard to local discussions and meetings, permission is granted to local Ordinaries to give the necessary approval of the Holy See on three conditions, namely, (a) that all communication in sacred functions is avoided, (b) that the treatment of matters at issue is duly examined and directed, (c) that at the end of each year a report is sent to the Sacred Congregation of the Holy Office as to the place of the conference and the experience derived from it. As to theological conferences, there is an added condition, namely, that a yearly report is sent to the aforesaid Congregation of the questions treated and the persons of each party present.

#15. In regard to interdiocesan, national, or international conferences, permission of the Holy See for each separate conference is to be obtained, and in the petition it must be stated what questions are to be dealt with and who are the participants. Before the permission has been granted, no external action towards convening the conference may be begun, nor any cooperation with non-Catholics if they begin to move in the matter.

#16. It is not forbidden to recite at the beginning or end of the conferences the Our Father [Lord's Prayer] or any other prayer approved by the Church.[11]

These edicts have been issued since my break with Rome, although the Franciscan Order has always had similar rules.

Father George Dunne, the Jesuit priest assigned to " refute " Paul Blanshard's *American Freedom and Catholic Power*, lives in Phoenix and was one of the three priests who remained friendly to me. I told him several times that his " refutation " of Blanshard refuted nothing.

Mr. Blanshard asked me to invite this priest to debate the book in the Catholic colleges on the west coast, particularly the Jesuit universities. " You know the bishops as well as I," the priest told me. " They will never consent."

This smug mental isolation and separatism explained to me a phenomenon in Roman Catholicism of which I became aware only after leaving the priesthood. There is a mass schizophrenia throughout Roman Catholicism — a blind justification of practices, customs, and rituals which, when practiced by non-Catholics, are condemned as stupid by Roman Catholics themselves.

As a priest, I had been guilty of this inconsistency, reading and preaching about the blessings of the rosary while sneering at the prayer beads of the Orient. The prayer flags and prayer wheels of the Tibetans seemed to me pagan foolishness, without any power to influence God — at the same time that I was selling eight-day votive lights to Catholics too busy to have time to pray.

This anomaly became clear to me in 1950 as I looked

[11] Davis, *A Summary of Moral and Pastoral Theology*, p. 31.

down at *Life* magazine in a neighborhood drugstore. On the cover appeared a leader of the Hindus carried on the shoulders of his followers, proclaiming the washing away of sins to all who bathed in the Ganges. Inside the magazine appeared the Pope, riding his throne on the shoulders of the Swiss Guard, extending the indulgences of the Holy Year to all who came to Rome. My fellow clergy and I many times had expressed disgust at the mass ignorance of the Hindus who believed that the dirty Ganges could wash away sin. Yet both of these episodes were pilgrimages; both leaders claimed to represent God; both promised forgiveness of sin — one with a word, the other with water. And I suspected that the shopkeepers along the Ganges, like the merchants in Rome, were more interested in the influx of currency than in the forgiveness of their customers' sins.

The Catholic Church belittles the Mohammedan trek to Mecca. But it encourages pilgrimages to Palestine and attributes great spiritual value to the Crusades. It perpetuates the Crusaders' temporary freeing of the " Holy Land," and their re-enactment of the last hours of Christ, by attaching special indulgences to praying at the fourteen "stations of the cross " which circle the walls of every Catholic Church. Why should Roman Catholics call idolatrous a shrine of Buddha while draping diamonds and rubies around a statue of Mary? Why call ignorant and parasitical the monks of Tibet while supporting the non-productive contemplative monks of America? Why be shocked at the pricking pins and chanting incantations of Voodoo priests while approving the sprinkling water and the hierarchy's solemn exorcism of the devil? It seems ill advised to condemn the Salvation Army's collection of old clothes as "big business" while permitting the nuns of Santa Clara to solicit funds for "Shares in God."

In Canton, Ohio, these nuns of the Santa Clara Shrine of Perpetual Adoration offer, for a financial investment, shares in "God and You, Inc." They promise as dividends "a perpetual novena by the nuns . . . a midnight hour of adoration and rosary every night of the year . . . special mass and Holy Communion on three appointed days each month . . . a share in all spiritual and penitential works of the community." They promise that the names of all shareholders are kept on file in "God's Files for Prayer." They leave the monetary assessment of the benefit up to the individual's conscience with these words: "I value each share at _____ and enclose my investment of _____." The Christmas 1953 issue of their magazine, *The Voice of Santa Clara*, lists the names of more than six hundred "shareholders" in Ohio alone.

The hierarchy usually attributes crass commercialization to maverick convents or monasteries that slip by the Church's controls. The *Arizona Register* of October 23, 1953, contained the following official advertisement of the Catholic Near East Welfare Association (480 Lexington Avenue, New York):

FATIMA REACHES OUT

With our modest, but constant efforts we keep trying to add more Near East lands to Our Lady's conquests by putting a FATIMA SHRINE CHAPEL in each land. Thus Fatima keeps reaching out. Slowly we gather the dollars for our next one in JOR-DAN. Your mite or block ($10) with others will be a great help.

OUR HOLY FATHER PLEADS FOR YOUR "MEMBERSHIP OFFER-INGS" DURING OCTOBER. ENROLL YOUR LIVING AND DECEASED NOW in all classes of membership. They share in 15,000 masses

each year, including a daily mass at the Vatican. Individuals —
annual $1, perpetual $20. Family — $5 and $100.

Given in the advertisement as the organization's president
is the name of Francis Cardinal Spellman.

The same Roman Catholic separatism may explain also
a moral phenomenon which puzzles non-Catholics and
which was forcibly brought home to me after I left the
Church. It is the paradox of a Roman Catholic, faithful in
attendance at Sunday mass, perhaps an officer of the Knights
of Columbus, whose behavior on Monday shames his wife
and stuns his neighbors, business colleagues, and his political associates. It explains the hypocrisy of those who attend early mass to save their souls, so stupefied after an all-
night drinking party that they sleep through the ceremony.

This peculiar dichotomy in moral values may produce
tragic family situations. A Catholic woman I knew lived
for years with a Jew but would not marry him because he
refused to bring up their children as Catholics. In late 1952
the papers carried the story of another man, who had murdered his estranged wife because the Catholic girl with
whom he was living refused to marry a divorced man.
These stories are not uncommon.

When I left the priesthood I found that many Catholics
whom I had befriended when they were accused of immorality and illegality — prominent Catholic public officials
whose marriages I had saved or had legalized — were no
longer my friends. According to their standards, my decision to leave the priesthood, to marry, and to think for
myself constituted a crime more serious than the drunkenness, adultery, theft, perjury, and bribery of which many
of them had been guilty.

I was certainly disappointed in these "friends," but I did not hate them. Hate takes energy — energy better devoted in these cases to pity and compassion for their inconsistency and ignorance.

The entire Roman Catholic system of "education," from its parochial grammar schools through its universities and seminaries, is by its very nature a concentric, inbred thing, feeding upon itself, forbidden to draw strength and mental nourishment from without its own narrow doctrinal world. Its teachers are, for the most part, priests and nuns, indoctrinated people who have studied virtually nothing that has not borne the *Imprimatur* ("Let it be printed "). Their own education is that of instruction by edict, not by research.

The most important qualifications for the lectors and the professors, the priests who teach priests, are not knowledge or teaching ability — but indoctrination, docility, and loyalty to the Pope of Rome. The following constitutions of the Franciscan Order are similar to the rules of other orders and of Canon Law:

269. No Lector shall be appointed who is not commended without reserve for his morals, faith and docility toward the Holy See.
270. The Lectors of Sacred Theology, Canon Law and Philosophy may not begin their office before they have taken, in the presence of the Minister Provincial or his delegate, the Profession of Faith according to the formula prescribed by the Holy See.

This Profession of Faith — in effect a "loyalty oath " against "Modernism " — must be recited annually, according to Canon 1406, by every teacher in a recognized Roman

Catholic university or college.   The Profession of Faith
contains these words:

> I condemn and reprove all that the Church has condemned
> and reproved. This same Catholic Faith outside of which no-
> body can be saved, which I now freely profess, and to which I
> truly adhere, the same I promise and swear to maintain and
> profess, with the help of God, entire inviolate and with firm
> constancy until the last breath of my life.

The textbooks, the subject matter, and even the lives
of the lectors themselves are carefully controlled lest the
young priests-to-be, future teachers of the Roman Catholic
laity, begin to think for themselves:

> 273. Therefore, they shall not only teach their pupils the re-
> quired sciences, but they shall also give them an example of
> exact and regular observance. They shall educate the youths
> committed to them in an ecclesiastical and truly Franciscan
> way, teaching them goodness as well as discipline and science.
> 278. The Lectors and all the Friars are forbidden, in virtue
> of holy obedience, to dare publicly or privately to teach, de-
> fend or approve any erroneous or suspect doctrine or opinion
> savoring in any way of Modernism, or contrary to sound
> morals. Nay more, let them beware of too much freedom of
> opinion, especially in doctrines pertaining to morality. Where-
> fore they shall be bound to follow the more common and ap-
> proved opinions of Catholics and to conform themselves en
> tirely to the decrees of the Holy Apostolic See.

I had always thought of myself as an educated person.
I had spent enough years in the seminary to justify a Ph.D.
degree. People flattered me for my " marvelous " background. I had studied many languages and could still
speak Latin and make my way in German and in Spanish.
I could astound people with dates and events in European
and world history. I could converse freely about Spinoza,
Immanuel Kant, Descartes, Darwin, Hume, Berkeley,

James, Marx, Schopenhauer, and other influential thinkers. I could speak spontaneously on many subjects, and years of practice had given me facility in writing sermons or essays.

But the reading I was now doing exposed me to myself as a fraud. I was not a learned man. I was merely a theological technician. I had been an unthinking marionette who thought, spoke, and moved when the Vatican jerked the strings. The isolation, the positive indoctrination, and the negative control of the *Index* had duped me thoroughly.

In the " education " of the American laity, the Vatican and even the lower parish clergy deliberately conceal or distort actual Roman Catholic teachings or rituals. They do this to prevent their own people from learning how un-American some doctrines are, or how ridiculous and petty some rules can be.

Lay Catholics hear little of the *Syllabus of Errors* of Pius IX, dated December 8, 1864, which condemned:

> The rights of democracies, the claims of science, the sanctity of free speech, the principles of toleration, man's freedom to choose his religion, Protestantism's possession of some share of Christian truth, belief that the Church should not use force or rule temporally, separation of church and state, state education of children — all these, and many other tenets of liberal democracy were condemned.[12]

As far as I know, no succeeding Pope has repudiated these pronouncements of Pius IX.

Lay Catholics are not taught of the Vatican's early opposition to the American labor movement, the battle over " trusteeship " (lay ownership of church buildings), or Pope Leo XIII's condemnation of the " heresy of Ameri-

[12] McKnight, John P., *The Papacy* (New York: Rinehart, 1952), pp. 203–204.

canism " in 1899.   They are not taught that a more recent Pope, Pius X, not only did not modify the antagonism of his predecessor but went further and in his condemnation of " Modernism " lumped together Americanism, pragmatism, and German philosophy.   These two Popes condemned American qualities, including the initiative, the " virtues," and the resourcefulness which, as part of American life itself, have helped to make America — and indirectly the American Catholic Church and therefore the Vatican itself — rich in material possessions.

In the field of labor, the hierarchy is as inconsistent as it is in interracialism.   "Liberal " students in American Catholic universities delight in the "labor " encyclical, *Rerum Novarum*, of Leo XIII, and in the publicized stand of American bishops that the working man must have a living wage.   Priests and bishops are appointed arbitrators in strikes, and union men, especially Roman Catholics, boast that the Church is a friend of the masses.

But my fellow Franciscan, the Rev. Kilian Pryor, was ordered out of Phoenix at the instigation of wealthy Catholics because he became " too friendly " with the unions. The Rev. George Dunne was ousted from the Los Angeles diocese when he openly upheld the actors and technicians in their strike against the movie producers.

Within Catholic circles, churches, schools, and hospitals are notorious for their " peon " wages.   Employees who complain are told that theirs is a service of love to God and that their reward will be in eternity.   Sisters' hospitals, employing thousands, are strongly antagonistic toward unions.   In the Phoenix Hospital Council, I recommended that all hospitals join in the union-sponsored survey of dietary costs and operations that we were conducting. Sister Mary Eucharia, the superintendent of St. Joseph's Hospital, objected strenuously. She said that the experience of the Sisters of Mercy with unions had been bad, that they dictated to the nuns in St. Mary's Hospital in San Francisco, and that co-operation with union officials even for a survey would give them a toe hold that would ruin the hospital. In late 1953 the nuns were supplementing the heavenly promises with cash salaries of 67 cents an hour for kitchen workers.

The hotel and restaurant employees' union drew public attention to this condition in its publication, the *Aces*, on February 27, 1953:

ST. JOSEPH'S TO HAVE NEW HOME, OLD WAGE SCALES

. . . The most disturbing factor, so far as Local 631 is concerned, revolves around those people employed by the hospital who come under the jurisdiction of our organization. In the past they have been very poorly paid, and will probably continue to be underpaid in their new quarters.

A recent survey made by officers of the local union indicated that the workers in the food department of the hospital receive only about 60 per cent of the wages prevailing in the hotel and restaurant industry in this area. It is a shame to think that workers in a new and modern hospital are required to work for such substandard pay scales.

The hierarchy knows that if the inconsistencies of its papal pronouncements, the archaic medievalism of its doctrines, the foolishness of some of its ritualistic practices, and the paramount role that money plays in dispensations were commonly known or realized, not only would the Church lose its intelligent members but its over-advertised growth through converts would cease.

The contention that the goal of Roman Catholicism is not

merely to maintain its status but to "make America Catholic" is not merely a figment of a mind like mine which has rebelled and might be considered biased or frightened. The lay member and the ordinary priest feel it a duty of charity to bring back the "separated brethren" to the "one fold and one shepherd." The hierarchy can see an extension of power and wealth. But all agree on the objective and are confident that it will be realized.

The strongest segment of the Roman Catholic press in America is the *Register* chain of weekly newspapers published in Denver. Special editions are printed for thirty-two dioceses and archdioceses in America. The boasted weekly circulation is in seven figures. The editor in chief is the Right Rev. Monsignor Matthew Smith. He wrote in his editorial in the issue of June 5, 1953:

ARMY OF CONVERTS RISES OVER YEARS

The number of converts has vastly increased with the passage of the years. In the 1928 *Directory* the figure was given as 33,991 for 1927. In the new 1953 *Directory*, the year's crop is given as 117,803. . . .

Experts in the field of conversion assure us, however, that the annual number ought to be vastly higher, and that it would be if there were more lay apostles urging non-Catholics to take instructions and there were better organized methods of letting non-Catholics know we are interested in their spiritual welfare.

Of one thing I am sure, however, as a result of a study of statistics. We are going ahead fast. The fact that the average Catholic family is larger than the non-Catholic, owing to the Church's attitude on birth control, will in time make the U.S. a Catholic nation.

On August 21, 1953, in the *Arizona Register*, Monsignor Smith again discussed the Church's aim in connection with immigration:

CHURCH CAN GROW WITHOUT IMMIGRATION

As for the Catholic Church, it does not need giant immigra-tion to keep growing. It is doing very well now, in my estima-tion, and it looks to me as if it is going to do a great deal better as times goes on. The U.S. will be ours because of the desperate influence of the birth control movement on so many of our "separated brethren," whom none of us like to see dwindle the way many of them are.

The leakage from the Catholic Church was dreadful during the heavy immigrant days. People who tore up their roots in Europe often lost their faith when they found themselves in the slums and mining camps of America. I fear that, if the truth were known, at least half the nation should be Catholic, though we know it is not.

It may be, however, in another generation or two, as a result of birth control among Protestants.

Understandably I have had a very personal interest in the mental tyranny of Roman Catholicism. I have seen the crushing of spirit and vitality within the monasteries, seminaries, and rectories.

We can all see the national anemia of Catholic nations. To me the outstanding example is Brazil, which is larger than the United States. Its colonization started more than a century before ours. Those who should know claim that its material resources in minerals, timber, agricultural po-tentials, and other categories are greater than those of the United States. We know the difference between the two countries at the present time. Is Brazil's relative backward-ness and the domination of a Roman Catholic hierarchy in that country for more than four centuries merely a coinci-dence? An intellectual twilight also prevails in Spain, Ire-land, and much of South America.

As Roman Catholicism spreads in America — or gives the

illusion that it is spreading — we see increasing instances of boycotts, reprisals, blacklistings of movies, prohibitions of books (even in public schools), control of library and school boards, and even dictated elections.

Even now American Catholics are being taught that our country's greatness stems from the Roman Catholic tradition. In our seminary, as mentioned earlier, we were actually taught that Thomas Jefferson and Benjamin Franklin received their inspiration for the Declaration of Independence from the writings of Cardinal Robert Bellarmine of Italy.

The discrepancy between history as taught in the public schools and the Roman Catholic version was the occasion for a successful plan to invade the Phoenix Union High School Board, when I was still a priest. I heard the reasons and the planning within the lounge of St. Mary's rectory.

Many graduates of St. Mary's two parochial high schools (for boys and for girls) who enrolled in the Phoenix Junior College complained to the clergy that their history textbooks did not agree with those they had studied at St. Mary's. They mentioned the decadence of the Papacy in the Middle Ages, the cruel tyranny of the Inquisition, Catholicism's share of the blame for Europe's religious wars, and many other embarrassing facts.

St. Mary's clergy reasoned that, if there were a Catholic on the secondary-school board (which controlled the Junior College as well as the high schools of the area), he could effect changes in the textbooks. The " Dad's Club," composed of some three hundred fathers of students in the Catholic high schools, therefore elected one of their members to the secondary-school board. So few people vote in a school-board election that the " Dads " and their friends had no trouble electing their candidate.

Fortunately the other board members were aware of the Catholic strategy. The history books were not changed.

In looking back, that attempted destruction of free thought through the control of books has made me appreciate those citizens who, in my thinking, have the highest privilege and the most awesome responsibility in America — the members of public-school boards.

I had never attended public schools. I had been taught that they were far inferior to parochial schools. I had been told that their buildings were lavish and their resources unlimited but that their discipline was bad. The teachers were not dedicated, like nuns, but merely young women who tolerated the children while they took their paychecks and prowled for husbands. The public schools were godless, with no crucifixes on the walls, no prayers before or after every class. Rumors circulated in Catholic schools that the chief avocation of public high-school students was sex, and that the perennial problem of the faculty was the disposition of girls who became pregnant.

But now I could see the public school as the great sanctuary of the free mind, before whose altar the lamp of free research, study, and inquiry must be kept burning and then passed on like the Olympic torch from generation to generation.

The hierarchy's determination to impose Canon Law upon America was clearly stated by the American Roman Catholic hierarchy in the Third Plenary Council of Baltimore (1884):

It is obvious in countries like our own, where from rudimentary beginnings our organization is only gradually advancing towards perfection, the full application of these [Roman Catholic] laws is impracticable; but in proportion as they become practicable, it is our desire, not less than that of the Holy See, that they should go into effect.

In 1953, eastern bishops had the power (and they bragged of it in the *Arizona Register* of June 19, 1953) to defeat for the thirteenth time a law that would have permitted doctors to give " necessary " contraceptive advice. I was reminded of Bishop Gercke's attempt in 1947–1948 to use me, as priest-secretary of the Arizona State Board of Health, to prevent birth control in Arizona.

I believe, however, that my experiences can augur well for America as well as for others who might follow me out of the priesthood. With humility I can echo St. Paul: " I have fought a good fight. I have kept the faith." My experience has proved that an ex-priest can overcome his own fears and survive the most concentrated attacks of Roman Catholicism. That experience proves also that the American non-Catholic public still believes strongly in freedom of thought, freedom of religion, and freedom of the right to change one's means of livelihood — and that it will support a man who exercises that right. There is no need for any disillusioned priest or nun to seek the protective anonymity of Los Angeles, New York, or Detroit. He needs only the courage of his new convictions, a willingness to work, a deep confidence in America, and a solid faith in God.

CHAPTER EIGHT

"Upon the Altar of God"

I believe that no one could have lived sincerely in the Roman Catholic faith for forty years and in a seminary and the priesthood for twenty-five years without, at times, feeling an intense nostalgia for its beauty, for the sacrificing sincerity of many of its members, and for real friends still within its fold. Even now, five years out of the priesthood, when I pass a Catholic church the occasional aroma of the incense of the benediction ceremony recalls the seminary chapel, the faces of boys who persevered from 1922 until we were ordained together, of friendly nuns who taught me the alphabet and drilled me in spelling, and of my father, who walked with me every Sunday evening to the benediction service in St. Francis Church in Sacramento. The incense even recalls the ice cream he bought me on our way home in the little drugstore at Twenty-first and H streets.

There is much that is good in Roman Catholicism. It has existed too long, it is too big, it includes too many people not to have many of the qualities that are good and noble in humanity — as I knew from my personal experience in the Franciscan Order.

After all, Roman Catholicism is a religion. It offers

the solace of the hereafter to the bereaved and to those who are " heavily burdened." It began as something that was thoroughly good — a group of simple, sincere people perpetuating the memory, the message, and the inspiration of Jesus of Nazareth.

In the world of beauty and art, the Roman Catholic Church has certainly provided the inspiration for much that is great. Through it, many artists have seen the ideals of humanity and the timelessness of Jesus and have crystallized those transfigurations into masterpieces of sculpture, painting, and music.

The symbolism of many Roman Catholic rituals contributes to this beauty. No one could find fault with the ceremony of the blessing of the Easter candle or with the observance of the " Tenebrae " — the Darkness — during which, as mournful psalms are chanted, twelve candles are gradually extinguished to recall the desertion of Jesus by his twelve apostles. These and the many other special ceremonies, as well as the routine words and actions of the mass, satisfy that need for ritual which (as Erich Fromm points out) is almost instinctive in man.

The Roman Catholic Church, too, has given " culture " to certain parts of the world. Even in the United States, parents who are not married " in the church," or who practice birth control, or who for some other reason are not attuned to the *sententia ecclesiae* — the spirit of the Church — will place their children in parochial schools because of a certain strictness of ethics that they presume lacking in a public school.

In social welfare there are Catholic movements that have contributed mightily to America's good. The Catholic Youth Organization, developed by Bishop Sheil in Chicago, and Father Flanagan's Boys' Town are merely two of the better-known examples of "south of the tracks" projects carried on by devoted priests in many cities.

Priests who inspire such work are certainly sincere and good. So too are most of the nuns in hospitals and schools. Their sacrifice of self is genuine and complete. I believe that my brother, the priest, and my sisters and my multitudinous cousins are sincere even in their condemnation of my "apostasy," and I hold no malice toward them. Nor have I any for my aunt who said that it would be preferable for me to have died than to leave the Church. For I too was sincere at the time when I believed as they still do. Now my feeling for them is one of compassion and an impatience for them to "arise from their sleep."

The genius of Catholic missionaries laid at least the foundations of civilization in the Philippines, South America, and Mexico. The old Spanish missions of San Luis Rey and Santa Barbara, in which I lived and studied, were surrounded with ruins of reservoirs, irrigation canals, granaries, and workshops. It was not the fault of those valiant pioneers that their successors failed to erect the superstructure.

Very few Roman Catholics like the strictness of the detailed prohibitions of their Church's moral code. But its dogmatic doctrine, presented with an authoritarianism that claims to have divine sanction, gives positive and definite answers to man's basic questions: Whence? Why? Whither? Catholic finality of doctrine is, in truth, the opiate of the masses of its people who are too lazy or too stupid to think, or who instinctively feel that because millions of people believe a doctrine it must therefore be true. Just as the Church's monasteries and convents provide physical and financial security to priests and nuns, so the simple

answers of the catechism offer solutions not even attempted
by the world's great philosophers. A Franciscan priest (for
many years a professor in St. Anthony's Seminary) told
an ex-priest whom I know: " I don't think, and I won't
read anything that might make me think."

On the other hand it is also true that the Roman Church
appeals to some " intellectuals." It boasts of the conversion
of G. K. Chesterton, John Henry Newman, Heywood
Broun, Louis Budenz, and the well-publicized followers of
Bishop Fulton Sheen. These people, usually caught on an
intellectual or emotional rebound, either are oblivious to
the Church's superstition, inconsistency, and power politics or ignore them as the " human element."

They have capitulated to Roman Catholic " apologetics "
— a " science " which purports to establish by reason, scripture, and history the " divine " establishment of Catholicism. Through apologetics, the candidate is not asked to
accept anything on faith except the consciousness of his
own existence. Twenty-one proofs are adduced for the
existence of God. From that point on, the close reasoning
proceeds through syllogism after syllogism with all the
mental precision of a textbook on geometry. Premise follows premise through the proofs for the existence of the
soul, its nature, its immortality, and its dependence on a
deity. The possibility of a divine revelation, and the possibility of miracles and prophecies as its supporting proof,
are established in a manner reminiscent of the old theorem:
when a straight line intersects two parallel lines the alter-
nate interior angles are equal. This " science " proceeds,
treating the Bible merely as history, to " prove " Christ's
existence, divinity, sacrifice, and establishment of a

"church." The Roman Catholic Church is then identified with it — and the Papacy as the line of Peter's successors.

The overwhelming weight of several hundred pages of logic, usually absorbed by one whose "intellectuality" cloaks an emotional desire to be convinced, conceals the weak premise of the whole chain — the "inspiration of tradition." Orthodox Protestantism teaches that the Bible is inspired and therefore infallible. Romanism also believes this but adds the "infallible" support of early Christian "tradition" to cover the historical vacuum of those first centuries.

After leaving the priesthood I learned to read. I found the sophistries in those syllogisms of "apologetics." The two principal theorems which rest on each other are these: (1) The Roman Catholic Church is infallible because the Bible says so. And how does anyone know the Bible says so? (2) The Roman Catholic Church says it does. No wonder this is commonly referred to as a case of "circular reasoning"!

In the final analysis, therefore, the "science" of apologetics is merely intellectual window dressing. For the intelligent, as well as for the illiterate, belief in Roman Catholicism can have only one ultimate basis — blind faith.

New Testament texts are distorted by the Church to "prove" that Christ established the ritualistic system of the seven sacraments:

How do we know that Christ instituted the seven sacraments?
The sacraments were established to give men the grace necessary for salvation. Because of the fact that the sacraments give grace it is necessary that they were instituted by Our Lord. If grace is so connected with the sacraments as to make them a

divinely effective and authoritative instrument of salvation, they must owe their existence to divine institution. Everything in the Church, moreover, that is essential and substantial was set up by Christ Himself on earth. The sacraments, an essential part of the Church, were, therefore, instituted by Our Lord.

The institution of the seven sacraments by Christ is of faith for Catholics. The Council of Trent declared: " If anyone shall say that the sacraments of the New Law were not all instituted by Jesus Christ, Our Lord, or that they are either more or less than seven, to wit, Baptism, Confirmation, the Eucharist, Penance, Extreme Unction, Holy Orders and Matrimony, or also that any of these seven is not truly and properly a sacrament, let him be anathema."

Is there historical proof for the institution of the sacraments by Christ?

Tradition proves the fact of the divine institution. Each of the seven sacraments is set forth in the New Testament.[1]

Some people call themselves " Catholics with reservations." They say they believe in most of the teachings of the Church and love her ritual and traditions, but they refuse to accept official doctrine on some specific point such as celibacy, divorce, therapeutic abortion, sterilization, confession, miracles, or indulgences.

Logically there can be no such thing as a partial Catholic, or one with reservations. Logically one must embrace Roman Catholic doctrine in its entirety or reject it completely.

The admitted foundation of Roman Catholic doctrine is its claim to have been established by Christ and its consequent infallibility in matters of faith and morals. If a person rejects any one dogma, such as that of the bodily Assumption of Mary into heaven, or any one moral prohibition, such as that of birth control, he has rejected infallibility as such — and the foundation is gone.

[1] Riordan, Linus, in *Arizona Register*, June 5, 1953.

My personal rejection of Roman Catholicism had not begun as a doctrinal repudiation. But it ended as such. It began as an instinctive feeling that the God of Truth and Justice could not be party to a lack of consistency between theory and practice; that the God of Nature could not approve a code of morals that distorted human nature; that an all-sufficient God did not require a masochistic formalism while his creatures, through man's inhumanity to man, lay " hungered, thirsty, and naked."

My official faith had been blind, illogical, and unreasoning. Now it had collapsed. It was my real faith that remained — the cornerstone.

My rejection of the priesthood and of the Roman Catholic Church did not leave as much of a void of faith as might be imagined. I had not rejected God or religion. I had merely shed the idolatrous trappings that had overgrown the concept of God and of religion. I still believed as strongly as ever in a God and in the religion that means love of God through love of man.

For a decade, and with increasing intensity of feeling, my approach to God had been through man and not through rituals and sacraments. To me, love of God could be expressed only through love of man, respect for man, help to man. This belief was the issue that caused my break with Romanism.

The Catholic Church, contending that such help to man was a worldly, material, irreligious activity unworthy of a priest, ordered me to leave it. To me this is the truest expression of religion and I refused to give it up.

In what terms can this " worldly " religion be evaluated? At Memorial Hospital, in terms of dollars, more than

$100,000 of medical care is rendered yearly. To measure love by arithmetic — an impossible task — twenty thousand people each year are treated without charge in the clinics and emergency facilities of our institution. Nor has there been any change in Memorial Hospital's interracial policy, which through example has helped to break down segregation in schools, restaurants, businesses, and hospitals throughout the city.

When I departed from Roman Catholicism, there was no void left to fill in my belief in God and my belief in man.

But I did need to adjust. I needed to learn a new life of freedom. I needed to overcome my fear of Roman Catholic reprisals. I needed to clarify my thinking about God, religion, and my relation to my fellow man.

The average Roman Catholic layman doesn't bother to think deeply about the nature of God. He is so busy concentrating on Mary and the saints in the anterooms and side chapels of the churches that he tends to forget the main room with its altar and the God to whom it is consecrated. Roman Catholic theologians delve into such abstractions as God's essence, substance, nature, and qualities. But lay Catholics leave him to his " namelessness " — the " Weh " of the Old Testament — and devote their praise and supplication to the " Sacred Heart " of Christ and " Mother " Mary, the " Mediatrix " of all divine grace, strength, and favors.

Roman Catholic theology strips man of his strength, ability, and powers as it builds up the limitless power, majesty, and inaccessibility of God. Man sinks lower than the dunghills of Job. He becomes nothingness or, at most, a slave,

subservient and abject to the fancied whims of a tyrannical divine master.

Leaving Romanism drew me closer to God. The symbols, the magic, the medals, the indulgences, the saints, the " mothers," the mechanical and human intermediaries were swept away, and I had nothing left but God.

I could reach God — not through the mediation of the Virgin Mary or the intercession of dead saints, but through the love of living men. That love was to consist not in words or maudlin affection but in concern for my fellow man, in a sympathetic understanding, respect, and desire for the existence and development of his physical, moral, and intellectual being.

I now found in the words of Jesus a startling confirmation of my own feeling that love of man must validate the worship of God: " If thou bring thy gift to the altar and there rememberest that thy brother hath aught against thee, leave there thy gift before the altar, and go thy way; first be reconciled to thy brother, and then come and offer thy gift."

St. Paul equated the love of man with the love of God: " For all the law is fulfilled in one word, even in this, Thou shalt love thy neighbor as thyself." The only norm of righteousness in the eyes of St. James was man's love of God through love of his fellow: " If ye fulfill the royal law according to the scripture, ' Thou shalt love thy neighbor as thyself,' ye do well."

Jesus told men to search for God in mankind: " The Kingdom of God is within you." He rejected the master-slave relationship of fear which characterizes Roman Catholicism. To Jesus, God was a " Father " — not a slave-owner.

Jesus rejected the taboos that have made Romanism (and some other denominations) a form of actual idolatry: " Not that which goeth into the mouth defileth a man but that which cometh out of the mouth, this defileth a man."

And to me, the two thousand proscriptions of the Code of Canon Law were swept away by the words of Jesus: " Woe to you hypocrites for ye shut up the kingdom of heaven against men; for ye neither go in yourselves, neither suffer ye them that are entering to go in."

The Master considered disrespect and ridicule of one's fellow man to be as serious as murder: " Ye have heard that it was said by them of old time, ' Thou shalt not kill '; and whosoever shall kill shall be in danger of the judgment; but I say unto you, that whosoever is angry with his brother without a cause shall be in danger of the judgment . . . but whosoever shall say ' Thou fool ' shall be in danger of hell fire."

Morals and ethics were reduced, for me, to a single concept: love of God through love of man, as I should love and respect myself.

I have not as yet joined another church. Someday I may join one. Through hospital and other civic contacts, I know most of the ministers and leaders of the Protestant denominations in Phoenix. I have attended services in many of their churches and been a guest speaker in several of them.

In the five years since I left the Roman Catholic Church, I have read more of the Bible, of religious books, and of church newspapers and magazines than I did during my fifteen years in the priesthood. My interest has been not that of a lost soul wandering and searching for God and a way of life but rather that of a person interested in religion and satisfied in his own soul's contact with God. I am a person enjoying "fellowship" with other people and the variety of their religious experiences.

Every Roman Catholic priest has been taught, as I had, not only that Protestants are largely to be consigned to hell in the next world, but that on earth they constantly disagree and divide and are united on only one point — opposition to Roman Catholicism.

Protestant groups certainly have their differences. Some are narrow and some are liberal. Many of them have their quota of taboos. Most of them have shameful memories of the religious wars of Europe, for which they were partially responsible, and of the witch hunts, the book burnings, and the inexcusable persecutions of one another in early America's colonial days.

To me the differences among Protestants, though doctrinal, are superficial and non-essential. Their unity is greater than their divergency. They have an unshakable belief in a common God. They have personal mental independence. They are subject to no pope. They are, in truth, captains of their own souls. Their ancestors in America fought against religious intolerance, and wrote guarantees of freedom of thought and worship into the Constitution of the United States, and developed the unique idea of separation of church and state.

To me, the outstanding characteristic of all Protestant forms of worship is their enthusiasm. Whether in a revival tent, in an ivy-covered church, or in an impressive cathedral, the members of the congregation show a spontaneity in praying, singing, and listening that does not exist in

Roman Catholic churches. The reason is obvious: Most Protestants go to church because they want to; Catholics generally are there because they are afraid not to be. Missing mass deliberately on only one Sunday is for Catholics a mortal sin and damns their souls to hell. The mass is a stereotyped Latin ritual that somehow is supposed to placate God. The Protestant service of any denomination, even the silent Quaker service, calls for an active and voluntary participation of all those present.

A Protestant minister's function in the worship service is strikingly different from that of the Roman clergy. He is not a sanctified high priest representing a remote deity.

The Protestant clergy — and I know many of them intimately — seem far more sincere and personally dedicated than the average Roman Catholic priest. This is probably because they are in the ministry through adult choice, not drawn into it when too young to know better. Protestants remain in the ministry because they wish to, not because they are bound irrevocably by laws of their churches or because of threats of divine and human reprisals if they leave the ministry.

In worship, in doctrine, and in morals the Protestant keynote is love. In Roman Catholicism it is fear. The hierarchy, of course, denies this. A good test would be the abolition of the penalty of sin for non-attendance at Sunday mass.

The aspect of Protestantism that impresses me most is its solicitude for its youth and the response of that youth.

A common complaint in the councils of the Roman clergy is that an undue proportion of its faithful communicants, at mass, confession, and communion, are old women. This is true even in parishes with elaborate school systems. But in Protestant services I am struck with the large proportion of young people in their late teens and early twenties. They are there through choice and also, I believe, because they are actually receiving the moral, religious, and social guidance that they seek. Through the program of the churches, Protestant youth learns the concept of love — love in the sense of human respect, mutual esteem, and the practical desire to help one another — religion at its best.

My impression is that most Protestants would rather educate young people in a proper way of life than build churches. The education should be broad, not confined within denominational restrictions. Even the church universities have no "index of forbidden books." As a girl, my wife studied the atheism of Omar Khayyám in Baylor University, run by the Southern Baptists in the "fundamentalist" state of Texas.

Roman Catholicism also has a school system, vast and expensive, enrolling millions of children and young people. But while Protestantism is solicitous for its youth, Roman Catholicism is solicitous for itself. It wants loyalty, not learning, in its members. In its colleges and universities the students are not educated; they are merely trained. They encounter not mental development but thought control. They are not permitted freedom of thought or of research. The *Index of Forbidden Books* rules their libraries.

Any Catholic who reads these words I have written will be automatically excommunicated.[2] He is forbidden to

---

[2] Bull of Pius IV, *Dominici Gregis*, March 24, 1564, confirming the twenty-fifth session of the Council of Trent. See *Canons and Decrees of the Council of Trent*, by H. J. Schroeder (St. Louis: B. Herder Book Co; 1941), p. 551.

think. He lets the priest think for him. But he does not realize that the priests do not think either. They, too, are forbidden to read.

Protestants have probably as many variations of doctrine and of worship as there are churches to house them. But all Protestants, whether fundamentalist or liberal, whether northern or southern, whether high or low, whether trinitarian or unitarian, agree in two common beliefs.

The first is the personal, independent, private interpreta.ion of the Bible. From this principle, according to Roman Catholic " observers," flow the bickering and cleavages of Protestantism. But from that principle also flows something the Roman Catholic " observers " have not seen — the freedom to think, to search, to probe, to believe the teachings of Jesus with the simplicity in which Jesus spoke them.

The second common belief of Protestantism stems from those simple teachings of Jesus. It is the belief that worship is subordinate to or a part of that thing called " fellowship " — an intelligent, helpful love of all men. Doctrine is much less important. " Whosoever imagines that a Methodist is a man of such and such an opinion," wrote John Wesley, " is grossly ignorant of the whole affair. The distinguishing marks of a Methodist are not his opinions at all. I am sick of opinions; give me a humble gentle lover of God and of man. . . . [Protestant] Christianity is essentially a social religion."

America must be grateful to John Wesley and other liberal leaders of Protestantism. Their belief in free thought and practical " fellowship " gave birth to American democracy. Only the preservation of those Protestant Christian liberal ideals will enable American democracy to continue to live. We are a religious nation, not in the sense that the great majority of us are constant churchgoers, but in the sense that we think freely and we love deeply — and thus come near and directly to God.

It is difficult for me to express my personal appraisal of American democracy without perhaps appearing to the critical intellectual mind to be maudlin and sentimental. I am sentimental about it. Before leaving Romanism I scorned the displaced Pole or German or Yugoslav who, when granted American citizenship, passionately clutched the American flag, kissed it, and openly wept. But I do not scorn him now. I feel just as passionate. Now I know what he left and what he has received. For the tyranny of totalitarianism is not confined to political states, and the emotional appreciation of America is not reserved only to those who reject a nationality to become its citizens.

I came out of the physical and mental confines of the Roman Catholic priesthood as a person who had lived in America but had never known it or been a part of it. Even in voting, I, like the rest of the clergy and the nuns and many of the laity, had been an automaton, placing my X where the best interests of the hierarchy would be served or where a politician had indicated it would be profitable to place it.

Now I was an adult examining, for the first time, the nation that was my own and marveling, not only at its physical make-up and resources, but at its moral, intellectual, and spiritual resources. I was consumed with an insatiable curiosity that wanted to know everything about everything. I read almanacs. I analyzed articles and books on every aspect of America. I studied road maps. And on vacations and weekends I drove to small towns and asked questions in cotton camps, country churches, and crossroad bars.

I not only saw America and its greatness but realized why it is great. I realized why its form of government is so enduring, why it is mentally and scientifically advanced, why it is the moral leader of the world.

Some Americans cheat and connive in business. Many of them dodge their bills. Some (relatively few) become criminals. But the outstanding characteristic that I found in my personal search of my country was love. I found it in the neighbors who come weekly to entertain our polio patients. I found it in people who, when we appealed, during a banana shortage, for a baby dying of diarrhea, brought bananas by the hundred. I could see love everywhere.

Never in the history of mankind have there been people who loved one another or loved the rest of the world more than the American people of the twentieth century. With an outpouring of time and of energy, they have attacked every enemy of human health. They have done it spontaneously, not under compulsion.

Literally millions of American citizens give their time as well as their money in our vast national crusades against tuberculosis, cancer, heart disease, cerebral palsy, asthma, and infantile paralysis.

America is not satisfied to nurture only her own children. Through church groups of all denominations, and through research, educational, and relief foundations, she sends medical teams into all lands and pours out additional millions to eradicate disease and misery from the hinterlands of the earth.

America's love has never been equaled in human history. She turns her cheek seventy times seven times. She fights only to defend her family. But when she has defeated her enemies she binds their wounds, feeds their children, pays their bills, and hands forth more billions of dollars to restore them to an honorable place among the nations of the world.

This is what American democracy means to me.

Five years have passed since the eventful evening when I stood in the rectory of St. Mary's Church in Phoenix and offered farewell to my fellow Franciscan priests. These years have been the happiest of my life, years of struggle, of work, of relaxation, and of love in an unbelievably happy marriage.

They have been years during which the Roman Catholic Church and my life within it have come into true perspective in my mind.

I have written this story not out of spite, nor of hatred, nor of vindictiveness. I have written it for three reasons. The first is to acquaint Roman Catholics themselves, if they will read it, with the truth of the secret inner workings of their hierarchy. The second reason is to inform non-Catholic America, from the viewpoint of one who has seen and who knows, of the nature of this growth that has spread so luxuriantly in the free and nourishing soil of our land, while at the same time choking freedom of thought in the lands it controls. The third reason is the most important of all. I have written this story because I felt I must.

Many sincere Roman Catholics are perturbed about their Church. It is their birthright, and they want to be proud of it. But, privately or among their close friends, they deplore its financial rapacity, its political alliances, its archaic doctrines which they either ignore or permit to ruin their lives and their marriages. They continue to hope that their

Church will change, that it will become more charitable, less aggressive, and more realistic in faith and conduct.

Thousands of priests and millions of the laity, realizing the futility of hope for a change, have done the only thing they could do. They have regretfully taken their hands from the plow and have looked back.

To non-Catholic America, I have attempted to portray life within the priesthood as it actually is. I have emphasized the long, narrow, effective mental indoctrination of the seminary, taking young boys from their families, walling them off from society, from world events, from modern education through the formative years of adolescence, and then turning them out into the "vineyard" after ordination as thoroughly dedicated as a Russian envoy to the United Nations. I have pictured the tyranny of fear that chains these men to their religious posts long after they have become disillusioned and yearn for the freedom and normal life of America. I have tried also to show, through my own experiences and through correspondence, the miasmic fog which the Church has intentionally spread to conceal the truth from the Roman Catholics who blindly follow it — stifling their freedom of thought, of worship, of action, and of life itself. I contend that this foreign thing is far more subtle, far less forthright, but just as inimical to the American concept of life as Communism itself. It is often the indirect cause of Communism by keeping whole nations in ignorance and poverty and by developing techniques of fear, indoctrination, and mental tyranny that the Kremlin exploits. The Inquisition led by the Catholic Church in the sixteenth century finds its parallel in the political persecution by the Communists today in Czechoslovakia, Poland, and Russia.

For myself, putting the thoughts of my life on paper

has proven a mental catharsis. It has enabled me to re-appraise my decision and its motives and its reasons. I now emphatically reaffirm that decision. Looking back, I see my years in the priesthood and in the seminary as time spent in a dungeon, a prison whose floor was the burning fire of hell, whose walls and roof were made of unyielding stones, whose air was not light and free but musty with medieval-ism.

My past five years have been those of a free man, a man restored to his birthright of American liberties, liberties which in his first forty-one years of life under the American flag he had not been permitted to enjoy.

It became almost a childlike pleasure to shop in a grocery store, to help plan a meal, to paint a door, to sleep late on Sunday, to plant a shrub in one's own yard, to choose one's clothes without restriction, to entertain friends without consulting a Superior, and to love and to be loved.

I am an American again, not a foreign subject on American soil.

I can love America, and without asking a bishop or a Superior I can enjoy her mountains and streams, her noisy cities and quiet prairies, and especially the sea, nature's own symbol of freedom.

I can love God and continue with freedom in the service of my fellow man. For that freedom is now my heritage also. It is the freedom of America, the freedom that I, too, with all free men must guard. Like Thomas Jefferson, I " have sworn upon the altar of God eternal hostility against every form of tyranny over the mind of man."

Index